T0340636

Building to Suit the Climate
A Handbook

Building to Suit the Climate

A Handbook

Gerhard Hausladen
Petra Liedl
Mike de Saldanha

Birkhäuser
Basel

Table of contents

Foreword

Worldwide economic growth and the associated boost to prosperity have led to considerably increased building activity, especially in Asia and the Arab countries, and also in Russia and South America. Because there is such a strong desire to improve the standard of living rapidly, architecture and urban development change within a few years, while building culture in "old Europe" developed over decades or even centuries.

The International Style, which was enormously popular in Europe and America, produced an architecture that was detached from climatic aspects, architecture that was concerned primarily with formal language, in a period that saw dealing with climatic demands through technology and energy as a demonstration of technical skill. Unfortunately this often led to unbalanced solutions that consumed enormous quantities of electricity and fossil fuels to meet ever-increasing demands for comfort. The aim today must be for architecture that responds to climatic conditions in a similar way to traditional building methods. It really does make better sense to meet climatic challenges through the approach to building, rather than dealing with them exclusively through technology.

In China, India or the Arab world, the main problem is comfort in summer, especially because of the intense sunlight. Another challenge is the high humidity in tropical and subtropical terrain. Here the air has to be dehumidified, which usually requires a great deal of energy and technology.

Using passive energy sources such as soil sensors for cooling, or regenerative active systems such as solar cooling, involves examining the ambient climatic conditions very precisely. When looking for appropriate solutions, it makes only limited sense to transfer concepts from Europe and North America to countries in other climate zones.

In order to be able to develop holistic concepts that work in other countries and climate zones, equal attention must be paid to both climatic and cultural matters such as religion and tradition, or requests relating to comfort. Other aspects are economic factors and also technical matters such as the availability of technology, for example, energy prices or the expertise available for maintenance and operation.

Climatic conditions that are often extreme have to be addressed intensively when seeking holistic approaches. Attempts should therefore be made even in the early stages of planning a building to include climatic aspects such as irradiation, air temperatures, humidity conditions and the wind situation in the concept for the building. If cultural aspects are to be addressed appropriately, it is essential to study traditional building methods and also to come to terms with current local trends.

Aims of this book

In international projects, the rapid development of building activity means that the time available for planning is increasingly short. There is often a lack of planning experience when it comes to considering climatic influences.

This book aims to support architects and engineers when planning buildings in an international context, especially in the conceptual phase. To that end it offers a comprehensive analysis of the interplay between the climate and the building structure and the exterior of the building, as well as with technology inside the building and the energy concept. It is also intended to provide a companion for students while studying, and to open up areas of work for them all over the world.

The book's principal focus is on detailed climatic analysis as a basis for architecture with a future. This demonstrates the challenges and potential for a particular location, and shows the relevance to planning of individual climatic elements such as solar radiation, temperature, humidity and wind. An architectural climate classification defines climate zones on the basis of air temperature and absolute humidity. These key factors enable a first general view of climatic aspects of building planning.

The climate as it relates to building is examined, taking the cities of Moscow, Munich, Shanghai, Bangalore and Dubai as examples – as typical representatives of their climate zones – and readers are given tips on planning strategies.

The structure of the book

Chapter 1 defines climate as the key value in climate-oriented architecture. This is followed by climatic classification through building-climatic criteria; these make it possible to draw consequences for spatial conditioning by combining the building-specific climate parameters air temperature and absolute humidity, providing a first general view for building planners. Climatic differences arising from latitude, closeness to the sea or height are also shown.

The interplay of climatic elements such as temperature, solar radiation, absolute humidity and wind speed is examined and presented in detail. In addition, comfort criteria in the interior climate in terms of temperature and humidity are explained, with particular emphasis on recommendations in the international standard ASHRAE-55.

In subsequent chapters, the cities of Moscow, Munich, Shanghai, Bangalore and Dubai are taken as examples of the five climate zones "cool", "temperate", "subtropical", "tropical" and "desert", and function as a basis for climate analysis. To make the material more accessible, the diversity of the ecozones (according to Schultz 2002) is described. This is followed by planning tips on the placing and cubature of buildings, and also facade construction. These chapters also offer suggestions for room conditioning concepts that can be implemented in the different climate zones. In conclusion, the energy-saving potential of each location is indicated. The climate graphs in these chapters are location-specific, and so relate only to the city given as an example, while planning strategies apply to the particular climate zone in general. Particular climatic features can be taken from the architectural climate classifications in the "Climate" chapter and the city tables in the appendix and related to the cities presented.

All the graphs in the book relating specifically to climate and location were created with the interactive *ClimateTool* from the global climate data base Meteonorm. This tool makes it possible to analyse climate factors such as solar radiation, temperature, humidity, wind and light from the point of view of building, and apply them in a way that is useful to planners for any location in the world. It also provides the basis for the building climatology-related climate classification presented in the book, and for the city tables in the appendix.

Chapter 7, "Economics", examines energy-relevant costs during the construction process, and lists typical costs for heat and sun protection measures, as well as room conditioning and energy generation components. In addition, special features arising from interaction with the climate are presented in terms of economics.

The glossary explains essential terms on the themes of "outdoor climate", "building energy systems", "building skin", "light", "indoor climate", "room conditioning" and "energy generation". A diagram puts the terms in context for each of these subject headings, thus providing a survey of the interplay between the individual aspects. Terms from the glossary can be found in the margin in each chapter, and the relevant term in the main text is identified by a preceding arrow.

We wish all our readers an exciting trip round the world!

Munich, June 2011

Gerhard Hausladen, Petra Liedl, Mike de Saldanha

Climate

Climate and building for the future

The 21st century is characterised by climatic and demographic alterations. The predicted climatic changes will have major implications for building planning in the future. The population explosion in comparatively young states will demand extensive construction projects, which the standard European concepts will be insufficient to meet. The architecture of the future will need to be based on detailed climatic analysis, taking into account the impact of solar radiation, temperature, humidity and wind on buildings. Only close attention to the climate and the local architectural tradition can produce fully adequate buildings and optimal energy concepts.

100 75 50 25 0

Nights per year with an average temperature lower than 20 °C [%]

Introduction

The word climate is derived from the ancient Greek verb *klínein* ("to incline"). It describes the tilt of the Earth's axis. Climate, as opposed to weather, refers to the state of the Earth's atmosphere as established by statistics, over a period of time, which may be as long as several decades. These statistics describe the climate elements relevant to a location, a region or the whole Earth. There are three different types of climate: macroclimate, mesoclimate and microclimate – distinguished mainly by the size of the area involved.

Climate elements and climate factors

The climate of the Earth is determined by the sun's radiation, without which life on Earth would not be possible. We describe the climate in terms of climatic elements. The most significant of these are ↙ air temperature, precipitation, ↙ air humidity, population, wind and ↙ solar radiation. Climate factors are processes and situations that produce, maintain or alter a climate. They include a location's latitude, the distribution of land and sea, the local and trans-regional wind systems, and altitude.

↙
outdoor air temperature p. 142

absolute air humidity p. 142

global radiation p. 142

Atmospheric circulation

The Earth's atmospheric circulation is determined by the radiation level, the rotation of the Earth, and the distribution of water and land masses. As the radiation balance varies between latitudes, there is a permanent temperature gradient between the equator and the poles. This creates differences in air pressure. The greater this difference in air pressure, the more air flows from the high pressure area to the low pressure area. This creates strong winds (Fig. 1.1). Coriolis force causes the air streams to flow to the right in the northern hemisphere, and to the left in the southern hemisphere. The circulation systems are more pronounced in the southern hemisphere due to the distribution of land and sea.

Macroclimate

A macroclimate exists over very large geographical areas and long periods of time. It is identified and assessed using solar radiation distribution, the terrain height, the distribution of land and sea, and global circulation. Areas with similar climates are grouped together as climate zones. Macroclimates interact closely, influencing each other in a variety of ways. The global climate is created by the dynamic interaction between macroclimates.

Mesoclimate

The spaces and units of time involved are significantly smaller for a mesoclimate than they are for a macroclimate. Regional climates – one form of mesoclimate – are characterised primarily by their natural and cultural features: mountains, valleys, coasts, islands, wooded areas, cities and villages. Climates determined by landscape or location features are described as landscape climates or location climates. The urban climate is very important from an architectural point of view.

Microclimate

A microclimate may exist for only a very short space of time, and is a climate in the smallest unit of space and in the lowest atmospheric layer. It is influenced by terrain, distance from the ground surface and the ground surface's composition and flora. In a city, it is primarily determined by construction materials, development density, vegetation, horizon obstruction, and air streams. The microclimate can be recorded and described by only taking measurements because it is constantly changing.

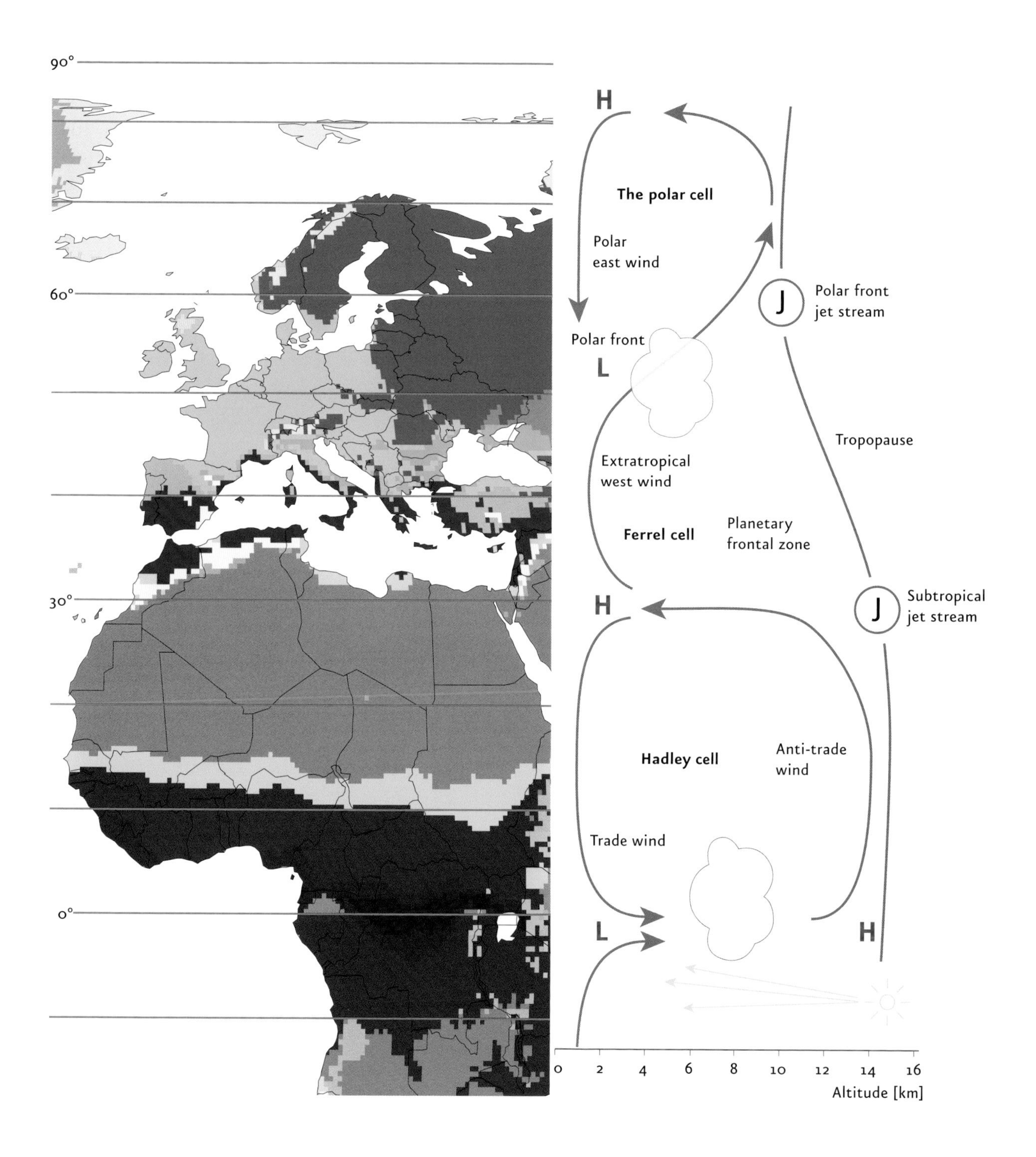

Fig. 1.1 The creation of climate zones

The sun is the motor that drives the climate. The different amounts of energy received by different places on Earth and the resulting wind systems create a variety of climate zones. Moist air rises from the equator, warmed by the high incidence of solar radiation. This creates an area of low pressure near the ground – the equatorial trough – combined with an area of high pressure at a very high altitude. As the air rises, the water vapour it contains condenses, creating clouds. If the water vapour saturation point is exceeded, it rains. This leaves masses of dry air, which flow towards the poles, sinking back to earth again when they reach the tropical regions. This results in an area of high pressure with little air movement – the horse latitudes. As the dry air masses descend, they warm up and absorb moisture – creating large, dry desert areas. At ground level, the air flows in the direction of the equator, creating the "trade winds" and closing the circle. This air circulation pattern is known as the Hadley cell (according to Schönwiese 2003). The colours denote the effective climate classification according to Köppen and Geiger, and show climate zones structured according to latitude.

Climate Elements

The climate is described in terms of climate elements. The climate elements that have an impact on architecture are solar radiation, air temperature, air humidity and precipitation, and wind.

Solar radiation

↙
heating energy demand p. 144
room climate p. 150
daylight provision p. 148
glazing percentage p. 146
global radiation p. 142
sun protection p. 146
solar cooling p. 154
photovoltaics p. 154
orientation p. 144

As a source of light and energy, solar radiation is an important planning factor – it reduces the ↙ heating energy demand, and is the major influence on the ↙ room climate in summer. A good plan should include sufficient ↙ daylight provision and good views, as well as controlling the effect of solar heating. The indoor daylight provosion is determined by the outdoor light levels together with the ↙ glazing percentage and the form of glazing used.

The ↙ global radiation level is composed of the direct solar radiation level plus the diffuse sky radiation level. Latitude is the major factor in changes in day length, the angle of radiation incidence (Fig. 1.2) and the type and intensity of solar radiation received throughout the year (Fig. 1.3). This influences the degree of shade from nearby structures and the amount of sun striking the facades, meaning that the latitude largely governs the daylight situation and the ↙ sun protection concept. The efficiency of solar heat gain, ↙ solar cooling and ↙ photovoltaic systems also depends on this. The azimuth and the angle of elevation of the sun in relation to the facade – and, therefore, the intensity of solar radiation received by the building – result from the building's ↙ orientation.

Temperature

The outdoor air temperature depends on solar radiation and the temperature of incoming air masses. The average temperature over the year influences a building's configuration, its heat protection and the ventilation and cooling systems required.

↙
night ventilation p. 152
concrete core activation p. 152
cooling tower p. 154
storage mass p. 144
earth piles/ groundwater utilisation p. 154
earth pipes p. 154

Changes in temperature throughout the day determine the practicality of passive cooling strategies such as ↙ night ventilation and ↙ concrete core activation with free ↙ recooling. Efficient night cooling requires low night temperatures and free ↙ storage mass. The frequency of days with extreme weather should also be taken into account, as it has implications for the effectiveness of passive cooling systems and for the configuration of the technology used.

A building's ability to make use of renewable heating or cooling may depend on the composition of the building ground and the soil layers beneath it. The major factor in the thermal utility of the soil is its moisture content: flowing groundwater is ideal.

The average annual temperature goes down into the soil to a depth of about 10–15 m. The soil temperature can be accessed as a source of heat or cold via tube registers, probes, ↙ piles or ↙ earth pipes.

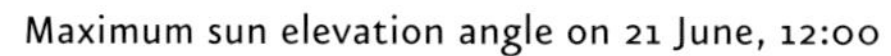

Maximum sun elevation angle on 21 June, 12:00
- Oslo (59° 55′ N): 53.5°
- Rome (41° 53′ N): 71.2°
- Bilma (18° 41′ N): 83.4°
- Kinshasa (04° 20′ S): 69.8°
- Cape Town (33° 55′ S): 32.5°

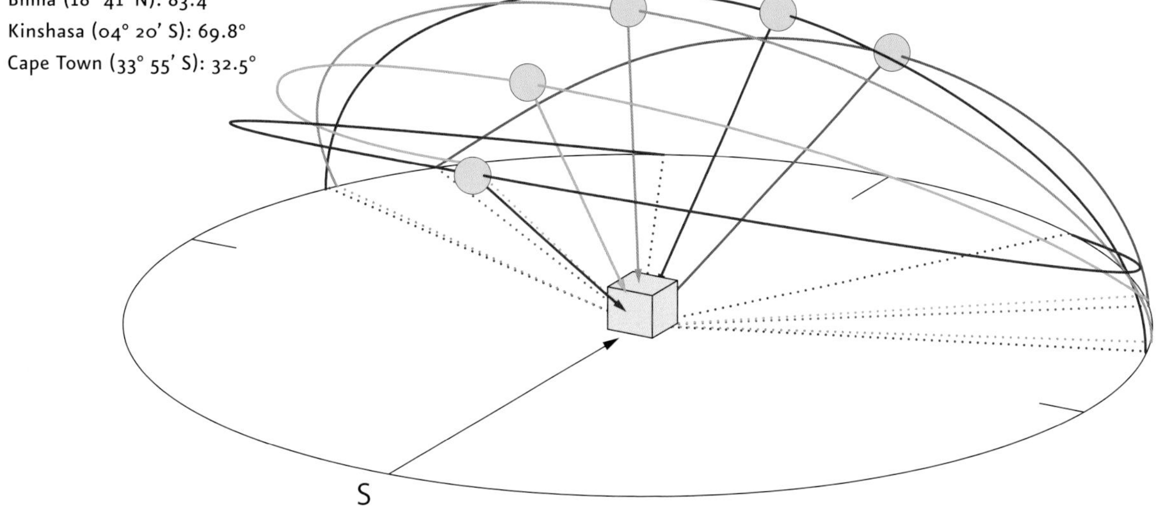

Maximum sun elevation angle on 21 December, 12:00
- Oslo (59° 55′ N): 6.6°
- Rome (41° 53′ N): 24.5°
- Bilma (18° 41′ N): 47.7°
- Kinshasa (04° 20′ S): 61.4°
- Cape Town (33° 55′ S): 79.1°

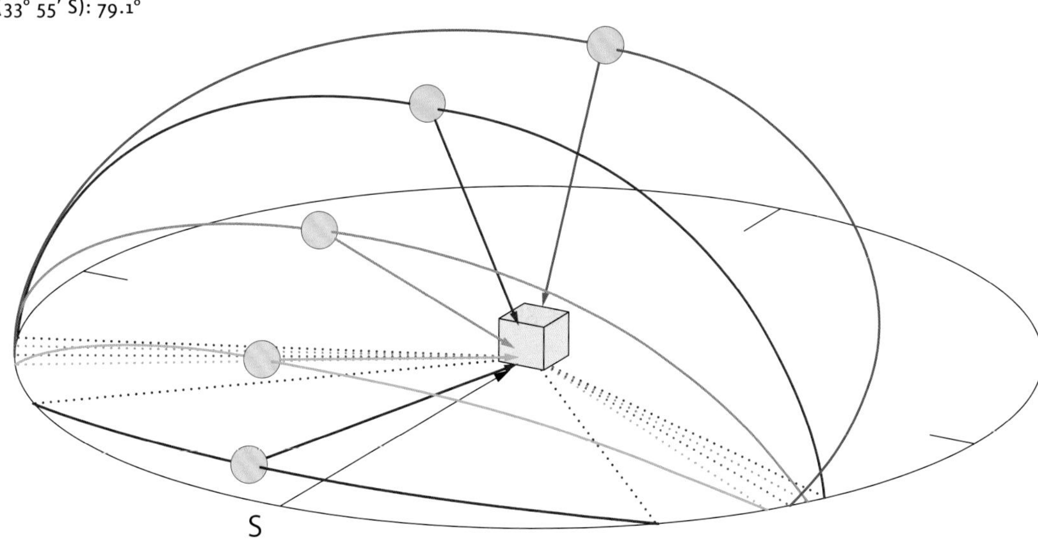

Fig. 1.2 Course of the sun
The course of the sun on 21 June (top) and on 21 December (bottom) with the sun's angle of elevation and azimuth angle for locations at different latitudes but similar longitudes.

Air humidity

There are two different measurements of air humidity: relative and absolute air humidity. Absolute air humidity, which is location-specific and is determined primarily by proximity to the ocean and by precipitation levels (Fig. 1.5), is an important factor in the room climate and in the outflow of moisture from indoor spaces. While the air's absolute water vapour content changes very little over the course of the day, relative air humidity is affected by the temperature. Minimum values of absolute humidity are reached on especially cold days, while maximum values occur at high temperatures.

↙
(de)humidifying
p. 150

dew point temperature
p. 142

decentralised ventilation system
p. 152

Whether air inflow has to be ↙ dehumidified or ↙ humidified depends on the absolute humidity level. ↙ Dew point issues can also significantly reduce the effectiveness of surface cooling systems, making dehumidifying the air inflow essential. Where the outdoor air is humid, ↙ decentralised ventilation system may require condensate drainage.

Depending on the location, the precipitation frequency, the monthly precipitation rate and the maximum precipitation levels may represent important planning data. Levels of solar radiation and cloud cover influence the temperature, particularly at ground level. During the day, clouds can reduce solar radiation incidence; on a cloudless night, the temperature goes down significantly.

Wind

The wind situation onsite is a critical factor in construction planning. The relevant aspect is the pressure and suction exerted by the wind on the building skin. The airflow around a building is determined by the prevailing wind situation, the building's shape and its surroundings. Meteorological data, however, provide only a generalised picture of wind direction and wind strength onsite. The major factor is the microclimate situation created by the terrain, the shape and proximity of the surrounding buildings, and the surrounding vegetation. The surrounding development can produce jet effects that increase ↙ wind speeds.

↙
wind speeds
p. 142

The areas acted on by the wind's pressure and suction can be incorporated into natural ventilation plans if ventilation and exhaust openings are positioned in aerodynamically optimised positions.

While the major wind systems recur with the seasons, regional winds are heavily influenced by the topography. The role of local winds is demonstrated by places that belong to a certain climate zone geographically having a significantly different local climate.

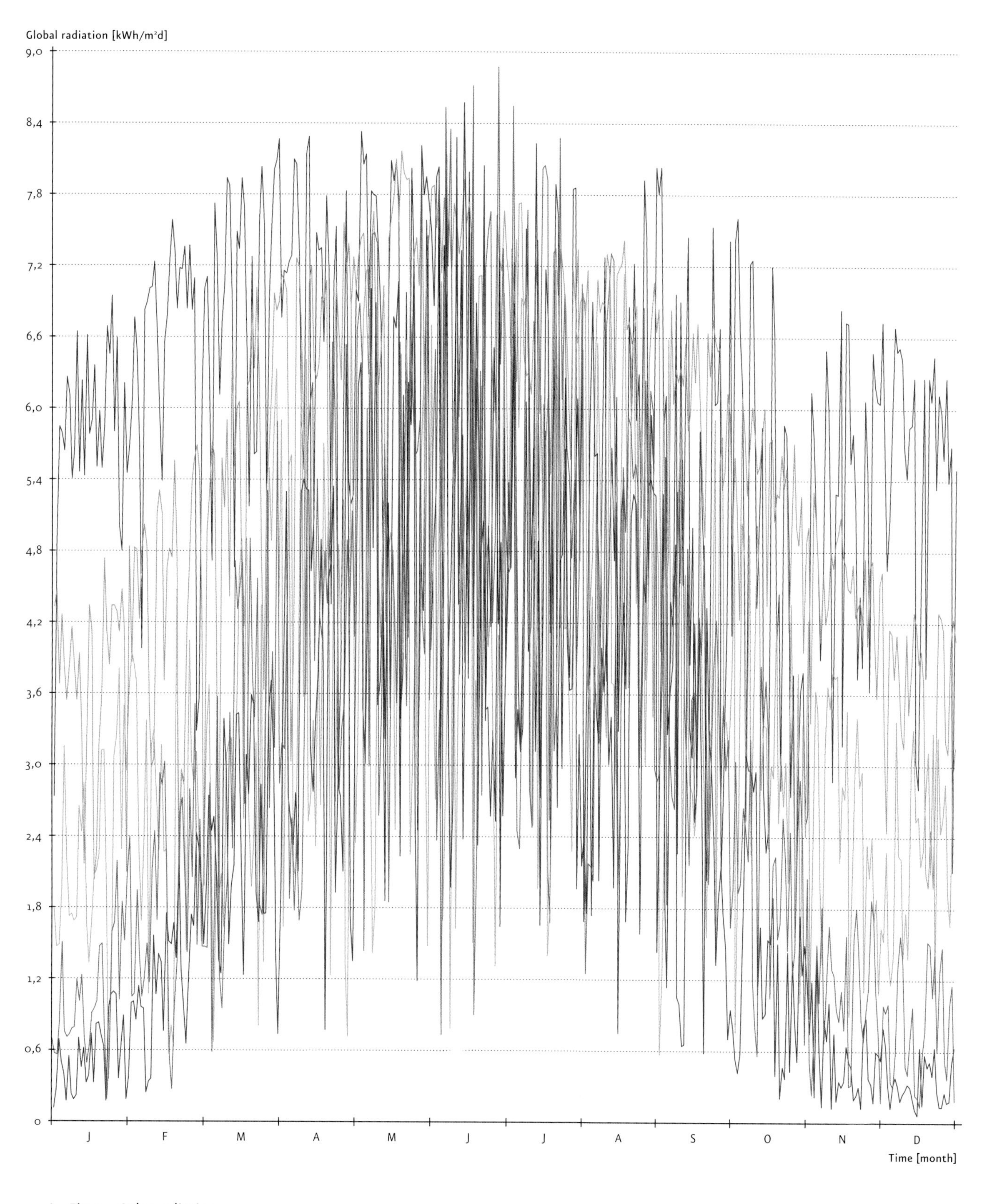

Fig. 1.3 Solar radiation

Typical changes in radiation energy levels in kWh/m²d over the course of a year in the cool (Moscow) and temperate (Munich) climate zones, the subtropics (Shanghai), the tropics (Bangalore), and the desert area in proximity to the sea (Dubai)

- Cool climate zone (Moscow)
- Temperate climate zone (Munich)
- Subtropics (Shanghai)
- Tropics (Bangalore)
- Desert coastal climate (Dubai)

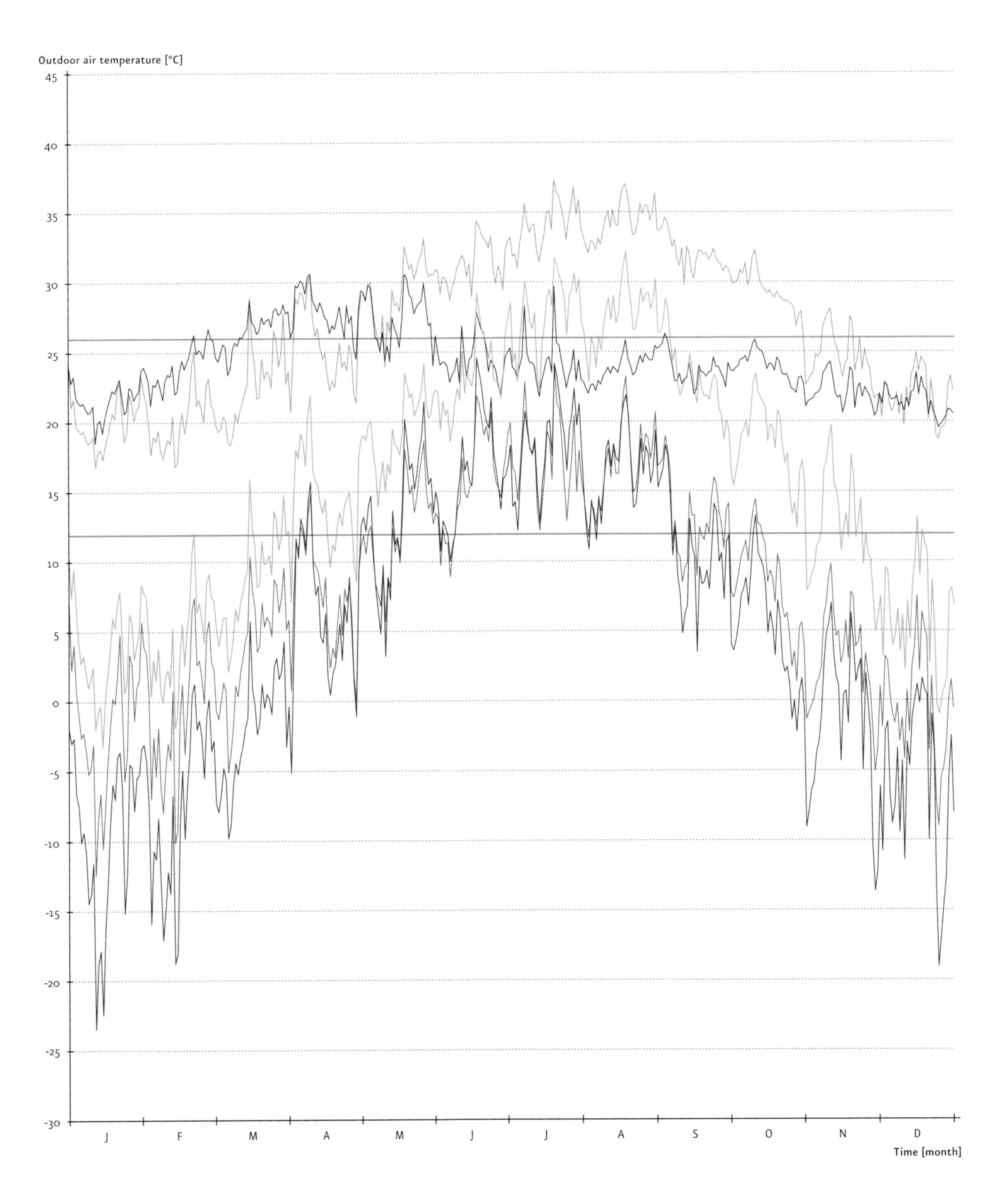

Fig. 1.4 Temperature

Typical changes in average daily outdoor temperature readings in °C over the course of a year in the cool (Moscow) and temperate (Munich) climate zones, the subtropics (Shanghai), the tropics (Bangalore), and the desert area in proximity to the sea (Dubai) Cooling may be required from 26 °C. Below 12 °C a heating system should be integrated.

- Cool climate zone (Moscow)
- Temperate climate zone (Munich)
- Subtropics (Shanghai)
- Tropics (Bangalore)
- Desert coastal climate (Dubai)

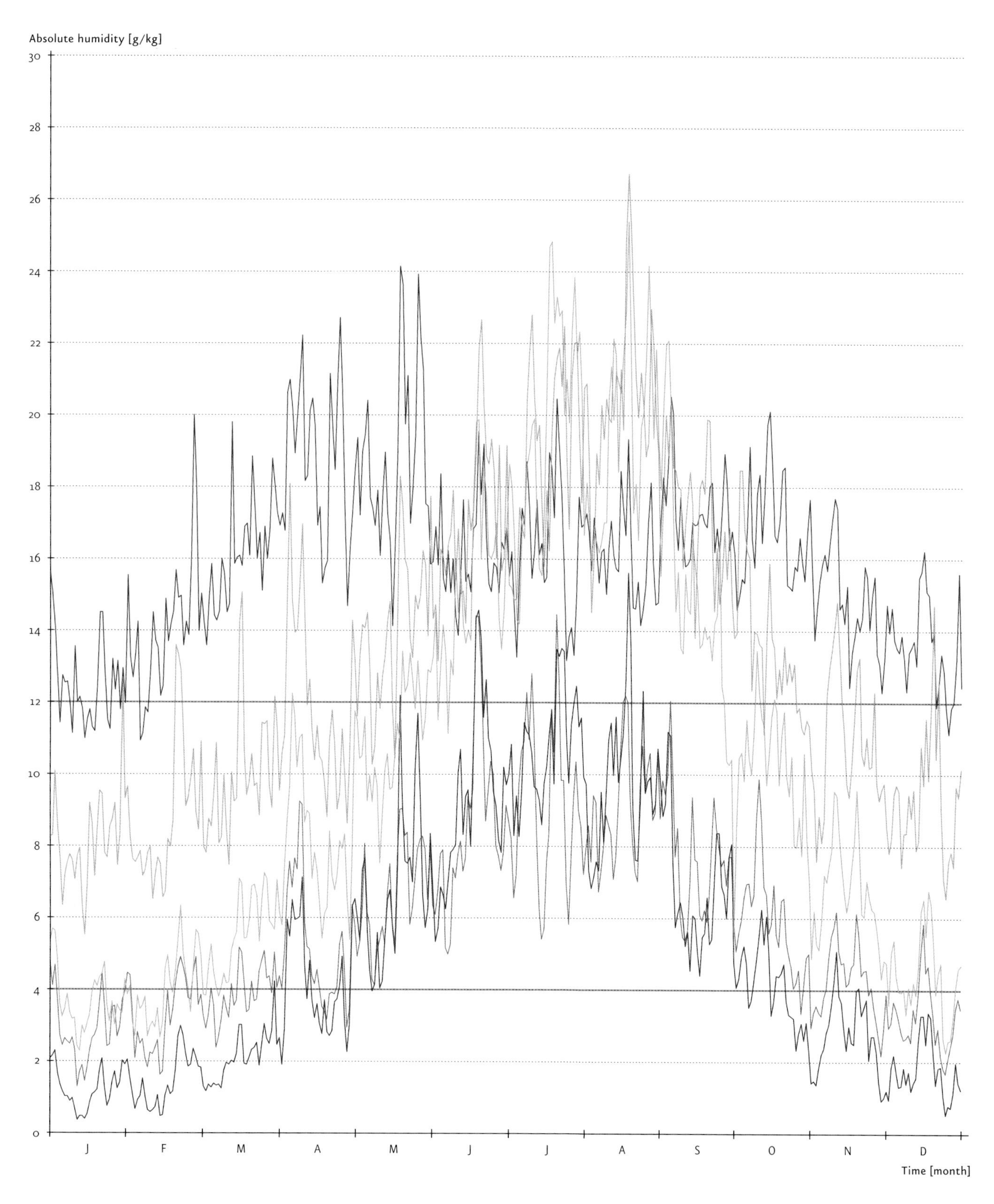

Fig. 1.5 Air humidity

Typical changes in absolute air humidity in g/kg over the course of a year in the cool (Moscow) and temperate (Munich) climate zones, the subtropics (Shanghai), the tropics (Bangalore), and the desert area in proximity to the sea (Dubai). According to ASHRAE-55, a comfortable level for daily absolute air humidity readings is defined as being no higher than 12 g/kg. Above this value, dehumidifiers must be provided. There is no lower limit, but absolute air humidity should be no lower than 4 g/kg.

- Cool climate zone (Moscow)
- Temperate climate zone (Munich)
- Subtropics (Shanghai)
- Tropics (Bangalore)
- Desert coastal climate (Dubai)

Climate Factors

Climate factors are processes and situations that produce, maintain or alter a climate. These include the latitude, the distribution of land and sea, the local and trans-regional wind systems and the altitude of a location. Terms such as "equatorial", "Mediterranean" and "polar" are used to describe the significant features of typical regional climates. The sun is the main motor that drives the climate. It determines daily and seasonal changes, and the intensity of solar radiation incidence is the major factor responsible for creating the Earth's climate zones.

Latitude

↙ **position of the sun** p. 142

A location's geographical position determines the ↙ position of the sun, the sun's course across the sky and the hours of sunshine it experiences (Fig. 1.6). The Earth's axis is inclined by just over 23.5°, meaning that at different times of year the southern hemisphere or the northern hemisphere is closer to the sun. The hemisphere closer to the sun experiences summer due to the higher incidence of solar radiation. The other hemisphere receives less radiation due to the shallow angle of radiation incidence and the fact that the radiation has to travel through a greater amount of the atmosphere. In the equator area, seasonal differences are negligible; they become more pronounced as one moves toward the poles. In the northern hemisphere, the sun travels across the southern half of the sky; in the southern hemisphere, it travels across the northern half of the sky. The Earth travels around the sun on an elliptical rather than a circular course, which means that its proximity to the sun changes over the course of a year. The earth is closest to the sun during the northern hemisphere's winter, and furthest from the sun during the northern hemisphere's summer. This is the reason why the northern hemisphere is less subject to seasonal changes in temperature than the southern hemisphere. The Earth's zone of highest sun radiation incidence migrates between the tropics over the course of a year. On the equator, the sun is at its zenith on 21 March and 21 September. On 21 June, the sun reaches its maximum height of 23.5° N on the Tropic of Cancer, and on 21 December, it reaches its maximum height of 23.5° S on the Tropic of Capricorn. As the sun gains height, the UV radiation level rises due to the reduction in the intervening atmosphere.

Differences in temperature over the course of a year depend primarily on geographical latitude. Maximum temperatures change throughout the year as the position of the sun changes. However, maximum temperature is not reached at the height of a hemisphere's summer (in June or December), although this is the time of maximum solar radiation. The soil, air and water need time to heat up, meaning that maximum temperature is reached one to four months later. Generally, maximum and minimum temperature values lie closer together in the southern hemisphere, because its large expanses of ocean have a balancing effect.

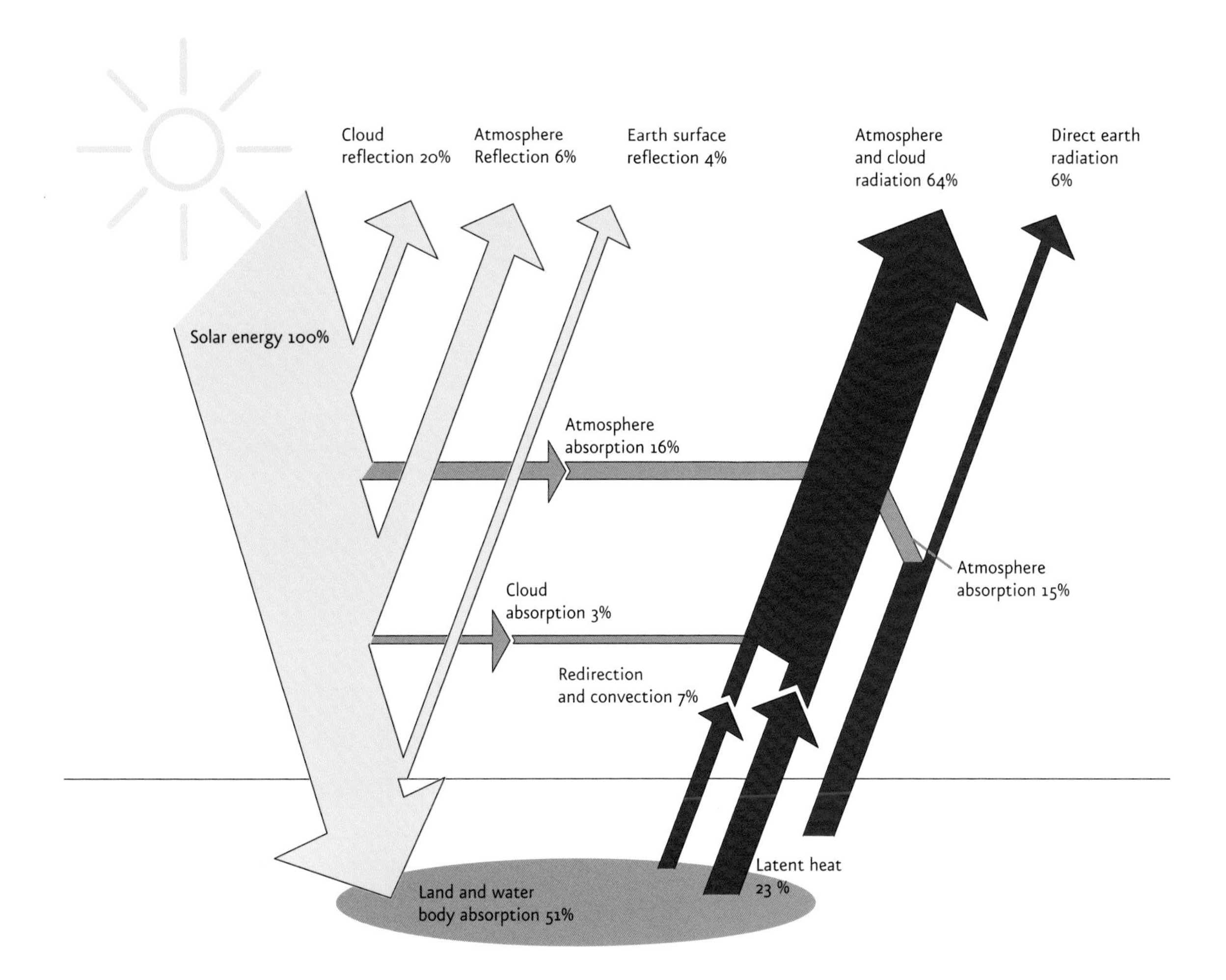

Fig. 1.6 The Earth's radiation balance

Solar radiation (yellow) warms the Earth's atmosphere and the Earth's surface, and is released as heat radiation (red). Part of the heat radiation is transmitted back to Earth by gases in the atmosphere, turning the atmosphere into a sort of natural greenhouse (according to NASA).

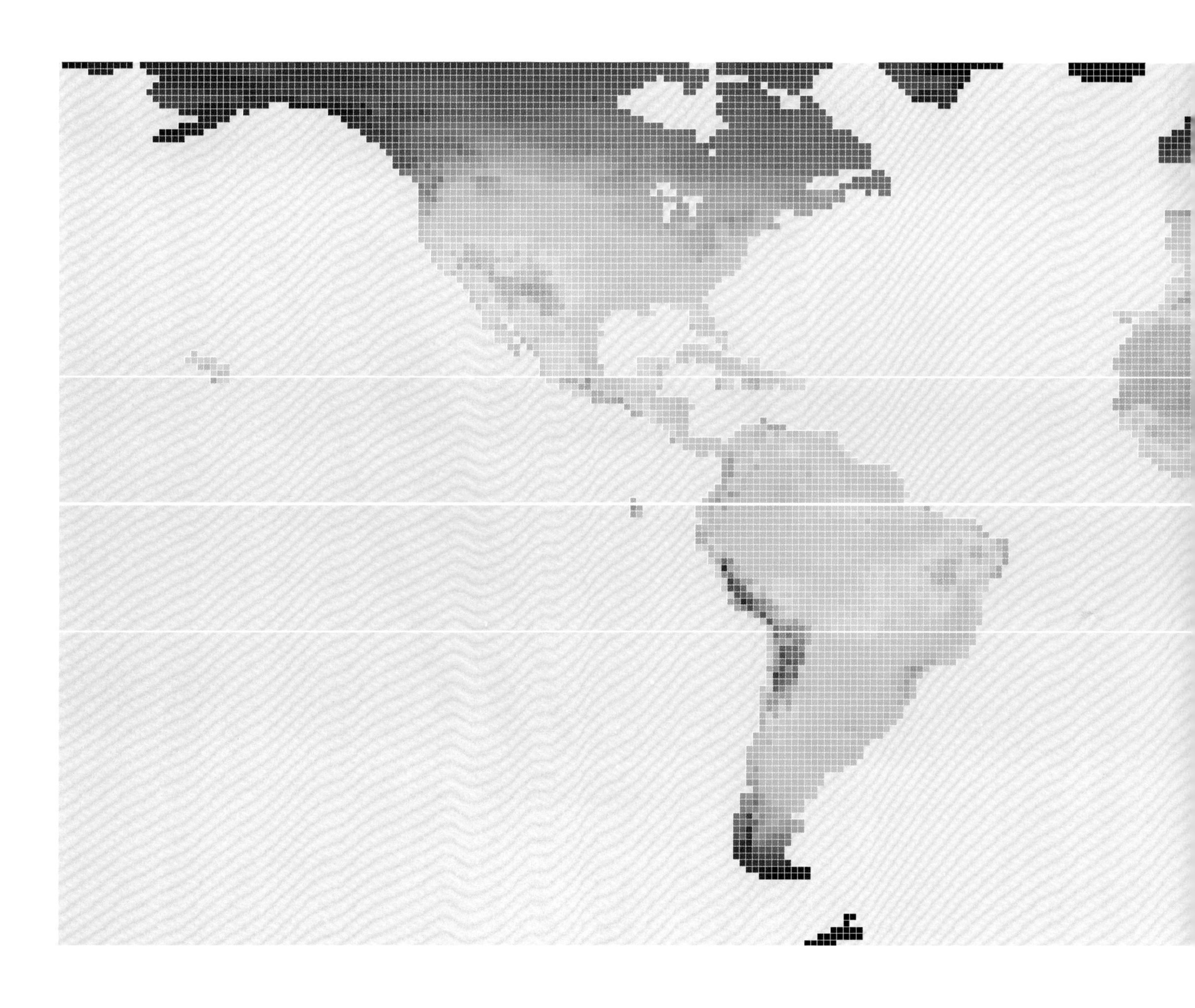

Fig. 1.7 Annual total global radiation relative to the horizontal

As one moves further away from the equator, the solar radiation's angle of incidence gets smaller and summer days get longer. The maximum daily solar radiation level received by the Earth's surface is found at the 30th and 45th parallels. Dry and hot regions receive the highest annual radiation levels due to their lack of cloud cover.

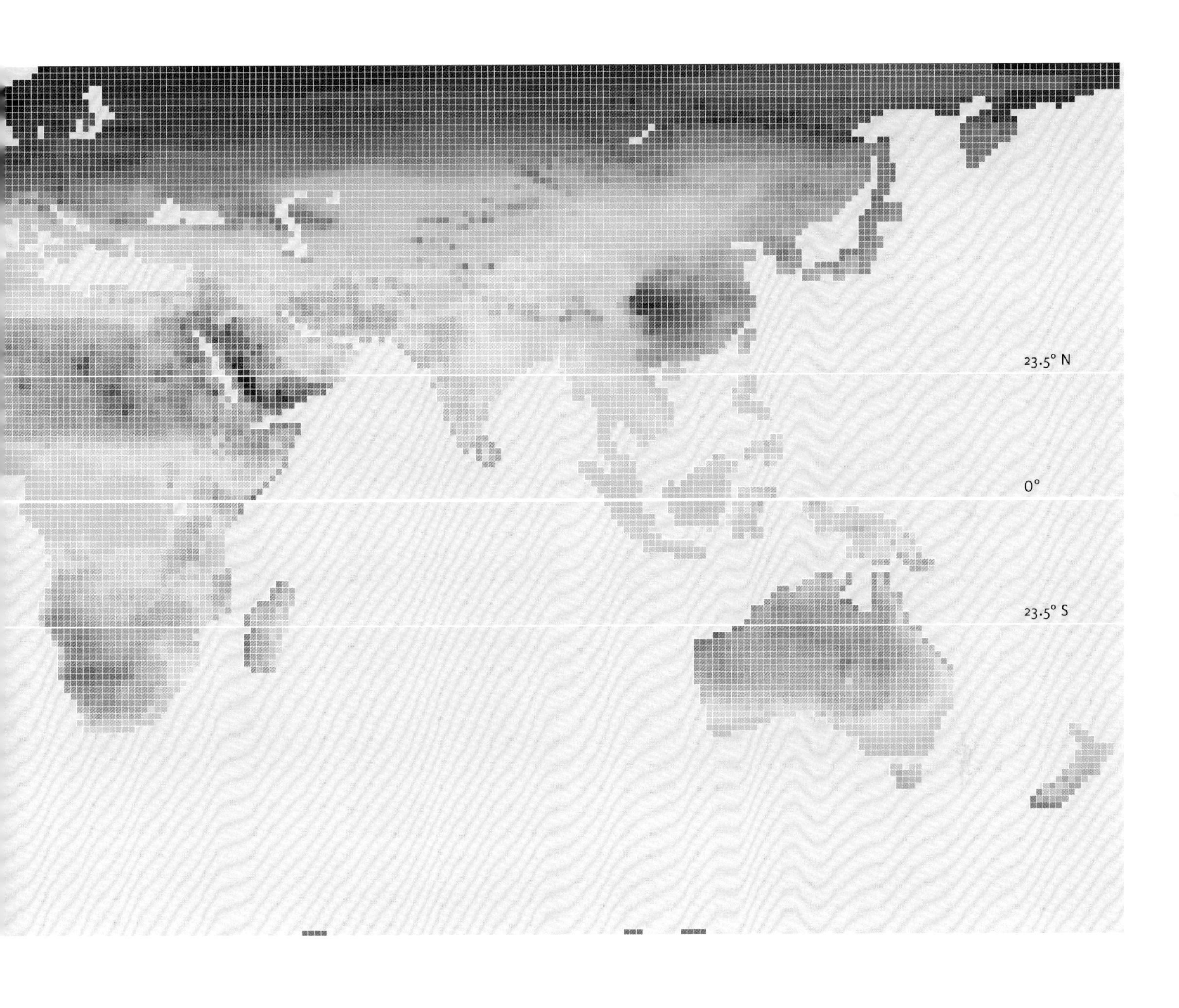

<700 <1,100 <1,500 <1,900 <2,300 ≥2,700 Energy radiation [kWh/m^2a]

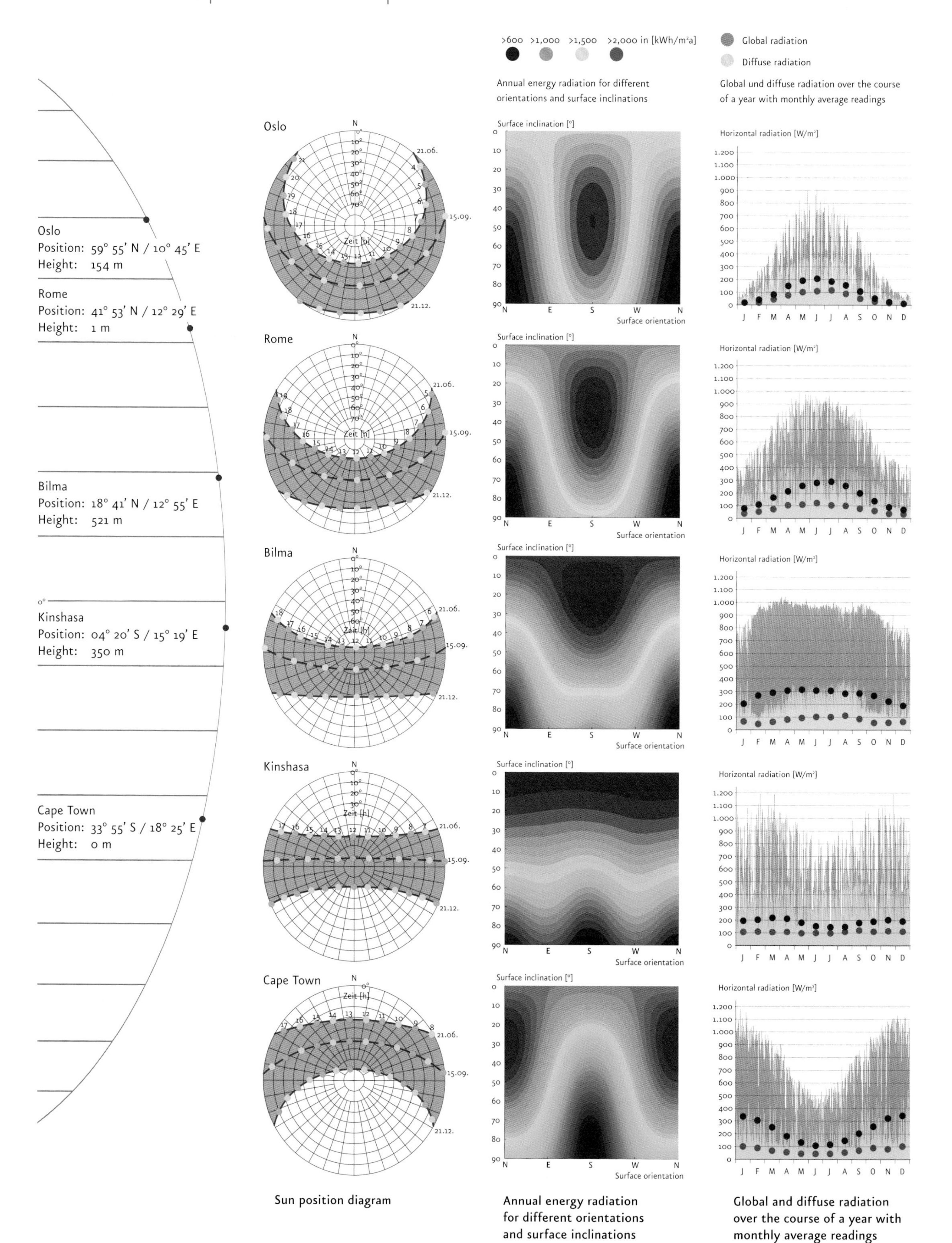

Sun position diagram

Annual energy radiation for different orientations and surface inclinations

Global and diffuse radiation over the course of a year with monthly average readings

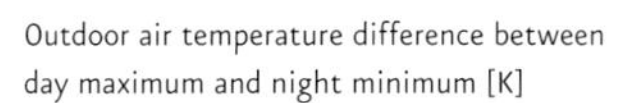

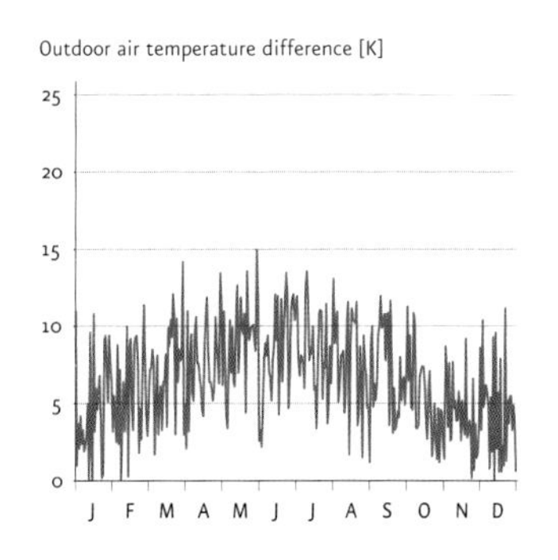

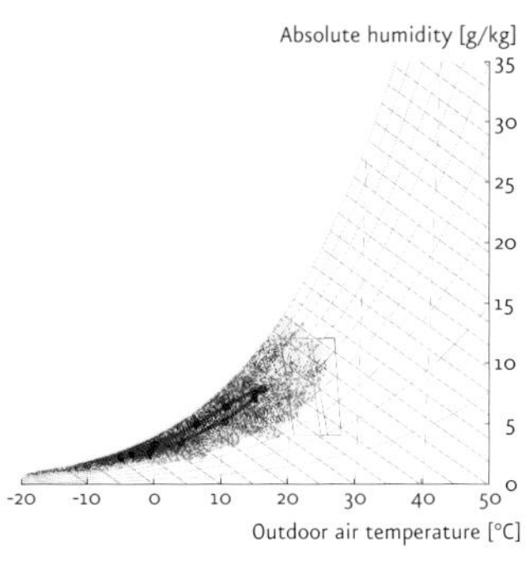

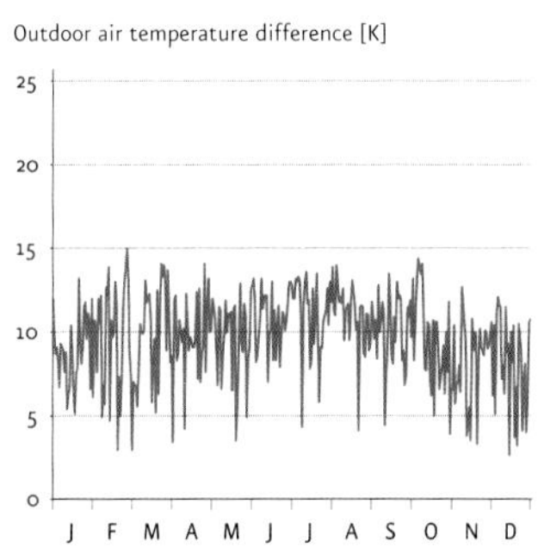

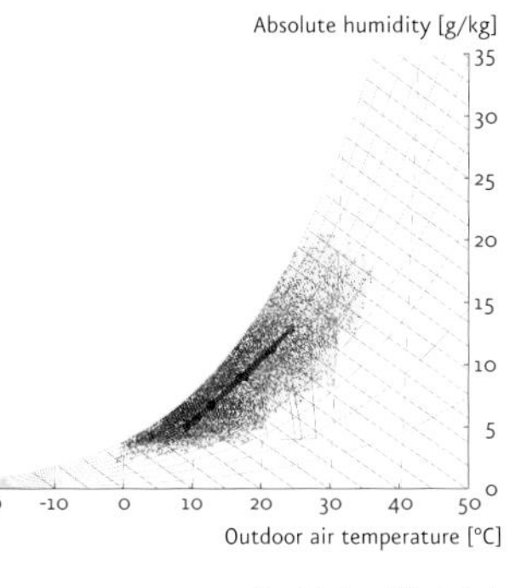

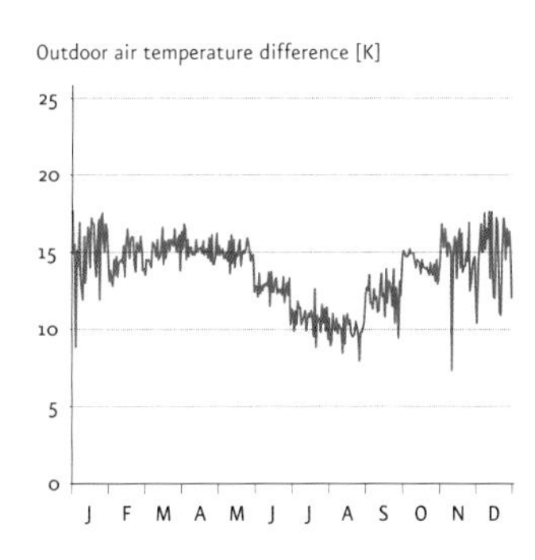

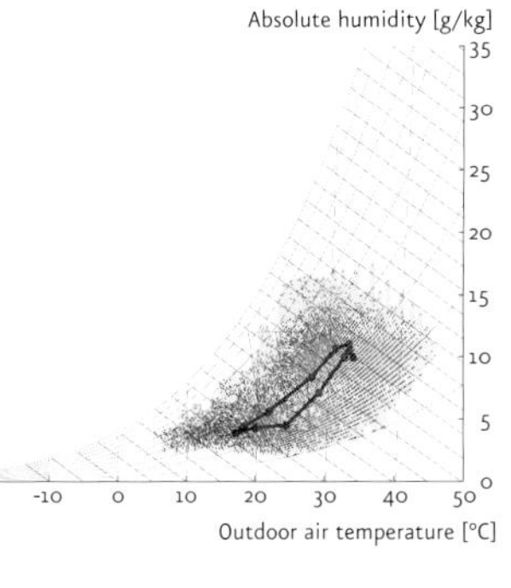

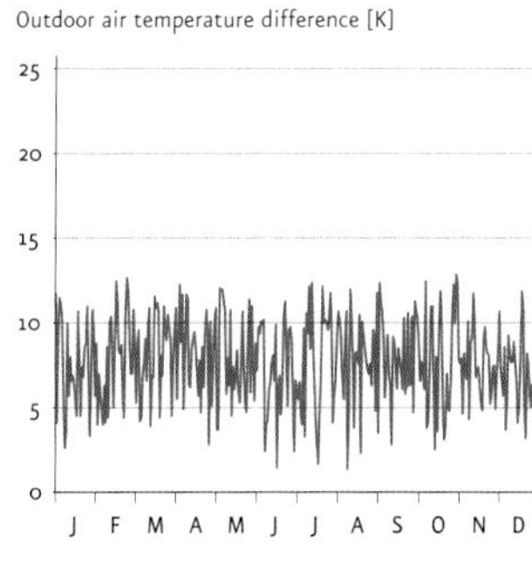

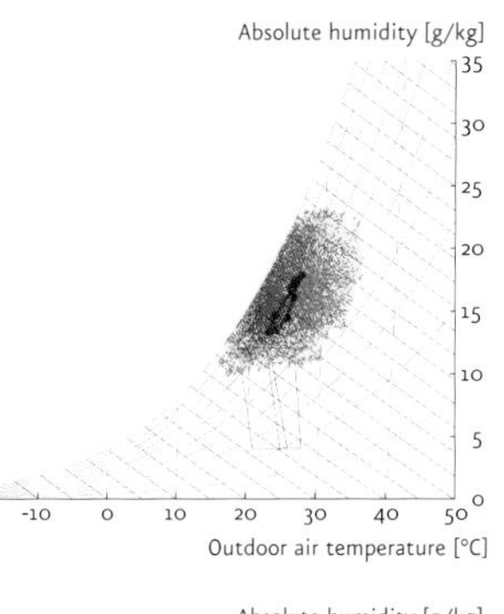

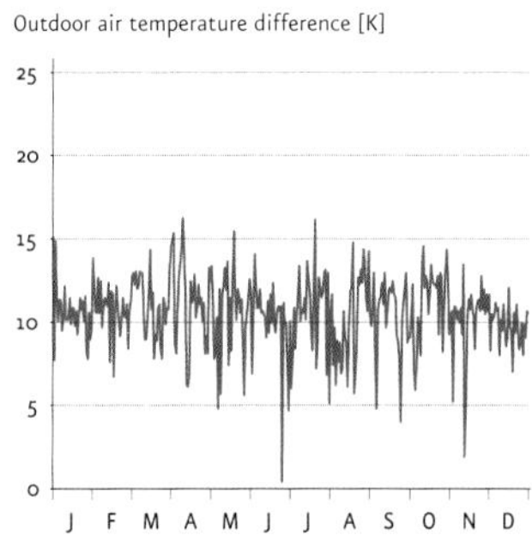

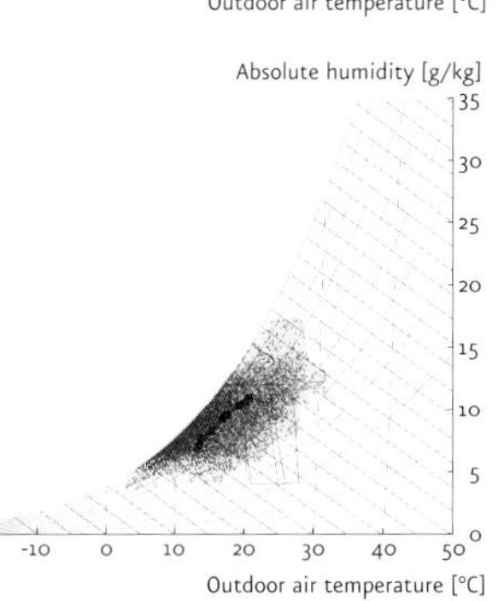

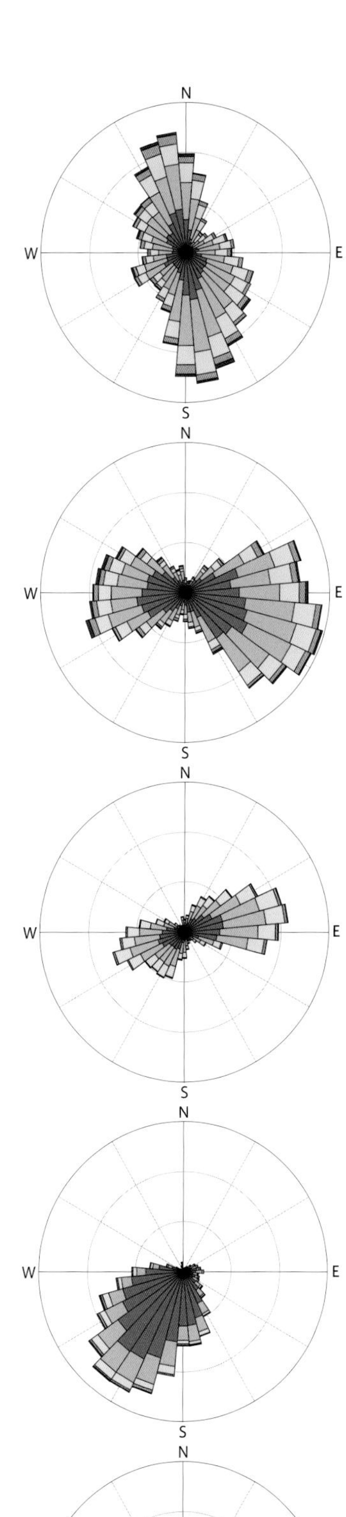

Outdoor air temperature difference

Psychrometric chart

Compass dial

Fig. 1.8 The influence of latitude

These five cities experience fundamentally different climatic conditions due to their differing geographical latitudes. In the northern hemisphere, the sun travels across the southern part of the sky from east to west, and in the southern hemisphere it travels across the northern part of the sky from east to west (column 1). The different latitudes of each location mean that their maximum sun heights and day lengths vary significantly throughout the year.

In Oslo, the climate changes significantly with the season. Oslo has a maximum of almost 19 hours of daylight in summer and about 5 hours in winter. In summer, the height of the sun varies between 5° and 55°. The closer a location is to the equator, the less difference there is between the seasons. In Kinshasa, for instance (directly on the equator), day lengths do not vary by more than one hour, and the height of the sun varies by only 10°.

The shallow angle of incidence in equatorial locations optimises the yield of solar energy. Orientation plays a secondary role. As one moves towards the North Pole, an increasingly steep angle of south orientation becomes optimal, and the same is true of a north alignment in the southern hemisphere (section 2).

The level of global and direct radiation is greatest in the tropics due to the low levels of cloud cover. At the equator, the precipitation levels can clearly be seen from the level of diffuse radiation and the gaps in the direct radiation. The fact that the sun is at zenithal position in Kinshasa in winter is shown by the highest radiation values occurring at this time (section 3).

The radiation level also determines the temperature and humidity conditions at any given location. Temperatures rise as one approaches the tropics. The equator, with its high precipitation levels and cloud cover, does not achieve the same maximum values as the dry deserts, while its annual temperature variation is lowest (section 5). The difference between day and night temperatures is also greatest in the deserts because of the high radiation during the day and the high heat loss due to a lack of cloud cover at night (section 4).

In Oslo, the need is for heat and humidity, whereas in Bilma the need is for coolness and humidity (with night ventilation as one option). In Kinshasa, the need is for coolness and a lack of humidity. The location with the most optimal climate is Cape Town, followed by Rome.

Wind direction and strength depend on geographical position and proximity to seas and mountains. This means that detailed observation is required.

Proximity to the ocean and continentality

More than 70% of the Earth's surface is covered by ocean. The average temperature of seawater is 3.8 °C. The climates of two locations at the same latitude can be very different depending on their relative distances from the sea, mainly due to the high specific heat capacity of water relative to land. This means that the air temperature at ground level fluctuates less where a large body of water is present – what is known as a maritime climate. In the centre of large continents, particularly at high geographical latitudes, the temperature fluctuations over the course of a year are very high. There is also a low level of condensation in continental situations, which lowers the air humidity.

The reflection capacity of surfaces – the *albedo* – is an important factor for the local climate. The higher the albedo, the more energy is reflected. On the continents, this value lies somewhere between 0 and 30%. Sand has a particularly high albedo value, with the result that continental desert areas have high radiation conditions with major fluctuations in temperature.

Due to the different thermal properties of land and water, the temperature over land changes significantly over the course of a day. Over water, the temperature remains almost constant throughout the day. Because of its much higher specific heat capacity, the sea warms up much more slowly than the land, but also stores the heat for longer. The warm air over the land is lighter than the cold air over the sea, causing it to expand and to rise, creating an area of low air pressure and causing the colder air above the sea to flow in over the land. The air cools down more quickly than the water during the night, thereby completing the circle: air rises above the water and sinks over the land, creating a reverse flow from over the land to over the water. The effects of the land/sea wind circulation can be felt many kilometres from the coast. As the sea wind moves inland, its direction is changed by the effect of the Coriolis force, which makes it blow perpendicular to the coast.

In warm and hot regions, the wind systems on the coast can be used to ventilate street space and buildings.

Altitude

Because of their expanse and height, mountains often act as a climatic barrier. Clouds form to windward of a mountain, resulting in precipitation that is known as orographic rainfall. For this reason, it is generally drier in their lee. The frequency of high ↘ wind speeds increases with altitude, and the ↘ solar radiation is also higher because the water vapour in the atmosphere decreases and cloudy weather is rarer. The temperature differences between day and night are greater.

↘
wind speed
p. 142

global radiation
p. 142

Air always changes temperature as it rises or falls, because, like any gas, it heats up under pressure and cools down when the pressure on it is released. As dry air rises from the Earth's surface into the higher, thinner air layers, it cools down by approximately 1 K per 100 m due to the lowering of air pressure. As air sinks, its temperature rises as the weight of the atmosphere exerts more pressure on it.

These thermal conditions create a local wind system, a cycle of alternating slope winds and mountain and valley winds that blow parallel to the valley. The mountain and valley winds change over the course of a day. During the morning, the east slopes are warmed by the sun, creating upslope winds. As the morning advances, this situation is changed by the much greater wind speed of the valley wind, which is created by the mountains and the foothills heating up at different rates. Mountain air cools down more quickly during the night, and streams towards the valley, closing the circle. In the hours before morning, both the mountain wind and the downslope wind blow outwards toward the valley, causing the impure valley air to be exchanged for clean mountain air, which has a lower particle content.

When choosing a location, the mountain climate should be assessed in detail. Locations at a high altitude have a greater ↘ thermal insulation requirement, while offering a high solar energy yield. Streams of cold air help to ventilate cities and to disperse emissions. A lack of wind in geographical basin locations can lead to a build-up of emissions. In summer, the heat cannot escape from such locations, leading to high temperatures, and in winter, fog and masses of cold air often form.

↘
thermal insulation
p. 146

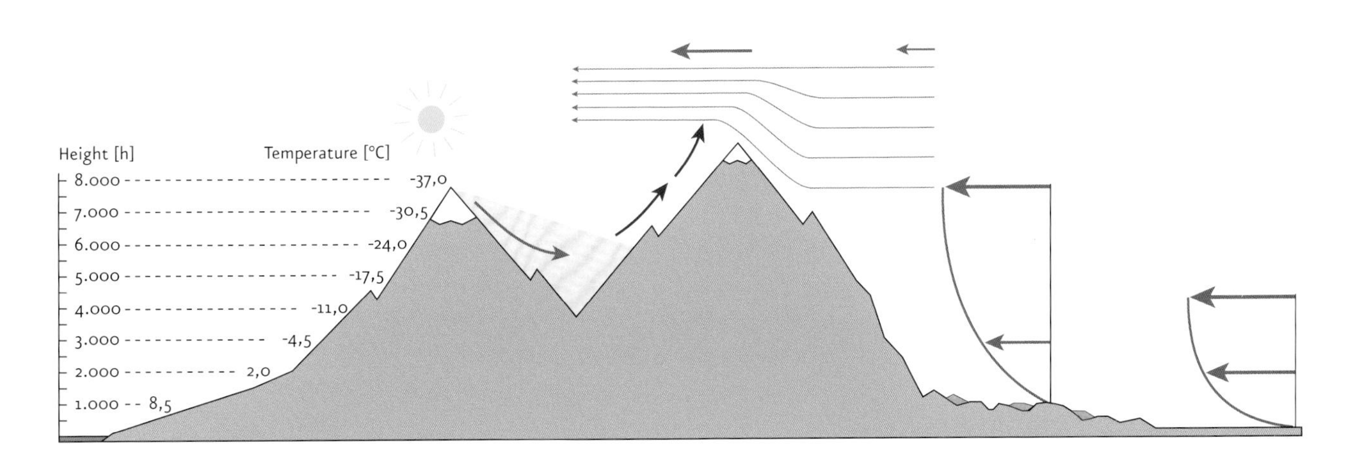

Fig. 1.9 Influence of altitude on the temperature and the wind system

On average, the air temperature decreases by approximately 10 K with every 1,000 m of altitude. In the morning, the east sides of the valleys receive more sunshine. This can create cold fall winds on the west slopes and warm, rising air masses on the east slopes. Wind speed can increase significantly on mountain peaks and hilltops and along valleys or corridors. Increased wind speeds can also appear over plains or the ocean due to the lack of surface features.

City climate

The climate in cities is different due to the impact of development. The city climate is determined by a mixture of natural and anthropogenic factors, with the result that there is no single, unified urban climate. Natural factors include geographical position, terrain, altitude and any natural, undeveloped areas. Anthropogenic factors include the nature and density of the city's development, the heat storage capacity of building components and the degree of surface sealing, and industrial, household and traffic emissions. A city's radiation and energy balance is different from that of the surrounding area, as are its temperature, humidity and precipitation levels. The wind also leads to differences in air quality that depend on the amount of air pollutants being released and the extent to which they are being thinned or dispersed. A city also affects the regional climate beyond its own boundaries.

A location's radiation balance depends on the sun's zenithal position and the opacity of the atmosphere. The gases and dirt and dust particles do not reach the higher atmosphere – they lie in a pall over the inner cities. Overall, a city's radiation level is lower than that of the surrounding country.

The inflow and outflow of air created by the wind determines a city's air quality. In calm weather, a city's higher temperature relative to the surrounding terrain and its heat islands can create a regional wind system. *Flurwinde* ("country breezes") are created by the warm air rising from cities and by the compression of the cooler rural air. The surface is rougher in developed areas than in undeveloped areas, meaning that ↙ wind speeds are lower on average in cities than in open country. Together with more frequent calm conditions, this produces less air exchange. When the wind is blowing in a particular direction, lee vortices can form to one side of buildings, creating strong gusts. Where there are gaps in the development or long, straight streets, jet effects may appear, which can significantly increase wind speed over a limited area and for a limited space of time. High-rise buildings that project high above the city's rooftops may divert stronger winds from higher atmospheric levels, causing powerful gusts and turbulence at ground level.

↙ **wind speed** p. 142

↙ Relative air humidity is lower in cities due to higher temperatures and limited evaporation. Fog is more infrequent during the summer months, and there may be more cloud formation in winter. Aerosols, gases and dust may be emitted in higher concentrations within cities. The condensation nuclei in the air lead to more cloud cover and precipitation.

↙ **relative air humidity** p. 142

Annual and daily air temperature measurements are higher in a city than in the surrounding area. This typically urban phenomenon is described as a heat island. The degree of heating is determined by the city's climate zone, terrain position, proximity to the coast, development density and construction type, and the state of technological development. Urban heat islands also depend to some degree on population numbers. The larger surface of the developments absorbs solar radiation, causing buildings to heat up. Sealed surfaces transmit more heat into the subsoil than natural ground surfaces (which act as an insulation layer, preventing the ground from heating up). Soil sealing also reduces the uptake of latent condensation energy by the atmosphere. In a mechanism similar to the greenhouse effect, the reflection of long-wave radiation is limited by the high particle concentration in city air. This results in warming processes outweighing cooling processes, so that cities consistently become warmer. The intensity of a heat island changes throughout the day and throughout the year. The temperature difference between a city and the surrounding area may be twice as high during a cold winter as it is during the summer. This is mainly due to building heating systems.

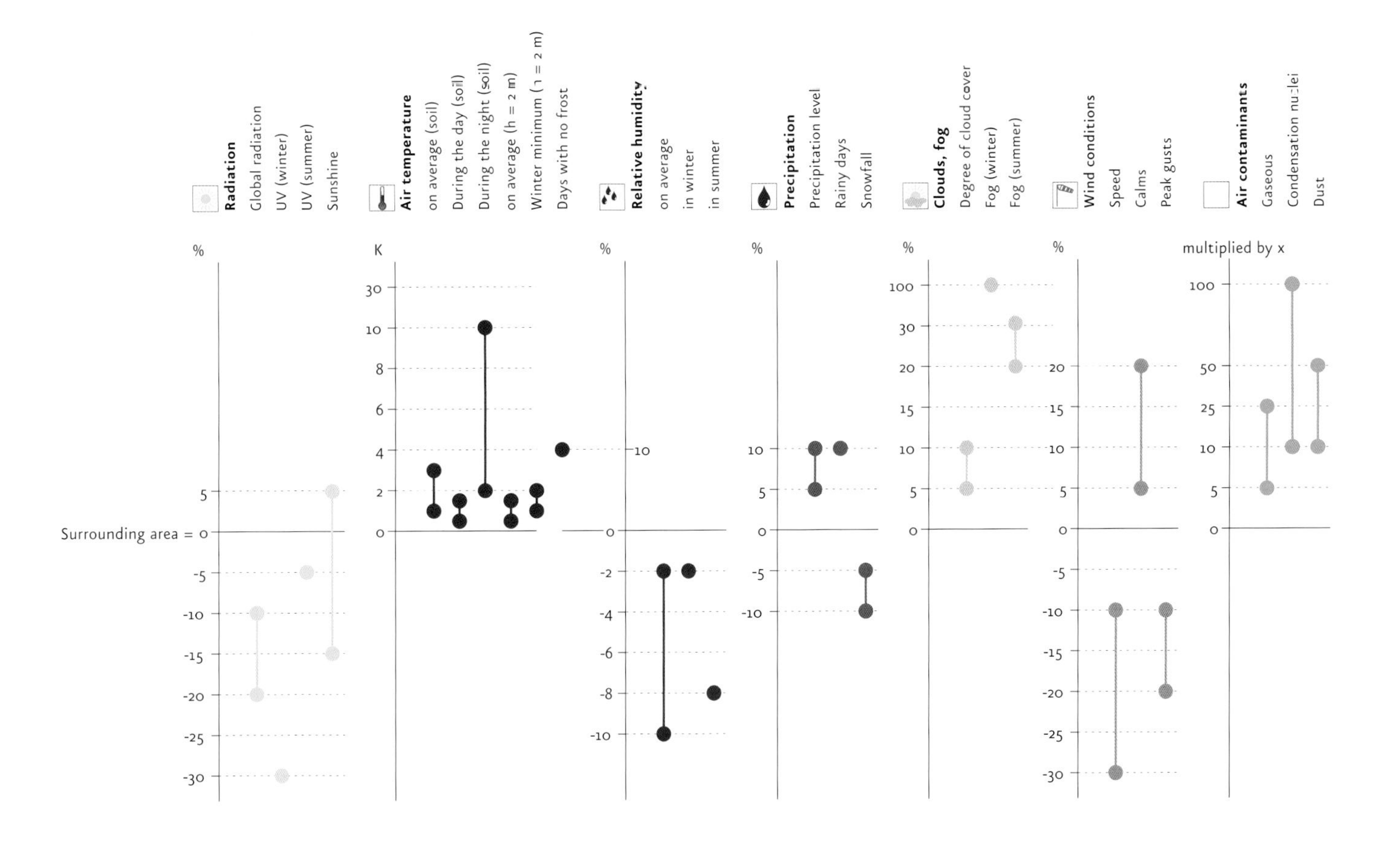

Fig. 1.10 Climatic differences between a city and the surrounding area
Scales show the differences between city and surrounding area in terms of radiation, temperature, moisture, precipitation, cloud cover, wind and pollution.

Climate Zones

Key values for room conditioning include the absolute air humidity and the temperature. Considering these construction-specific climate parameters in combination allows us to understand how the climate affects room conditioning needs. This involves displaying the values for the outdoor air temperature and the absolute humidity for the 8,760 hours of a year in a ↙ psychrometric chart. This provides an outline of a location's climate that shows whether heating or cooling, humidifying or dehumidifying is required and whether or not we are dealing with a temperate climate which places no major demands on building climate systems; and whether a comfortable room climate can be achieved using passive measures. ASHRAE-55 – an international standard – is used to define a comfort area for low wind speeds.

↙
psychrometric chart
p. 142

The world atlas (Fig. 1.12, see page 34f.) shows the standardised climate zone divisions as relevant to building climatology systems, indicating geographic factors such as latitude, altitude and proximity to the ocean. By combining these with the ↙ heating and cooling degree days and the humidifying and dehumidifying gram days, we can calculate to what extent passive measures will be sufficient, and whether active cooling or heating will be necessary to keep the room climate comfortable all year round (Fig. 1.13).

Cool climate

This climate is characterised by highly differentiated seasons. Four climate subtypes with different characteristics can be identified. They are mainly to be found in the northern hemisphere. Degree of continentality and latitude are the main causes of climatic differences within this zone.

This climate is characterised by cold winters and warm or hot summers. The ↙ heating and humidifying energy demand during the winter is the major demand. The higher, the more northerly and the more continental the location is, the greater these demands are. The lower ↙ outdoor air temperatures largely restrict the ↙ natural ventilation in winter. In the summer months, most of the ventilation can be provided by windows, and night ventilation is also possible. The lower cooling energy demand can easily be met by renewable cooling sources. For the more southerly areas close to the ocean, cooling and dehumidifying energy demand are also relevant, as the high humidity levels can restrict natural ventilation. In mountain areas, heating and humidifying is a significant element of room climate conditioning. The level required varies with altitude and latitude. Windows can be used for ventilation at times.

↙
heating energy demand
p. 144

outdoor air temperatures
p. 142

natural ventilation
p. 146

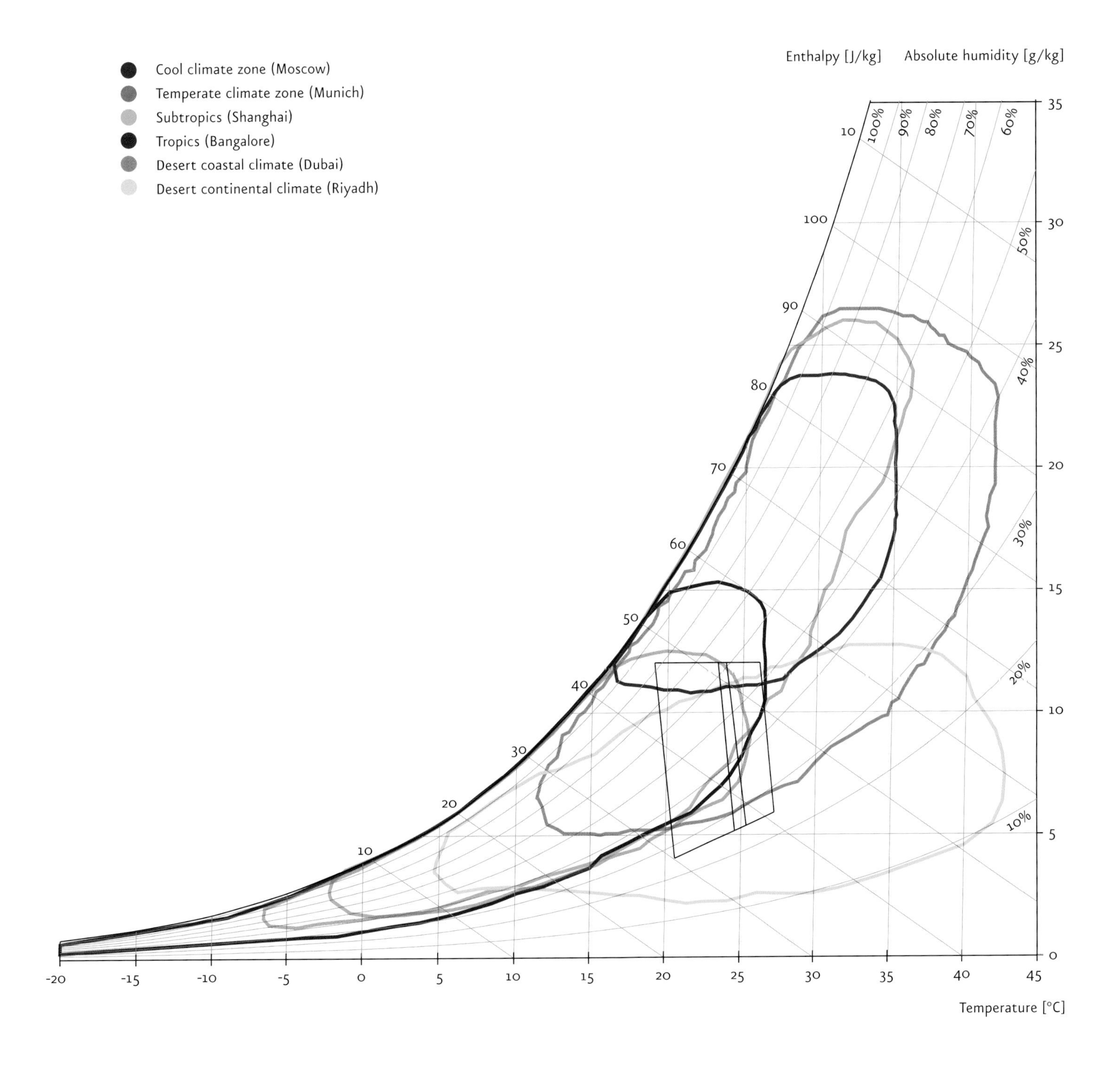

Fig. 1.11 Climate zones for building climate systems and room conditioning, shown in psychrometric chart format

Showing the overall trend given by 8,760 hourly average values for outdoor air temperature and absolute humidity in the tropics and subtropics, deserts in proximity to the ocean and inland and for the temperate and cool climate zones.

Temperate climate

Locations that are representative of this climate are characterised by seasons with transitional periods and without extreme values in terms of outdoor air temperatures and air density. Four climate subtypes with different characteristics can be identified. Their geographical latitude, proximity to the sea and altitude determine climate differences in equal measure.

↙ **heating energy demand** p. 144

natural ventilation p. 146

This climate is characterised by warm summers and cold or cool winters. The critical factor is the ↙ heating energy demand. The cooling energy demand can easily be met by passive measures such as night cooling. The cooling and dehumidifying energy demand are very low. Ventilation can be comfortably provided by windows for almost the whole year round, with only the outdoor air temperature in winter restricting ↙ natural ventilation. There is no cooling energy demand in northerly locations in summer. Proximity to the sea reduces the heating energy demand and the humidifying energy demand in winter.

The subtropics

This climate is characterised by short transitional periods between the seasons. Five climate subtypes with different characteristics can be identified. They lie mainly between the 25° and 45° northerly and southerly latitudes. Distance from the sea and geographical latitude are the main causes for these climatic differences. Altitude is always an important factor.

↙ **dew point temperature** p. 142

This climate is characterised by hot and humid or warm summers, and wet and cold or cool winters. The cooling energy demand and the dehumidifying energy demand are the major factors during the summer, particularly in areas in the northern hemisphere and on the east coasts of open oceans. The frequently high outdoor air temperatures and the high absolute humidity restrict window ventilation. Surface cooling systems are affected by ↙ dew point issues. Window ventilation is possible during transitional times, particularly in high latitudes. In areas outside the tropics, the heating energy demand is low during the winter, and the humidifying energy demand is almost non-existent. The extent of the energy demand cannot be established with any certainty simply by looking at the location.

The tropics

This zone is characterised by outdoor air temperature and absolute humidity values that remain almost constant. However, five climate subtypes with different characteristics can be identified. Proximity to the equator and altitude are the main reasons for these climatic differences. The cooling energy demand and the dehumidifying energy demand are the critical factors for a comfortable room climate.

This climate is characterised by high outdoor air temperatures combined with high absolute humidity throughout the year. The cooling energy demand and the dehumidifying energy demand are the critical factors for a comfortable room climate. The lower and closer to the equator a location is, the higher these will be. The high absolute humidity values restrict the effectiveness of natural ventilation. Surface cooling systems are affected by dew point issues. At higher elevations or on the periphery of the tropics, ↘ window ventilation is effective for more of the time.
In this situation, night ventilation should be considered. The outdoor climate and the soil offer very limited cooling possibilities. In mountain situations above 2,000 m, the cooling energy demand and the dehumidifying energy demand are significantly reduced. At extreme altitudes, the humidifying energy demand and, especially, the heating energy demand increases dramatically.

↘
natural ventilation
p. 146

Deserts

This climate is characterised by extremely high outdoor air temperatures combined with very high or very low absolute air humidity. Five climate subtypes with different characteristics can be identified. Aside from latitude and altitude, proximity to the ocean is the main reason for these climatic differences. In desert areas that are near to the sea, buildings have to be cooled and dehumidified almost all year round. In continental desert areas, no ↙ dehumidifying is required.

What all desert areas have in common is that they experience hardly any rainfall all year round. There are, however, significant differences between different desert locations that affect building climate systems. In desert areas that are near to the sea, buildings have to be cooled and dehumidified almost all year round. Evaporation cooling is impossible, although window ventilation and ↘ night cooling are possible in the winter. The ↘ cooling energy demand is the major factor in all deserts, including tropical coastal deserts, although the dehumidifying energy demand decreases significantly in such locations. This increases the percentage of the day and night during which natural ventilation is possible.

↘
night ventilation
p. 152

cooling energy demand
p. 144

In continental desert areas, no dehumidifying is required. Evaporation cooling and night cooling are easily practicable. Within the tropics, considerable cooling and occasionally a small degree of heating is needed. In locations outside the tropics, the cooling energy demand reduces with increased altitude, while the heating and the humidifying energy demands increase significantly with altitude.

40°–60°, north, with a high degree of continentality

30°–45°, north, close to the sea

around 60°, north, coast

from approx. 30°, north, from 1,000 m

Fig. 1.12 Building specific climate classification types

- 40°–50°, north, continental, up to 500 m
- 35°–40°, north, continental, up to 1,000 m
- 45°–55°, north, continental, up to 500 m
- 50°–60°, north, coast
- 20°–25°, north, east coast
- 30°–35°, north, east coast
- 25°–40°, coast
- 30°–45°, coast
- 20°–30°, coast
- approx. 30°, close to the sea, 0–500m
- approx. 25°, continental, 500–800m
- 30°–35°, 500 up to 1,300m
- from 35°, north, 500 up to 2,000m
- 0°–15°, up to 150 m
- 0°–20°, up to 800 m
- 0°–15°, up to 2,000 m
- from 20°, from 150 m
- 0°–20°, from 2,000 m

City	Latitude [°]	Longitude [°]	Height above sea level [m]	Average temperature [°C]	Maximum temperature [°C]	Minimum temperature [°C]	Max. daily variation [K]
Moscow RU	55.750	37.700	152	5.0	30.6	-25.5	17.9
Beijing CN	39.930	116.400	30	11.8	36.4	-14.3	15.1
Helsinki FI	60.220	25.000	12	4.7	27.1	-24.8	16.2
Lhasa CN	29.653	91.119	3.650	7.5	25.5	-12.9	18.7
Budapest HU	47.500	19.080	130	11.0	34.6	-12.2	18.3
Madrid ES	40.410	-3.710	608	13.9	37.5	-2.4	16.0
Munich DE	48.130	11.580	536	8.0	28.7	-15.2	15.4
Glasgow UK	55.850	-4.250	56	8.4	23.1	-7.8	15.3
Taipeh TW	25.020	121.450	419	19.8	32.5	5.1	12.6
Shanghai CN	31.230	121.470	8	15.8	36.3	-4.7	14.0
New Orleans US	30.000	-90.050	0	20.7	34.4	-1.2	19.3
Melbourne AU	-37.750	144.970	82	14.1	36.6	-0.4	22.7
Singapore SG	1.280	103.850	30	26.5	33.5	20.8	10.3
Bangalore IN	12.970	77.580	762	24.2	36.6	14.3	14.7
Brasília BR	-15.920	-47.670	960	21.3	32.7	9.3	16.9
Santa Clara CU	22.420	-79.970	102	25.8	35.5	12.0	14.3
Bogotá CO	4.630	-74.080	2.560	13.3	23.6	2.0	20.0
Dubai AE	25.230	55.280	0	27.1	43.6	11.9	13.4
Cairo EG	30.050	31.250	84	21.3	39.6	5.1	15.4
Riyadh SA	24.650	46.770	701	25.5	43.9	4.9	16.8
Las Vegas US	36.170	-115.170	680	19.5	44.9	-3.4	18.8
Kabul AF	34.516	69.195	1.800	12.1	37.4	-11.0	21.7

Fig. 1.13 Climatic analysis of typical examples of the building specific climate classification types

Average humidity [g/kg]	Maximum humidity [g/kg]	Minimum humidity [g/kg]	Average radiation [W/m^2]	Maximum radiation [W/m^2]	Sum of radiation [kWh/m^{2}a]	Heating degree days [Kd/a]	Cooling degree days [Kd/a]	Humidifying gram days [gd/kga]	Dehumidifying gram days [gd/kga]
5.1	17.7	0.0	113.7	914.0	996.0	5,100.8	196.7	926.7	167.0
6.9	23.9	0.5	169.2	917.0	1,482.2	3,222.3	903.7	806.7	501.0
4.8	13.6	0.4	110.2	847.0	965.4	5,148.6	91.9	861.4	69.2
5.5	16.5	0.6	219.6	1,306.0	1,923.7	3,894.5	100.8	902.5	194.9
6.0	16.4	1.2	137.5	978.0	1,204.5	2,989.7	497.2	657.2	113.6
7.1	16.7	2.5	187.6	1,028.0	1,643.4	2,175.9	712.6	460.9	179.6
5.8	15.1	1.1	131.7	970.0	1,153.7	3,895.6	177.1	683.4	113.1
5.8	13.1	1.9	99.3	936.0	869.9	3,662.1	18.3	598.5	35.6
13.7	24.1	5.2	155.2	1,094.0	1,359.6	349.7	1,160.3	15.9	1,554.3
10.2	27.6	1.9	146.3	1,009.0	1,281.6	1,922.9	971.1	359.9	990.1
11.5	23.7	2.2	189.3	1,133.0	1,658.3	443.1	1,518.2	156.3	1,053.5
7.1	20.8	3.3	176.4	1,162.0	1,545.3	1,435.8	605.1	384.2	174.8
18.9	25.0	13.2	186.3	1,080.0	1,632.0	0.0	2,714.8	0.0	2,993.7
15.9	26.7	9.4	231.2	1,168.0	2,025.3	0.0	2,350.7	0.0	2,160.8
12.3	21.0	5.2	204.6	1,259.0	1,792.3	0.0	1,721.4	26.2	1,155.3
16.3	26.0	7.8	185.8	1,156.0	1,627.6	0.0	2,639.6	0.0	2,202.4
10.1	14.3	5.4	179.4	1,310.0	1,571.5	262.9	121.1	2.3	641.9
13.3	30.3	4.6	231.3	1,031.0	2,026.2	0.0	3,122.1	32.0	1,341.2
8.5	17.8	3.3	228.5	1,104.0	2,001.7	81.7	1,799.0	290.8	313.4
6.0	19.9	2.3	249.9	1,101.0	2,189.1	119.7	3,033.7	660.6	37.5
4.0	15.2	1.2	234.6	1,080.0	2,055.1	1,245.6	1,914.0	1,126.6	16.4
5.8	13.2	1.4	225.4	1,192.0	1,974.5	2,964.2	846.5	720.4	66.8

Outdoor Climate and Room Climate

The requirements imposed on room conditioning by the outdoor climate and changes in the moisture content of air are shown in the psychrometric chart, which corresponds to Richard Mollier's h-x diagram. It is also known as the Carrier chart – after the inventor of the air conditioning unit, Willis Carrier.

Representation

The temperatures of international locations are given on the X-axis, while their absolute humidity levels are given on the Y-axis. The graph curves represent levels of relative humidity. The isotherm line is almost vertical, while the enthalpy lines run diagonally from top left to bottom right. The ↙ dew point temperature can be calculated from this graph by moving a point horizontally to the left until it meets the curve representing a relative air humidity of 100%, and by then shifting this point along the isotherm line towards the x-axis. The ↙ limit of cooling temperature can be calculated by moving a point along the enthalpy line as far as the curve representing a relative air humidity of 100% and then moving the curve along the isotherm line
as far as the X-axis.

↙ **dew point temperature** p. 142

wet bulb temperature p. 142

Room conditioning

If we define the comfortable zone by the international ASHRAE-55 standard, this gives the following room conditioning measures for situations where the wind speed is low. Where the ↙ room temperatures are below this comfort zone, it is too cold and heating should be provided. If internal heat loads or passive ↙ solar gain bring the temperature up to almost the minimum value – approximately 20 °C – but outdoor temperatures are low, conventional heating systems must be provided. Any higher than a temperature of approximately 26 °C, and the air is too warm. A number of strategies are available, with the best strategy to deploy largely depending on air humidity. ↙ Efficient sun protection must be included in the plan.

↙ **room temperature** p. 150

solar gains p. 144

sun protection p.146

In principle, air with a water content higher than 12 g/kg is too humid, and should be dehumidified. There is no lower limit given for air humidity, but the uncomfortable effects of low water content should be considered. If humidity is within comfortable parameters and the temperature is above 26 °C, passive cooling measures such as the use of storage mass and ↙ night ventilation can be used. Evaporation cooling can be used where temperatures are high and humidity levels are low.

↙ **night ventilation** p. 152

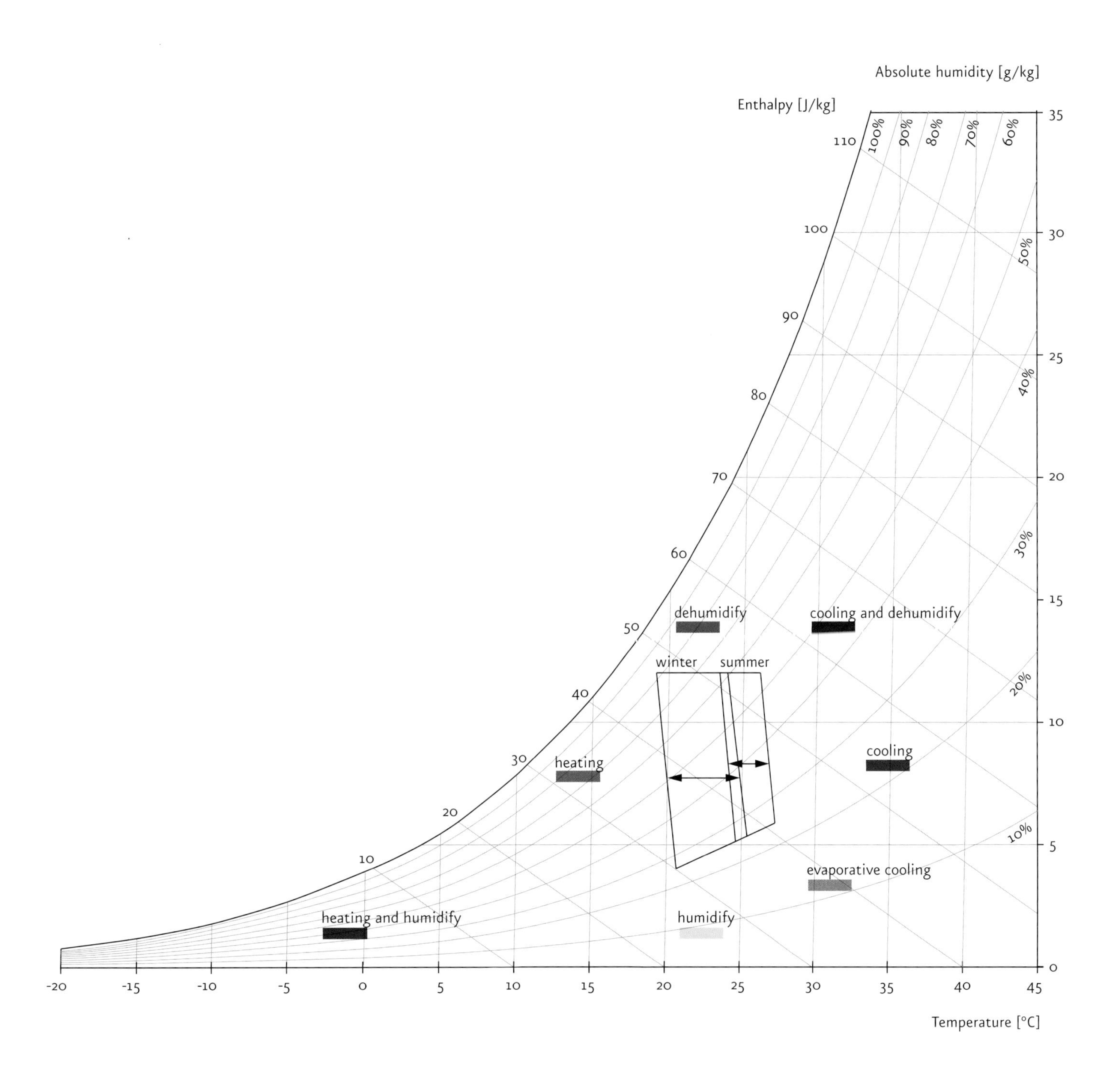

Fig. 1.14 Room climate conditioning methods, shown in psychrometric chart format

In order to create a comfortable room climate, a number of different room climate conditioning measures may be advisable, depending on air temperature and absolute air humidity. The graph shows the comfort zones for winter and summer according to ASHRAE-55.

Climate and Building Concepts

The following climate elements have a bearing on building concepts: temperature, solar radiation, absolute air humidity and wind speed. Rather than work from calculations of average annual temperature, one must analyse temperature changes over the course of a month or a day and the incidence of extreme values. It is not enough to look at individual parameters in isolation – the occurrence of two or more values at certain times may be relevant.

The location of a planned building depends on the climate in the wider area, the local climate and the microclimate. The radiation situation and the air currents around the building, which are determined by the urban context, significantly influence the energy-related and room climate-related aspects of building planning. Adapting the building concept to local conditions saves energy and makes the building more comfortable for the user.

Facade concepts

The building skin is the interface between interior and exterior; if it is well adapted to the climatic conditions, less technology and energy will be needed to make it comfortable inside. The need to combine heat protection, sun protection and daylight with passive solar gain in winter and a comfortable room climate in summer can create conflicts. Certain parameters – ↙ glazing percentage, window geometry, ↙ sun protection and heat protection – should be adjusted to satisfy energy, room climate and daylight-specific requirements. Differentiated openings are required to ensure efficient and comfortable ventilation. Important values that cannot be quantified include the building's relationship to its surrounding environment and the way individuals adjust the ventilation and sun protection.

↙ **glazing percentage** p. 146

sun protection p. 146

In climate zones with heating energy demand, the main priority is to minimise ↙ transmission and ↙ ventilation heat losses and to take advantage of passive solar gain. This is achieved by a combination of good thermal insulation, extensive airtightness and a versatile sun protection concept. Where ventilation is achieved via windows, a comfortable inflow of air in winter should be ensured. In warm and hot climate zones, solar radiation must be counteracted and heating caused by incoming air should be restricted. The glazing percentage should therefore be moderate, and the window lintels should be as high as possible. The sun protection should exclude direct radiation while allowing sufficient ↙ daylight provision. Where air flows in through the facade, the fact that the interface with the external air is close to the facade will lead to a higher inflow temperature.

↙ **transmission heat loss** p. 146

ventilation heat loss p. 146

↙ **daylight provision** p. 148

An optimised facade is the basis for simple room climate conditioning strategies and the utilisation of renewable energy sources.

Room conditioning concepts

The room climate conditioning concept that should be used depends on the building's function, the facade type and the location's outdoor climate conditions. The comfort requirements, the internal heat loads and the fresh air requirements depend on the building's function. The facade influences solar heat input and the potential for natural ventilation. Whether the building needs to be heated or cooled, humidified or dehumidified depends on the outdoor climate.

Where there is a high air requirement, or humidifying or dehumidifying is required, mechanical ventilation must be installed. The same is true if noise, dust or outdoor air temperature levels are high. To conserve energy, ventilation should not exceed the airflow rate required for health purposes – 25–30 m^3 per person per hour. To achieve this, rooms should be heated or cooled using water-based systems.

Where there is an increased ventilation heating requirement, a ↘ heat recovery system should be provided. Otherwise, window ventilation should be preferred because it does not require any operating energy, and because it creates a good relationship with the outdoor space and allows people to adjust the ventilation for themselves. If air inflow temperatures are limited due to energy generation, a surface heating system is necessary.

↘
heat recovery
p. 144

Where there are high heat loads or high outdoor air temperatures, cooling is necessary. Source or displacement ventilation can dissipate only low heat loads. Mixed ventilation provides a high degree of cooling, but comfort should also be borne in mind. Surface cooling is more comfortable than convective cooling. Dew point issues may make air inflow dehumidifying necessary.

Energy generation concepts

The energy generation system that should be used depends on the heating, cooling and dehumidifying demands, the required capacities and the ↘ system temperatures of the room conditioning. Location-specific factors include the intensity and duration of solar radiation, the outdoor air and ↘ soil temperature and the absolute humidity of the air.

If the soil or the groundwater is at a certain temperature, it can be used to heat or cool incoming air. If the soil temperature is sufficiently low, it can drive a surface cooling system or an incoming air cooling unit directly. In winter, a ↘ heat pump can be used to warm a building by extracting heat from the soil. Where outdoor air temperatures and air humidity permit, the lower night temperatures can be utilised via a ↘ recooling plant to remove the load from a ↘ concrete core activation system. Hot water energy demand can readily be met by solar thermal ↘ collectors. With the right level of heating energy demand and solar radiation conditions, these can also be used to meet part of the heating energy demand. ↘ Solar cooling is a good way of meeting cooling or dehumidifying energy demands. Where there is also a winter heating energy demand, the collector field can remain in operation all year round, increasing efficiency. Desiccant cooling works well where there is a dehumidifying requirement. Where the solar radiation system is favourable, integrated ↘ photovoltaic systems may be an intelligent addition to the system. One should check how their performance will be affected by exposure to dust and by rises in temperature.

↘
system temperatures
p. 152

soil temperature
p. 142

refrigeration unit
p. 154

cooling tower
p. 154

concrete core activation
p. 152

solar thermal system
p. 154

solar cooling
p. 154

photovoltaics
p. 154

Outdoor air temperature minimal/maximal

Moscow	-25.5 / 30.6 °C
Munich	-15.2 / 28.7 °C
Shanghai	-4.7 / 36.3 °C
Bangalore	14.3 / 36.6 °C
Dubai	11.9 / 43.6 °C

Maximum temperature variance over a year

Moscow	56.1 K
Munich	43.9 K
Shanghai	41.0 K
Bangalore	22.3 K
Dubai	31.7 K

Maximum daily temperature variation during the summer

Moscow	14.8 K
Munich	15.4 K
Shanghai	10.3 K
Bangalore	14.7 K
Dubai	13.4 K

Annual wind average

City	Wind
Moscow	3.6 m/s
Munich	3.1 m/s
Shanghai	2.0 m/s
Bangalore	1.9 m/s
Dubai	3.4 m/s

Precipitation in a year

City	Precipitation
Moscow	655 mm/a
Munich	956 mm/a
Shanghai	1,112 mm/a
Bangalore	907 mm/a
Dubai	128 mm/a

Absolute humidity minimal/maximal

Moscow	0.0 / 17.7 g/kg
Munich	1.1 / 15.1 g/kg
Shanghai	1.9 / 27.6 g/kg
Bangalore	9.4 / 26.7 g/kg
Dubai	4.6 / 30.3 g/kg

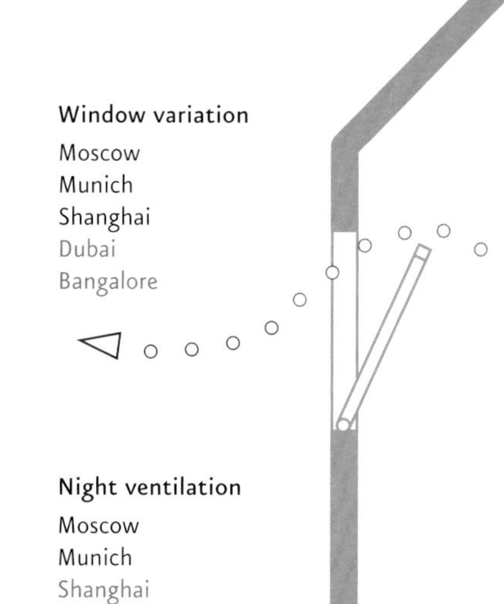

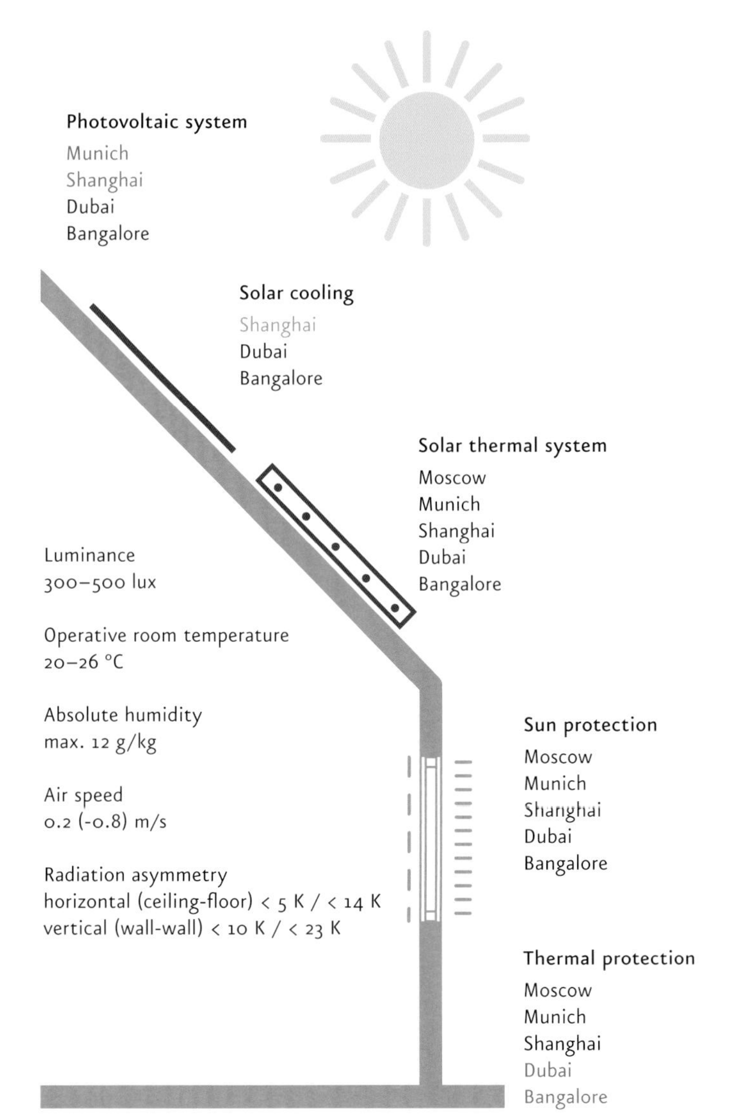

Maximum global radiation [W/m²]	
Moscow	914
Munich	970
Shanghai	1,009
Bangalore	1,168
Dubai	1,031

Hours of daylight minimum/maximum [h]	
Moscow	57° / 10°
Munich	65° / 18°
Shanghai	82° / 35°
Bangalore	100° / 53°
Dubai	88° / 41°

Sun height at 12:00 noon on the 21 June / 21 December	
Moscow	7.00 / 17.33
Munich	8.21 / 16.04
Shanghai	10.07 / 14.11
Bangalore	11.22 / 12.53
Dubai	10.34 / 13.42

Percentage of diffuse radiation [%]	
Moscow	51
Munich	53
Shanghai	65
Bangalore	38
Dubai	39

Average illuminance over a year [lux]	
Moscow	12,366
Munich	14,406
Shanghai	16,283
Bangalore	25,888
Dubai	25,488

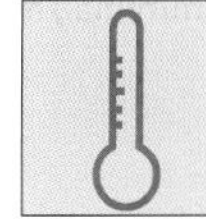

Soil temperature from approx. 10 m deep [°C]	
Moscow	5.0
Munich	8.0
Shanghai	15.8
Bangalore	24.2
Dubai	27.1

Fig. 1.15 The interaction of climate, building, technology and energy

Climate factors decisively influence the building configuration, the indoor space conditioning measures and any energy generation systems needed to achieve a comfortable room climate.
The outdoor climatic conditions produced by climatic elements (solar radiation, temperature, humidity and wind) in Moscow (cool climate), Munich (temperate climate), Shanghai (the subtropics), Bangalore (the tropics) and Dubai (desert areas in proximity to the ocean) are shown here. The comfort requirements according to ASHRAE-55 are given, together with the measures that must be taken to create comfortable conditions within the cities. The implementation of solar and renewable energy systems is also shown. City names written in black stand for a recommended measure, and those in grey stand for a measure that can be recommended only where circumstances permit.

Cool

Moscow, the perceived centre of Russia

Moscow has a typical cool temperate climate. The city lies within the extratropical west winds zone. Rain falls all year round, with maximum rainfall in summer due to areas of low pressure accompanied by high temperature, as opposed to the areas of high pressure accompanied by low temperatures that form in the winter. Due to the city's continental position, summers in Moscow are warm, with maximum temperatures of over 30 °C, and winters are cold, with temperatures dropping as low as -25 °C. In summer, the difference between maximum and minimum temperature over the course of a day may be as much as 15 K. The city's thaw begins in mid-March, and summer lasts from the beginning of June to mid-August. Frosty nights may begin as early as mid-September, and the first snow falls at the end of October.

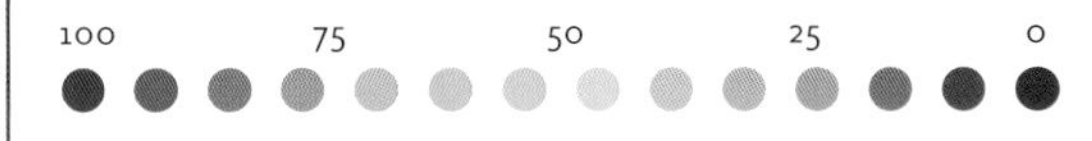

Nights per year with an average temperature lower than 20 °C [%]

Climate in the Cool Climate Zone

A cool temperate continental climate with full humidity is found only in the northern hemisphere, as the southern hemisphere has no correspondingly large land masses. Such a climate exists between the latitudes of 40° north and 60° north.

Temperature fluctuations between summer and winter temperatures are very high in continental locations, increasing as one moves farther from the ocean. Temperature differences within a single day are far greater in summer than in winter.

Precipitation occurs all year round, but mainly in summer due to the heat balance of the land masses, which heat up sufficiently to cause warm air to rise, leading to convective rainfall. In winter, the land masses cool down considerably, causing the cold air to draw together and sink. The low levels of precipitation that occur in winter fall mainly as snow.

The hours of sunlight per day vary significantly throughout the year. For a certain period of time, the long summer days compensate for this zone's low levels of solar radiation incidence compared to areas nearer the equator. However, because this is the case only for a short period of the year, air temperatures in this zone remain lower than at the equator. The very short path of the sun across the sky in winter means that only the south sides of buildings receive particular elements of the sun's radiation.

The main forms of vegetation in continental locations are boreal pine forests, or taiga.

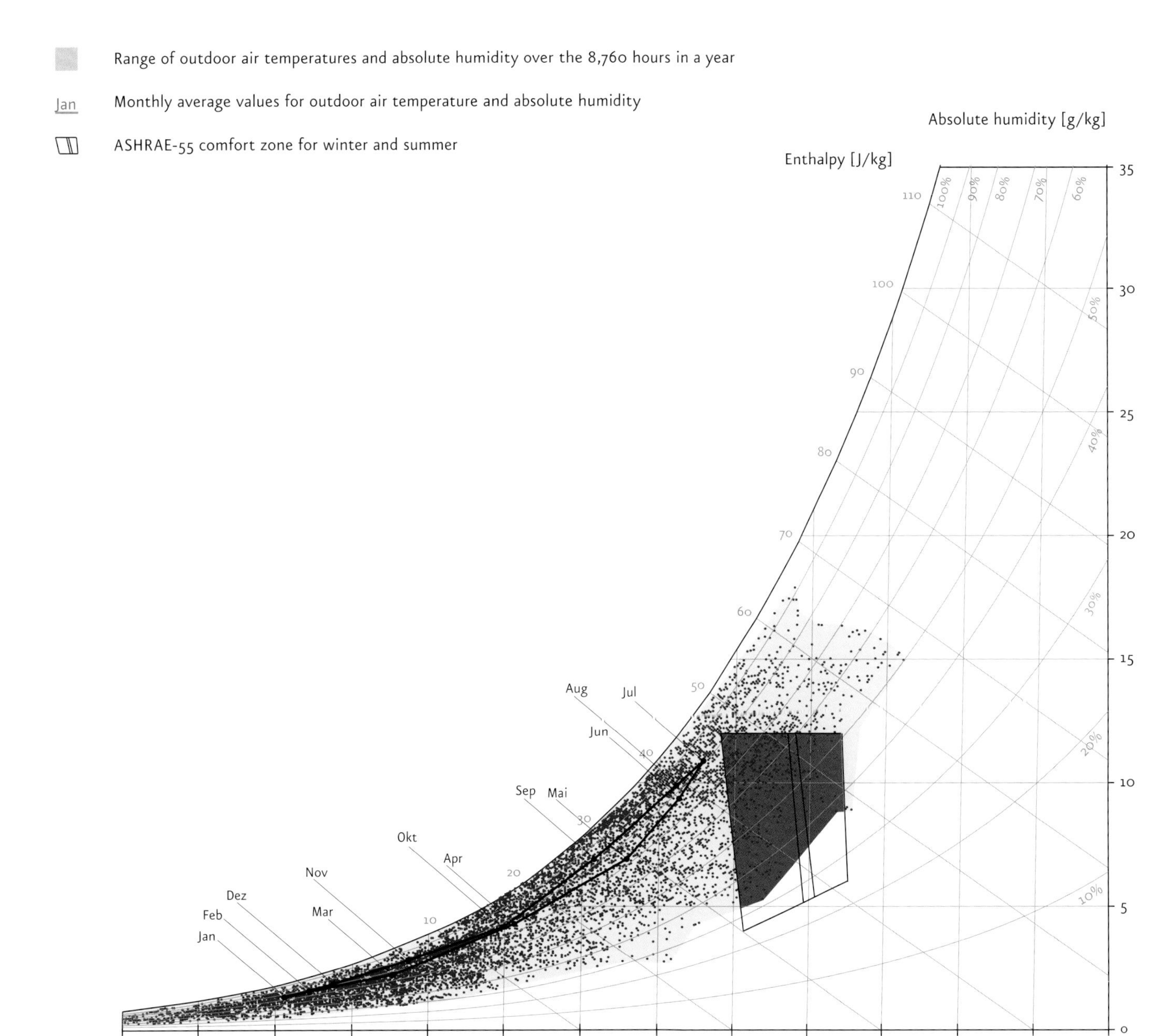

Fig. 2.1 Range of outdoor air temperatures and absolute humidity for the Moscow area, with ASHRAE-55 comfort zone superimposed

Moscow's climate features very low winter temperatures (as low as -25 °C) and summer temperatures of 25 °C. From October to April, incoming air must be humidified to create a comfortable degree of humidity in the indoor space. Air dehumidifying is barely necessary, as average humidity levels over a month do not exceed 12 g/kg. The main focus is the heating energy demand.

Climate and Construction

Moscow's climate is typical of a cool temperate continental climate zone. It shows very pronounced fluctuations in temperature and solar radiation throughout the year. This means that a high level of energy is required to heat buildings in this area (Fig. 2.1). The more northerly and continental a building is and the higher its altitude, the greater the ↙ heating energy demand. The location's low cooling energy demands can readily be met by renewable cold sources, with cooling and dehumidifying energy demands more important for coastal areas in low latitudes. A description of climatic conditions in Moscow for the purpose of constructing buildings adapted to the Moscow climate is given below (Fig. 2.2).

↙ **heating energy demand** p. 144

Temperature

Over the course of a year, temperatures fluctuate between -25 °C (in winter) and 30 °C (in summer). ↙ Natural ventilation is impractical in winter due to the low outdoor air temperatures and the uncomfortable thermal situation they create. Although the outdoor air temperatures are high during the summer, changes in temperature over the course of the day (which are particularly pronounced in continental locations) make passive cooling possible. The low overall temperature throughout the year means that the soil is a serviceable cooling source. The temperature level is too low for heat to be effectively extracted from the ground using a ↙ heat pump.

↙ **natural ventilation** p. 146

refrigeration unit p. 154

Humidity

In the winter, the air is generally so dry that humidifying is required. The absolute humidity level is never so high during the summer that it is necessary to dehumidify the incoming air. ↙ Surface cooling systems are effective; as the ↙ dew point temperature is 18 °C or a little over, there are no dew point issues.

↙ **heat/cold transfer** p. 150

dew point temperature p. 142

Global radiation

The ↙ global radiation rate is 996 kWh/m²a. The highest absolute values are reached in summer between the end of May and the middle of July – corresponding closely with the period of maximum precipitation. Diffuse and direct radiation are in equilibrium. ↙ Solar thermal energy can be used to heat the domestic hot water supply, or as an auxiliary heating source during transitional periods.

↙ **global radiation** p. 142

solar thermal system p. 154

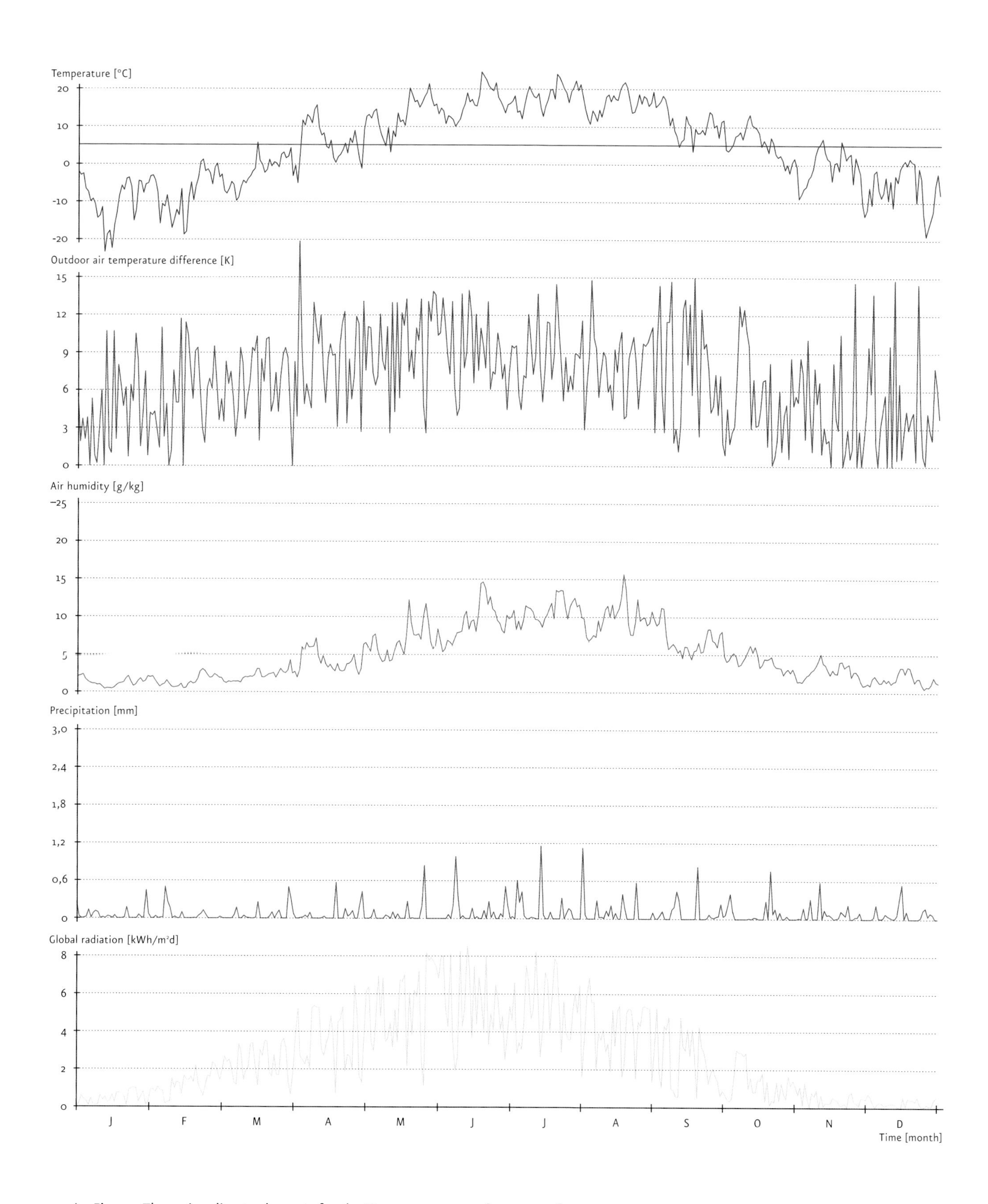

Fig. 2.2 The major climate elements for the Moscow area over the course of a year

Showing average daily outdoor air temperatures (1st line), with soil temperatures at a depth of 10–12 m (red horizontal line), and the outdoor air temperature difference between the maximum temperature during the day and the minimum temperature at night (2nd line). Also included are the average daily absolute air humidity (3rd line) and precipitation (4th line) values, as well as the amount of energy relating to a horizontal surface received in a day (5th line).

Solar radiation

Due to this location's high latitude, its day lengths, angle of radiation incidence and solar radiation intensity vary significantly throughout the year. This impacts on the radiation to which variously oriented facades are exposed (Fig. 2.3). During winter and transitional periods, solar radiation is welcome as it helps to reduce the heating energy demand.

The level of radiation energy absorbed by roofs and east or west facades is at its highest in June, due to the long hours of sunlight and the higher position of the sun during this part of the year. In summer, the east, south and west facades all receive a similar level of radiation, whereas in winter, almost all radiation is diffuse. Radiation received by the north sides of buildings is largely irrelevant.

Winter days are significantly shorter than summer days, resulting in a significant illumination energy demand. It is unfortunate for a building to be shaded on the south side by other buildings because this reduces ↙ daylight provosion and prevents the desired ↙ solar gain in winter.

↙
daylight provision
p. 148

solar gains
p. 144

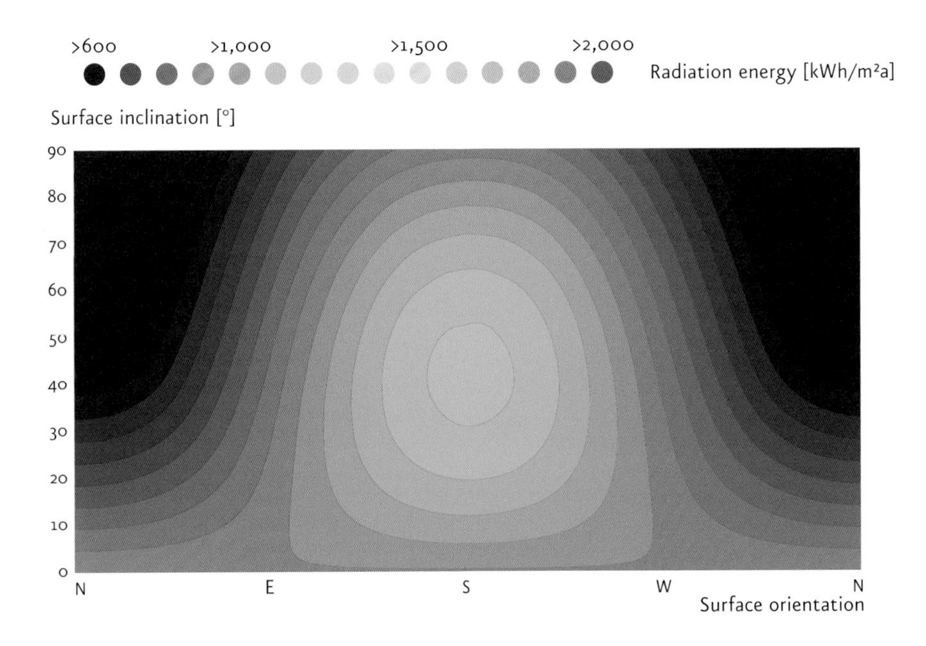

Fig. 2.3 Radiation energy received in kWh/m²a correlated with orientation and angle of inclination, to be used for evaluating the alignment of solar power systems in the Moscow area

Measured on the horizontal plane, the global radiation level is 996 kWh/m²a. At the optimal angle of inclination (42°) and with a south-facing orientation, the level of energy received is 1,212 kWh/m²a.

>0 >40 >80 >120 >160 >200

Energy radiation [kWh/m² per month]

75
40
32
32
61
39
35°
92°
60
38
105
48

March

167
77
64
50
104
58
58°
137°
116
59
94
58

June

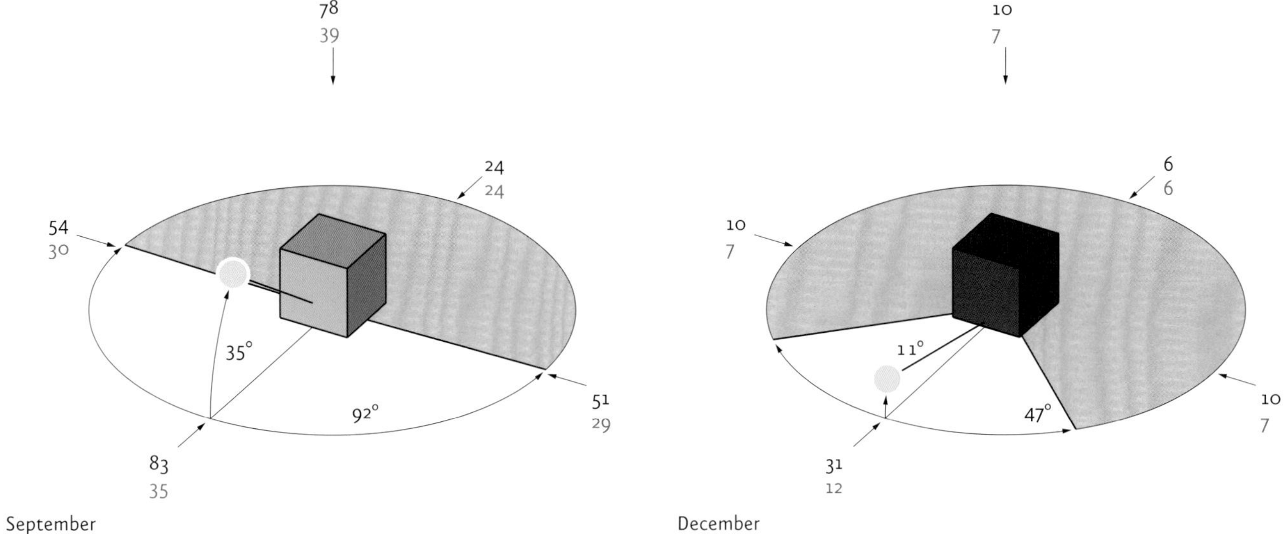

Fig. 2.4 Solar radiation and path of the sun for the Moscow area

The sides of this cube show the amount of energy received in kWh/m² for a given month. The numbers in black quantify the overall radiation level, and those in grey the diffuse radiation level. Also included are the maximum elevation angle and azimuth angle of the sun for the 21st of the month.

Building Structure

↙
transmission heat loss
p. 144

cubature
p. 144

heating energy demand
p. 144

orientation
p. 144

solar gains
p.144

daylight provision
p. 148

In the cool climate zone, ↙transmission heat loss is a significant factor due to low outdoor air temperatures and the long heating period. This makes a compact configuration advisable. A low ↙surface-to-volume ratio can be achieved by a compact arrangement of three sections in parallel or reducing the outer shell surface by planning atria or buffer zones. Very high buildings suffer from increased wind loads, which may have an adverse effect on the ↙heating energy demands in winter. They also place more demand on technical systems, requiring large building systems shafts.

A north-south building ↙orientation is best, as it optimises ↙solar gain in winter and avoids solar input in summer (Fig. 2.6). In summer, the south facade can easily be shaded by means of a horizontal sun protection element, without restricting the view or available daylight. Shading by nearby buildings should be avoided; due to the sun's low position in winter, it is better if any other buildings on the building's south side are a good distance away. In summer, it is advantageous for the building to be shaded by other buildings on its east and west sides (Fig. 2.5), as long as this does not restrict ↙daylight provision.

Clear space around building 20 m

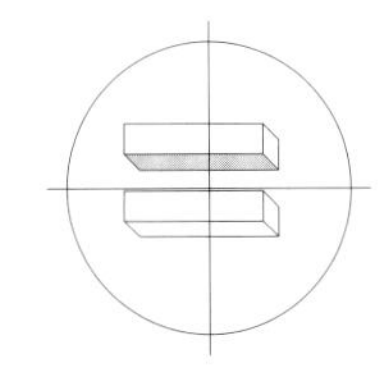

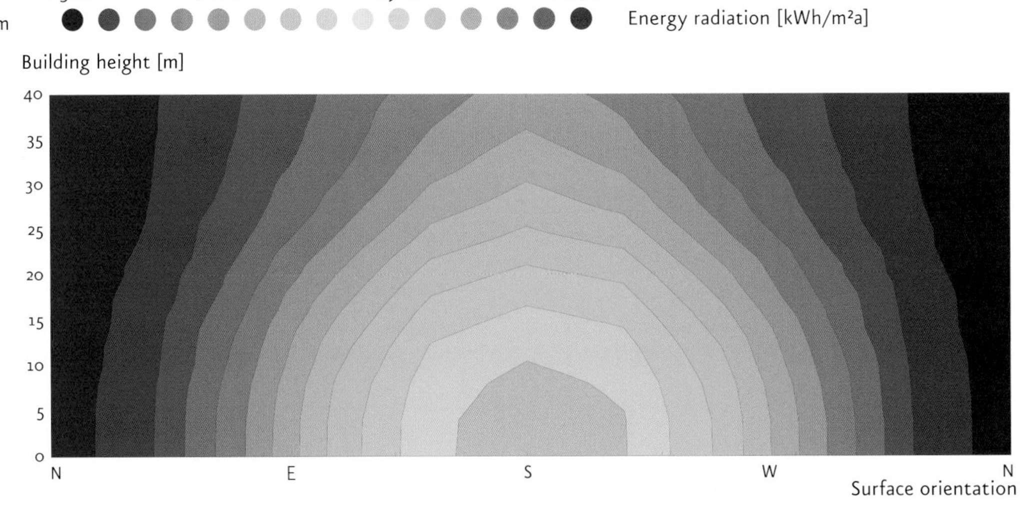

Fig. 2.5 Radiation energy [kWh/m²a], as an average value, received by the facade, correlated with its orientation and the height of a building 20 m away in the Moscow area

This simulation is based on a typical office block, 70 m x 15 m x 20 m (l x w x h). The height of the shading block 20 m away is variable. In Moscow, the solar radiation received by a south-facing facade where the neighbouring development is 20 m high (900 kWh/m²a) is about half as high again as that received by east-facing or west-facing facades (600 kWh/m²a).

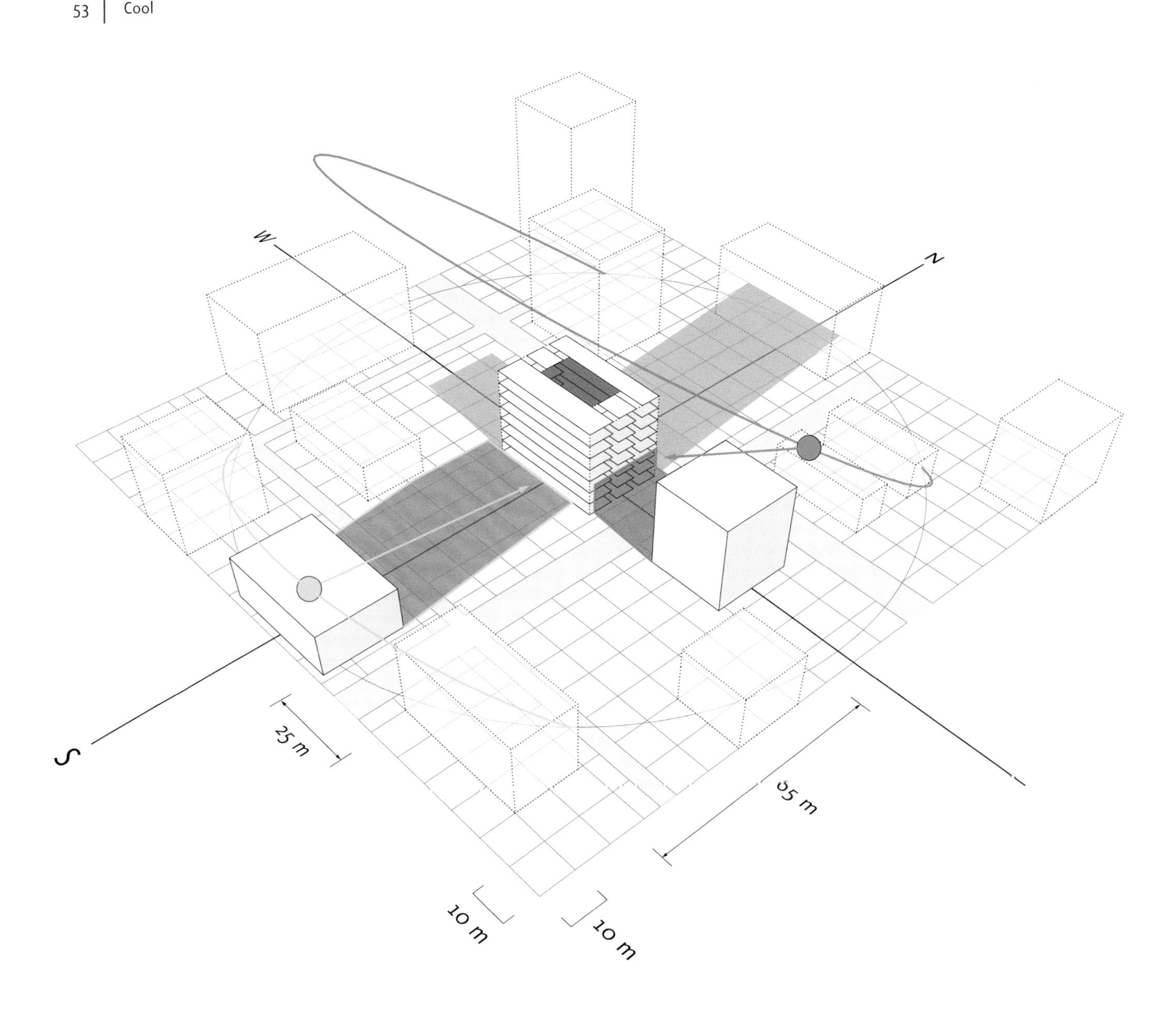

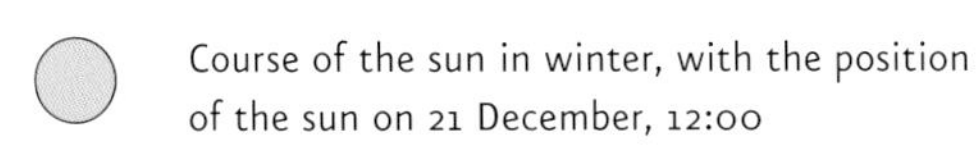

Course of the sun in winter, with the position of the sun on 21 December, 12:00

Course of the sun in summer, with the position of the sun on 21 June, 8:00

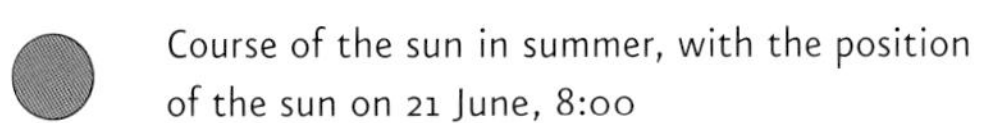

Shade at midday on 21 December. To keep the south facade free of shade in the winter, the nearest building on the south side should not be closer than about three times the building's height.

Shade in the morning on 21 June. With appropriate space left for daylight, east-to-west shading of the building in summer is only possible for the lower storeys. In some cases, taller buildings in a north-west position may provide shading for the west facade during the use period.

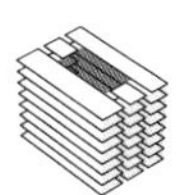

A north-south oriented block with external atrium. The energy advantages of a compact construction and the need for optimal use of daylight must both be considered. In this respect, a double-loaded floor plan arrangement represents a good compromise. A glazed atrium on the south side of the building takes advantage of solar gains and acts as a climate buffer. In some cases, the atrium can be incorporated into the ventilation concept. Projections are a simple way of providing shade for the south facade in summer.

Fig. 2.6 Building structures for a cool climate
A compact construction is suitable for Moscow. The south facade should not be shaded by any nearby buildings, but shading of the east and west facades can be an advantage. A minimum distance should be maintained to ensure good daylight provision.

Building Skin

↙
solar gains
p. 144

sun protection
p. 146

A facade concept for a cool climate zone must minimise heat loss and enable passive ↙ solar gain in winter while avoiding thermal gain in summer. Ideally, external sun protection should be provided. Where the window surface areas are small, internal sun protection systems may be adequate. ↙ Sun protection coatings are an inefficient strategy.

Glazing percentage

↙
glazing percentage
p. 146

daylight provision
p. 148

The best ↙ glazing percentage depends on the transmission heat loss, the solar gains in winter and the solar input in summer. Ideally, the glazing percentage on the north, east and west facades should be between 30% and 40%. A south facade glazing percentage of up to 50% has a positive impact on the heating energy demand. A high window lintel or a skylight should be included to ensure sufficient ↙ daylight provision.

Sun protection

↙
sun protection
p. 146

Mobile ↙ sun protection works better than sun protection coatings because it does not prevent the desired solar gains during the winter. The east and west facades receive the highest radiation incidence in summer, meaning that the sun protection has to block out a low sun. For the south and north facades, internal sun protection is sufficient. It can also function as glare protection.

Glazing

↙
glazing
p. 146

U-value
p. 146

Heat protection glass is preferable to sun protection ↙ glazing if one wishes to benefit from passive solar gain in winter and not to reduce the available daylight in winter further. A daylight-responsive artificial light control system is also a good way of reducing the artificial light energy demand. Triple heat protection glazing with a ↙ U-value of lower than 0.7 W/m^2K is ideal.

Insulation

↙
insulation
p. 146

thermal bridge
p. 146

Good ↙ thermal protection for the building skin is necessary to avoid transmission heat loss in the winter. An insulation layer 20–30 cm thick is recommended. ↙ Thermal bridges should be avoided.

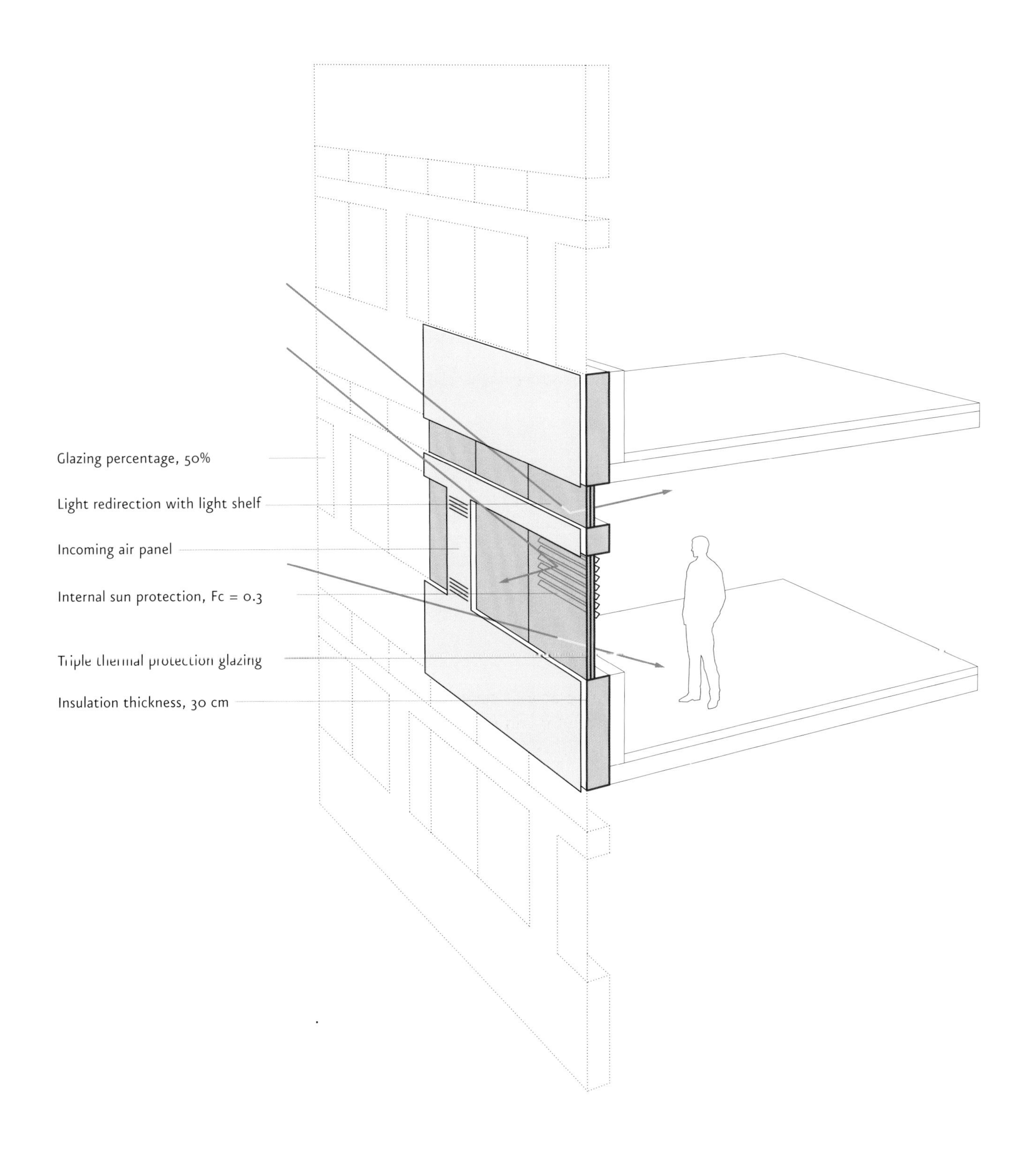

Fig. 2.7 Facade concept for the cool climate zone

Strategies for a south facade with optimised energy, room climate and daylight features. One possible alternative would be a sheltering projection combined with internal sun protection. The glazing percentage for the east-facing and west-facing facades should be between 30% and 50%, and the sun protection should block a low sun. The glazing percentage on the north-facing facade should be kept below 30%. Internal glare protection is sufficient for a building's north side.

Building Systems

In the cool climate zone, heat provision is the major consideration. If the amount of fresh air required is above a certain level and humidifying is necessary, mechanical ventilation with a ↙heat recovery system should be provided – to ensure ↙comfort, among other reasons. If cooling is necessary, renewable sources should be used.

↙ heat recovery p. 144
comfort p. 150
earth pipe p. 154
photovoltaics p. 154

In winter, the relatively high temperature of the soil can be used to warm incoming air via underground registers or ↙earth pipes. Where hot water is needed, the solar thermal system can be expanded and also used to provide auxiliary heating during the transitional periods. Due to the low overall temperature all year round, the soil is a potential renewable cooling source (Fig. 2.2). In an ideal installation situation, a ↙photovoltaic system's yield is about 180 kWh/m²a (Fig. 2.3).

Radiator

↙ natural ventilation p. 146

If the comfort demands are not high and simple technology is required, ↙natural ventilation with radiator heating can be used. Provision should be made for a comfortable inflow of air – casement windows, baffle plates or ventilation radiators. Night ventilation openings should be included to improve the room climate in summer. Thermal activation of the storage masses should be possible; this concept is appropriate where only a small amount of air exchange is required. Mechanical ventilation can potentially be used to cool indoor spaces to some degree.

Heating/cooling convectors

↙ convector p. 152

If active cooling is required in a small space, one possibility is to use a cooling convector combined with natural ventilation. A ↙convector can also be used to heat a space. The climates of individual rooms can be effectively regulated in this way. For moderate to high cooling loads, the cooling convector could also be combined with mechanical ventilation.

Concrete core activation

↙ system temperatures p. 152
storage mass p. 144
earth piles/ groundwater utilisation p. 154
cooling tower p. 154

If renewable cooling sources are to be used, a concrete core activation system is ideal; its moderate ↙system temperatures and ↙storage mass-related phase shifting enable effective deployment of renewable cooling systems that use sources such as ↙groundwater or night ↙recooling (Fig. 2.2). In winter, basic heating needs can be covered by concrete core activation with comparatively low ↙inflow temperatures. For comfort and heat recovery, mechanical ventilation should be provided in the winter.

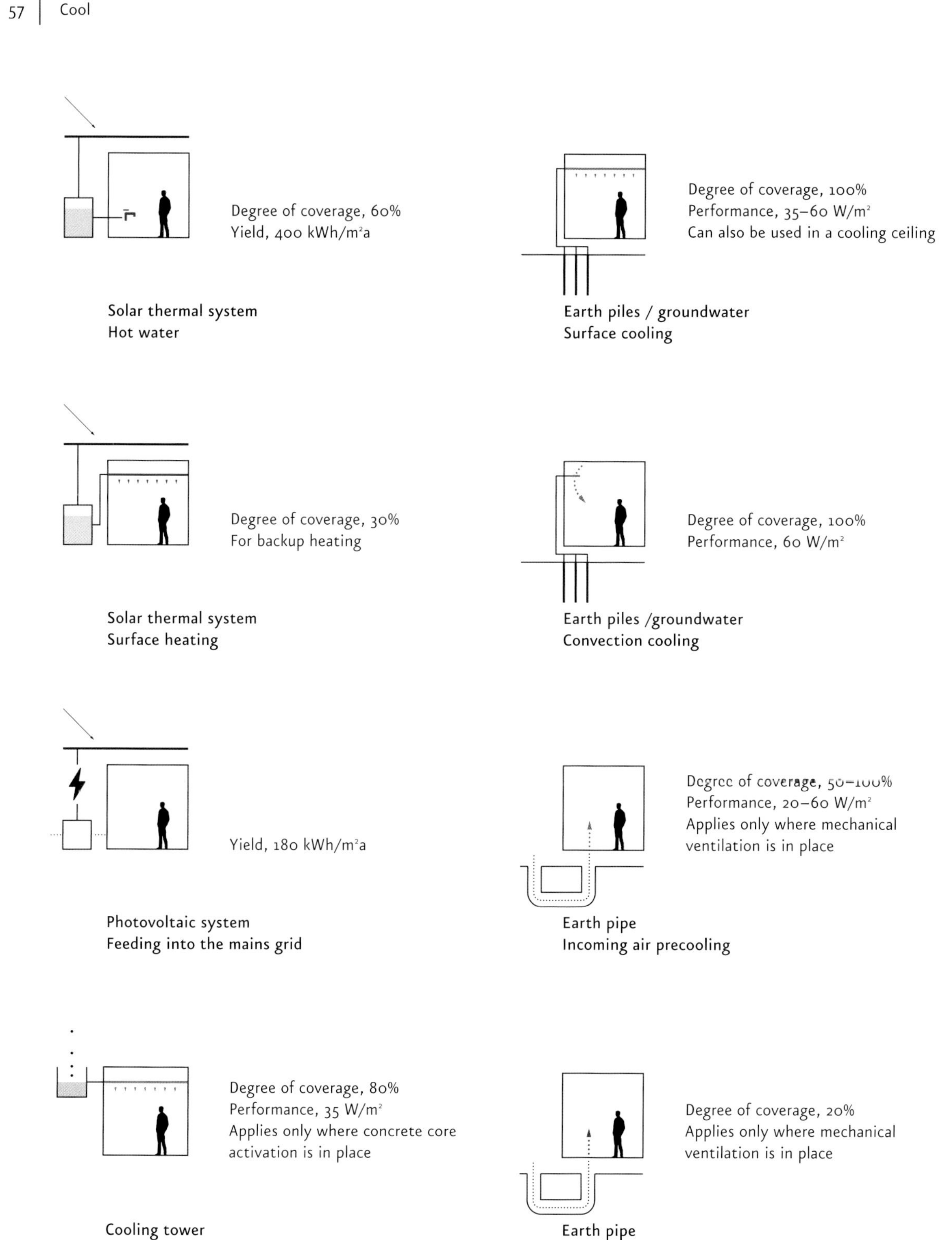

Fig. 2.8 Room conditioning concept in combination with renewable energy generation systems for the cool climate zone

Suitable system combinations. The degree of coverage represents the proportion of renewable heat or cooling provided. The diagram gives the annual yield for a solar power system in an optimal installation position and the specific heating or cooling performance of the room conditioning systems.

Planning Rules for Moscow

In the cool temperate continental climate zone, a very high degree of heating and a very low degree of cooling are required. It is not necessary to dehumidify the air, and there is a low humidifying energy demand in the winter. For Moscow, these factors give the following strategies:

Heating and humidifying

↙ **glazing** p. 146

Due to the long winters with low outdoor temperatures, the building skin must have very good thermal insulation. This should include ↙ heat protection glazing. In winter, extensive use of daylight for illumination is required, while solar radiation may reduce the heating energy demand. For these reasons, sun protection glass should not be used.

↙ **glazing percentage** p. 146

heating energy demand p. 144

heat recovery p. 144

The heating energy demand involves a significant amount of energy – approximately 40–60 kWh/m²a. Approximately 10% of this is required for humidifying. The influence of the ↙ glazing percentage on the heating energy demand is low for unshaded south facades. In the right circumstances, larger window surface areas can improve the availability of daylight indoors and the building's connections with its surroundings. Extensive window surfaces on the other facades can increase the heating energy demand. A room's orientation has a major impact on its ↙ heating energy demand, changing it by about 30%.

If the external walls' thermal insulation is optimal, and triple heat protection glazing and a mechanical ventilation system with ↙ heat recovery are in place, then the heating energy demand can be reduced to as little as 20 kWh/m²a.

Cooling

↙ **sun protection** S. 146

night ventilation S. 152

storage mass S. 144

If active cooling is not included in the plan, a comfortable summer room climate can be created by a combination of a moderate glazing percentage, external ↙ sun protection and efficient ↙ night cooling. ↙ Storage masses have a positive impact. A dehumidifying energy demand is not a factor.

The results of the thermal simulation are accurate for a standard office space with typical internal loads. Unless stated otherwise, the space is a light construction facing south, with a glazing percentage of 50%. The glazing has a g-value of 0.6 with internal sun protection. The U-value of the outer wall is 0.3 W/m²K.

Opportunities and strategies

In the cool temperate continental climate zone, an optimised building and facade concept is needed to reduce the heating energy demand in winter and the indoor heat gain in summer. Triple heat protection glazing and a facade with 20–30 cm of thermal insulation are ideal for this. The ideal glazing percentage varies depending on the facade's orientation. To ensure comfort, mechanical ventilation is recommended. The heating energy demand can be reduced significantly by a heat recovery system. In winter, the soil's relatively high temperature can be used to warm incoming air, by means of underground registers or an ↘earth pipe. ↘Solar thermal systems can be used to heat water and to provide auxiliary heating during transitional periods.

A combination of construction measures – a medium glazing percentage, external sun protection and night ventilation with extensive storage masses – renders a refrigeration or cooling system unnecessary provided that the building's heat loads are not excessive. Potential renewable cooling sources such as free ↘recooling at night and cooling by means of ↘groundwater or underground registers can be harnessed without complications. A ↘concrete core activation system is also suitable.

↘
earth pipe
p. 154

solar thermal system
p. 154

cooling tower
p. 154

earth piles/ groundwater utilisation
p. 154

concrete core activation
p. 152

Temperate

Munich, the "northernmost Italian city"

Munich is a typical temperate climate location. As far as the people of Munich are concerned, there are five seasons in the year: spring, summer, autumn, winter and the "Wiesn" – the Oktoberfest, held in autumn. Winters are cool, with temperatures under freezing point, while summers may be as warm as 25 °C. In September, the *Altweibersommer* or Indian summer brings the city pleasant temperatures, fragrant air and a few last days of sunshine under a blue sky with white clouds. One peculiarity of this Alpine upland is the *Föhn*, a fall wind created by dry, warm air streaming over the Alps. The clear air conditions this wind creates make the mountains appear to be within touching distance of the city. Rain falls all year round, and the first snow falls in early November.

100 75 50 25 0

Nights per year with an average temperature lower than 20 °C [%]

Climate in the Temperate Climate Zone

Wet temperate zones occur mainly in the northern hemisphere. Their distribution is non-uniform – they include areas between the 35th and 60th parallel in the east part of North America and in the west of the Eurasian land mass. Temperate locations are oceanic or continental depending on how far they are from the sea.

Primarily because of thermal conditions, the climate in the wet temperate zones lies somewhere between the adjoining northerly and southerly zones, causing it to be described as a temperate or intermediate climate.

Day length varies between 8 and 16 hours depending on the latitude. The seasons are pronounced and distinct, with relatively long springs and autumns.

As one moves closer to the coast, winters become warmer and summers become cooler, and the growing season also lasts longer. This is described as a maritime climate. In continental locations, in comparison with sites near the sea, much greater temperature variations are possible in the course of a year.

High levels of rainfall, particularly on the coasts, create the right conditions for intensive agriculture and forestry. While most of the inland rain falls in summer, rain – and, to a lesser extent, snow – generally falls in coastal areas in winter.

Flora varies, ranging from deciduous and mixed forests to evergreen rainforests.

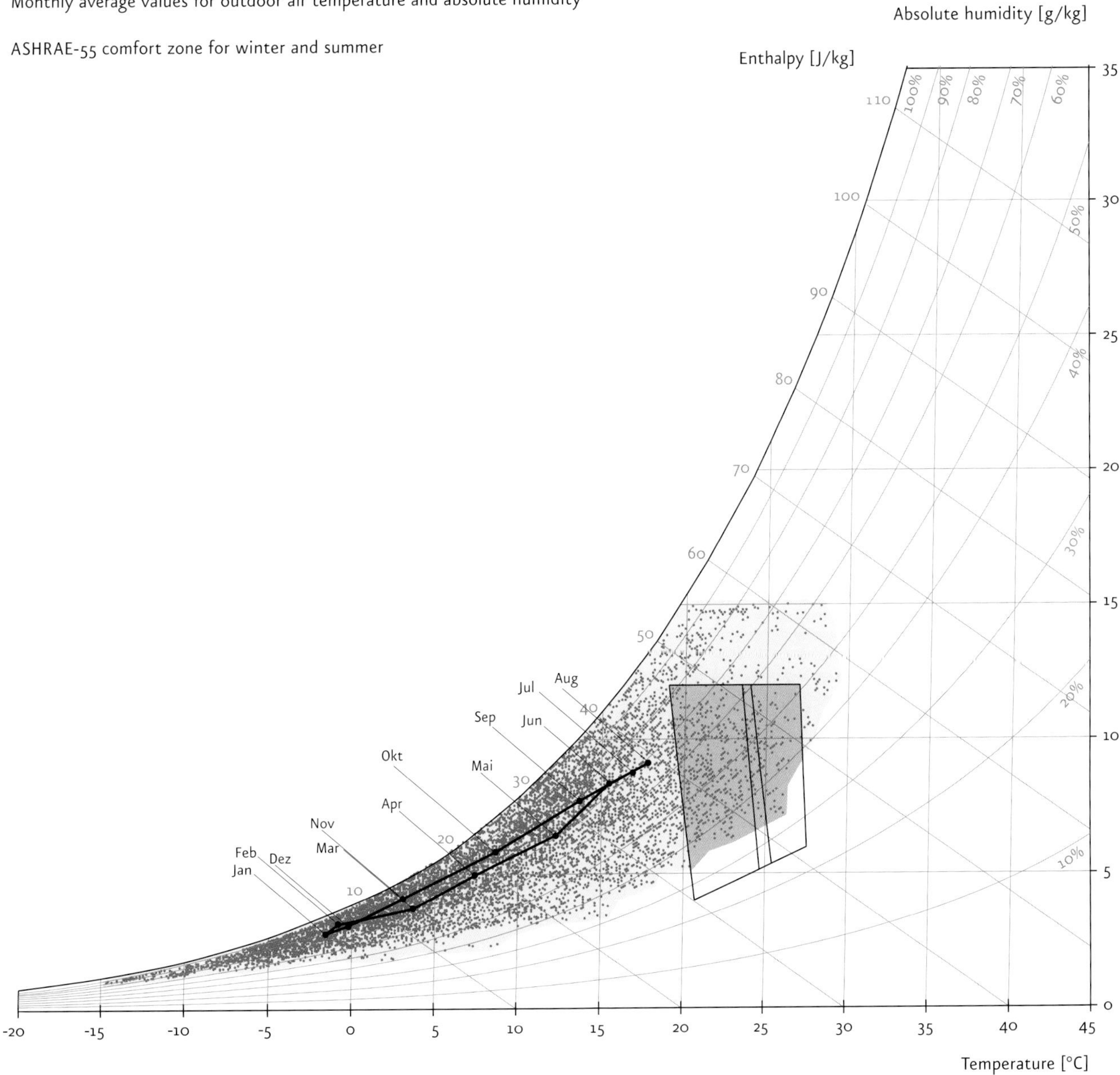

Fig. 3.1 Range of outdoor air temperatures and absolute humidity for the Munich area, with the ASHRAE-55 comfort zone superimposed

The Munich climate reaches temperatures as low as -15 °C in winter. In summer, the temperature may be about 20–25 °C. In winter, heating is needed. In summer, passive cooling measures are sufficient to create a comfortable room climate, as long as solar radiation input is restricted. It is not necessary to humidify or dehumidify incoming air, and natural ventilation is practical almost all of the time.

Climate and Construction

Munich's climate is typical of a temperate climate zone. Temperature and solar radiation fluctuate considerably throughout the year. Energy is required for heating – and also for cooling (Fig. 3.1). A description of climatic conditions in Munich for the purpose of constructing buildings adapted to the climate is given below (Fig. 3.2).

Temperature

↙ **heat recovery** p. 144

refrigeration unit p. 154

Over the course of a year, temperatures vary from -15 °C in winter to 25 °C in summer. Natural ventilation is possible almost all year round, but ↙heat recovery is advisable as a way of conserving energy. In summer, the outdoor temperatures rise, but the lower temperatures at night can be used to provide cooling. The soil can be used for renewable cooling or as a source of heat for a ↙heat pump.

Humidity

↙ **heat/cold transfer** p. 150

dew point temperature p. 142

Humidifying or dehumidifying systems are not required. ↙Surface cooling systems can be used without complications. If the cooling surface temperature is low, there may be ↙dew point issues on warm and humid days.

Global radiation

↙ **global radiation** p. 142

solar thermal system p. 154

photovoltaics p. 154

The ↙global radiation received is 1,147 kWh/m²a. The highest absolute temperature values occur in June and July. The proportion of direct radiation is higher than that of diffuse radiation. During transitional periods, ↙solar thermal systems can be used to heat water and to provide auxiliary heating. Integrated ↙photovoltaic systems are also suitable.

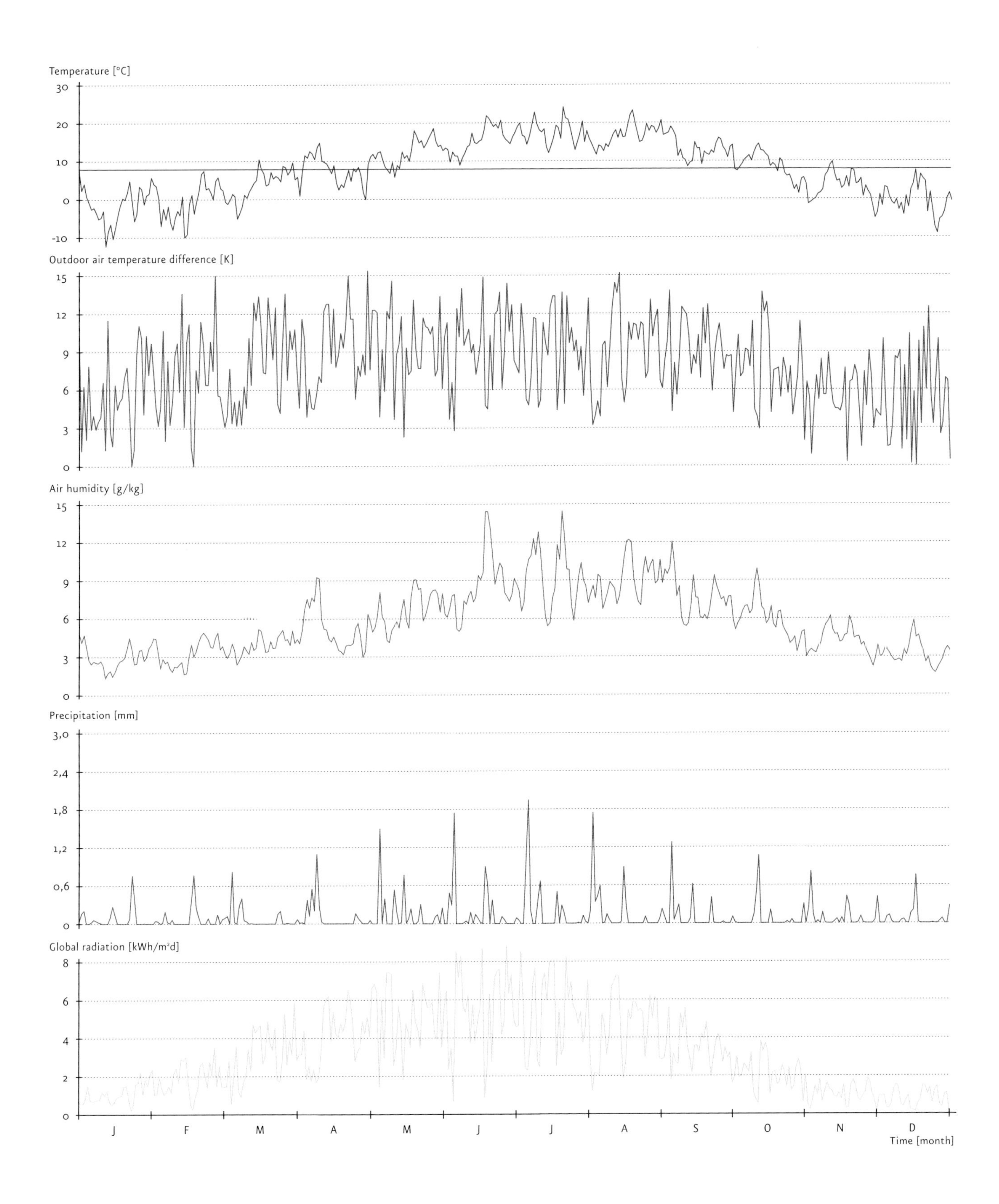

Fig. 3.2 The major climate elements for the Munich area over the course of a year

Showing average daily outdoor air temperatures (1st line), with soil temperatures at a depth of 10–12 m (red horizontal line), and the outdoor air temperature difference between the maximum temperature during the day and the minimum temperature at night (2nd line). Also included are the average daily absolute air humidity (3rd line) and precipitation (4th line) values, as well as the amount of energy relating to a horizontal surface received in a day (5th line).

Solar radiation

Over the course of the year, the day length, the angle of daylight incidence and the intensity of solar radiation change. This changes the radiation situation for the facades (Fig. 3.4). In summer, high radiation yields are to be expected, particularly on the east and west facades. In winter, solar radiation on the south facade is desirable because it reduces the ↙heating energy demand.

↙ **heating energy demand** p. 144

In summer, the level of radiation energy on horizontal surfaces and on east and west facades reach the highest values, with a certain amount of direct solar radiation also occurring on north facades. In winter, the only useable solar gains occur primarily on south facades.

Winter days are shorter than summer days and provide less illumination, creating a need for more artificial light. Due to the reduced ↙daylight yield and the need for ↙solar gains in winter, shading of a building's south side by other nearby buildings is undesirable.

↙ **natural lightning** p. 148

solar gains S. 144

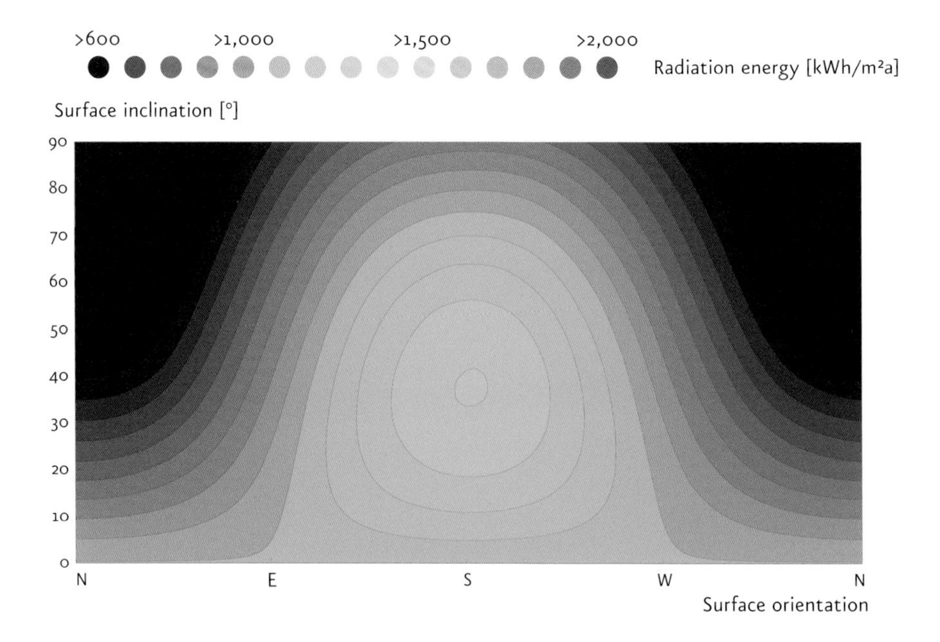

Fig. 3.3 Radiation energy received in kWh/m²a correlated with orientation and angle of inclination, to be used for evaluating the alignment of solar power systems in the Munich area

Measured on the horizontal plane, the global radiation level is 1,147 kWh/m²a. At the optimal angle of inclination (38°) and with a south-facing orientation, the level of energy received is 1,352 kWh/m²a.

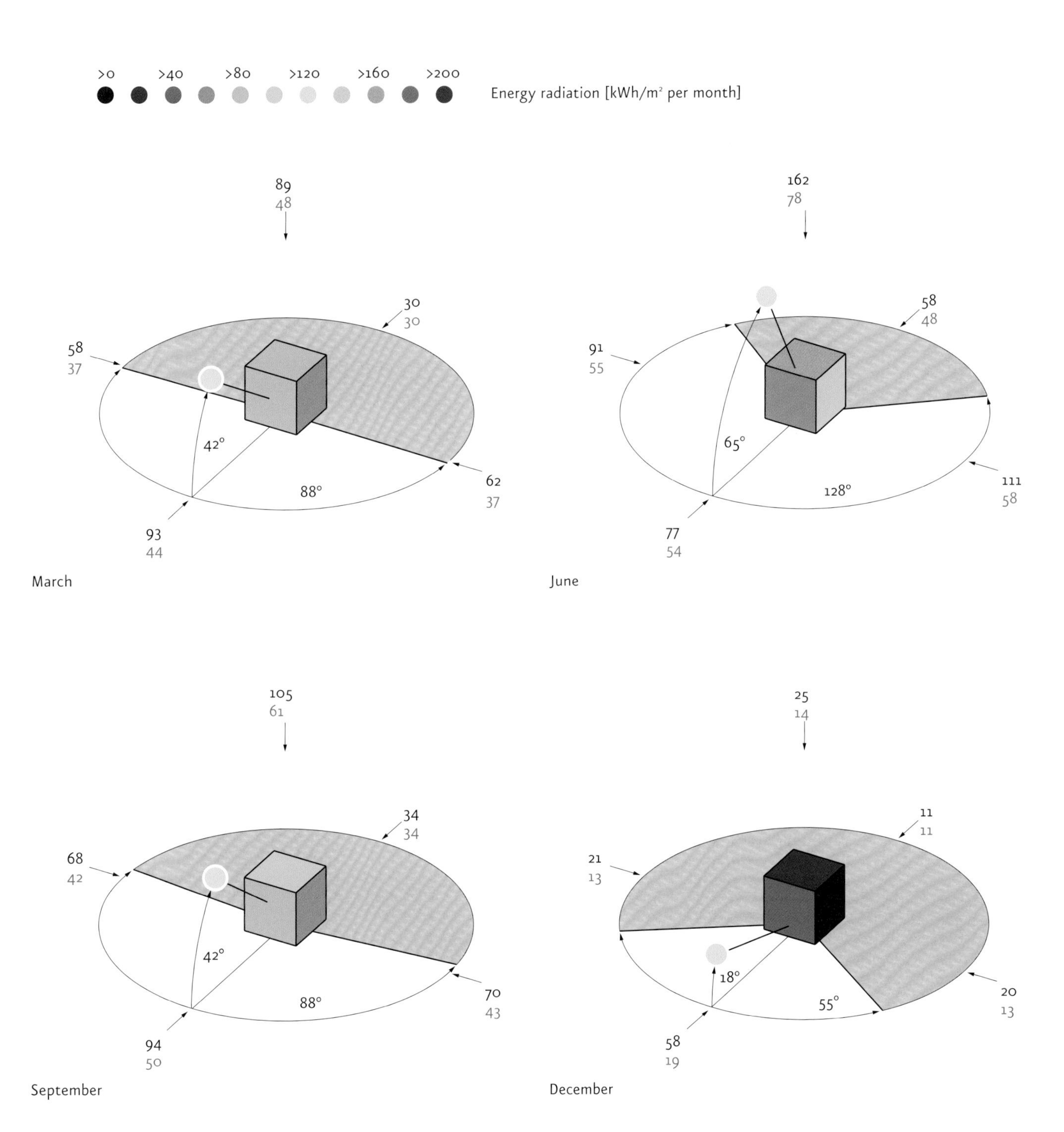

Fig. 3.4 Solar radiation and path of the sun for Munich

The sides of this cube show the amount of energy received in kWh/m² for a given month. The numbers in black quantify the overall radiation level, and those in grey the diffuse radiation level. Also included are the maximum elevation angle and azimuth angle of the sun for the 21st of the month.

Building Structure

↙
cubature
p. 144

transmiossion heat loss
p. 144

daylight provision
p. 148

natural ventilation
p. 146

orientation
p. 144

solar gains
p. 144

In a temperate climate zone, it is important to find a ↙ surface-to-volume ratio compromise between ↙ transmission heat loss, ↙ daylight provision and ↙ natural ventilation. A moderate depth of building is generally advisable. Atria and conservatories can be used to reduce heat transmission loss from the outer shell surface by creating a thermal buffer zone. Very high buildings have increased wind loads, making natural ventilation more difficult. They also place more demand on technical systems, requiring larger shaft areas.

Building ↙ orientation and the height of nearby buildings both have a major impact on the solar radiation received by the facade (Fig. 3.5). A north-south alignment is advisable because it optimises ↙ solar gain in winter and reduces undesired solar radiation incidence in summer (Fig. 3.6). It also allows good shading of the south facade by means of horizontal slats. The clearance space should be a little greater on the south side, while close proximity to other buildings on the east and west sides reduces solar loads in summer. The minimum distance from other buildings depends on the need for daylight.

Clear space around building 20 m

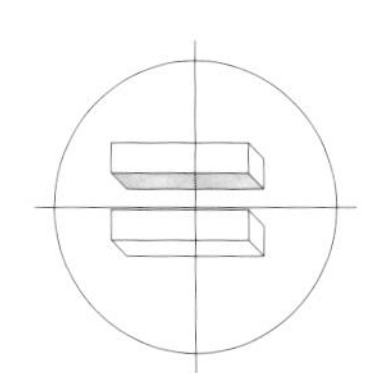

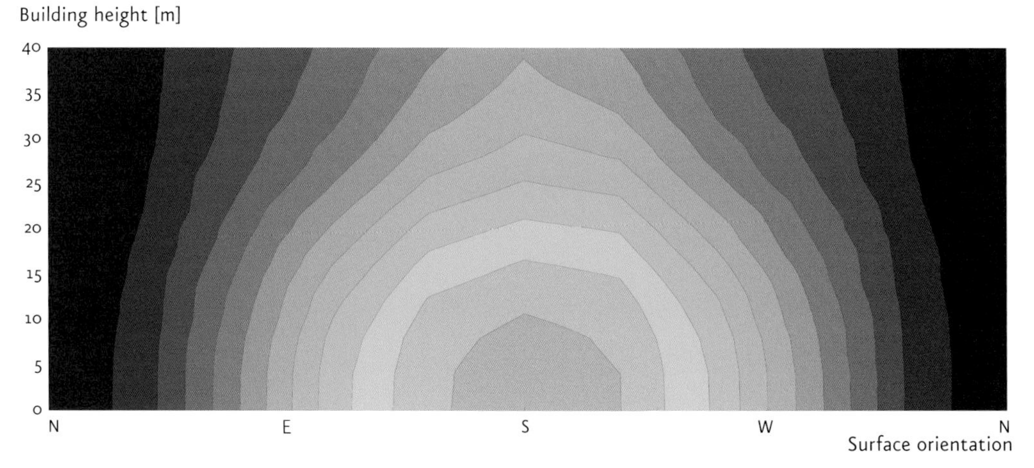

Fig. 3.5 Radiation energy [kWh/m²a], as an average value, received by the facade, correlated with its orientation and the height of a building 20 m away in Munich

This simulation is based on a typical office block, 70 x 15 x 20 m (l x w x h). The height of the shading block 20 m away is variable. As the angle of obstruction increases, it is primarily the radiation received by the south facade that is reduced. Where the neighbouring development is 10 m high, the south-oriented building surfaces receive half again as much energy as it would if the neighbouring development were 35 m high.

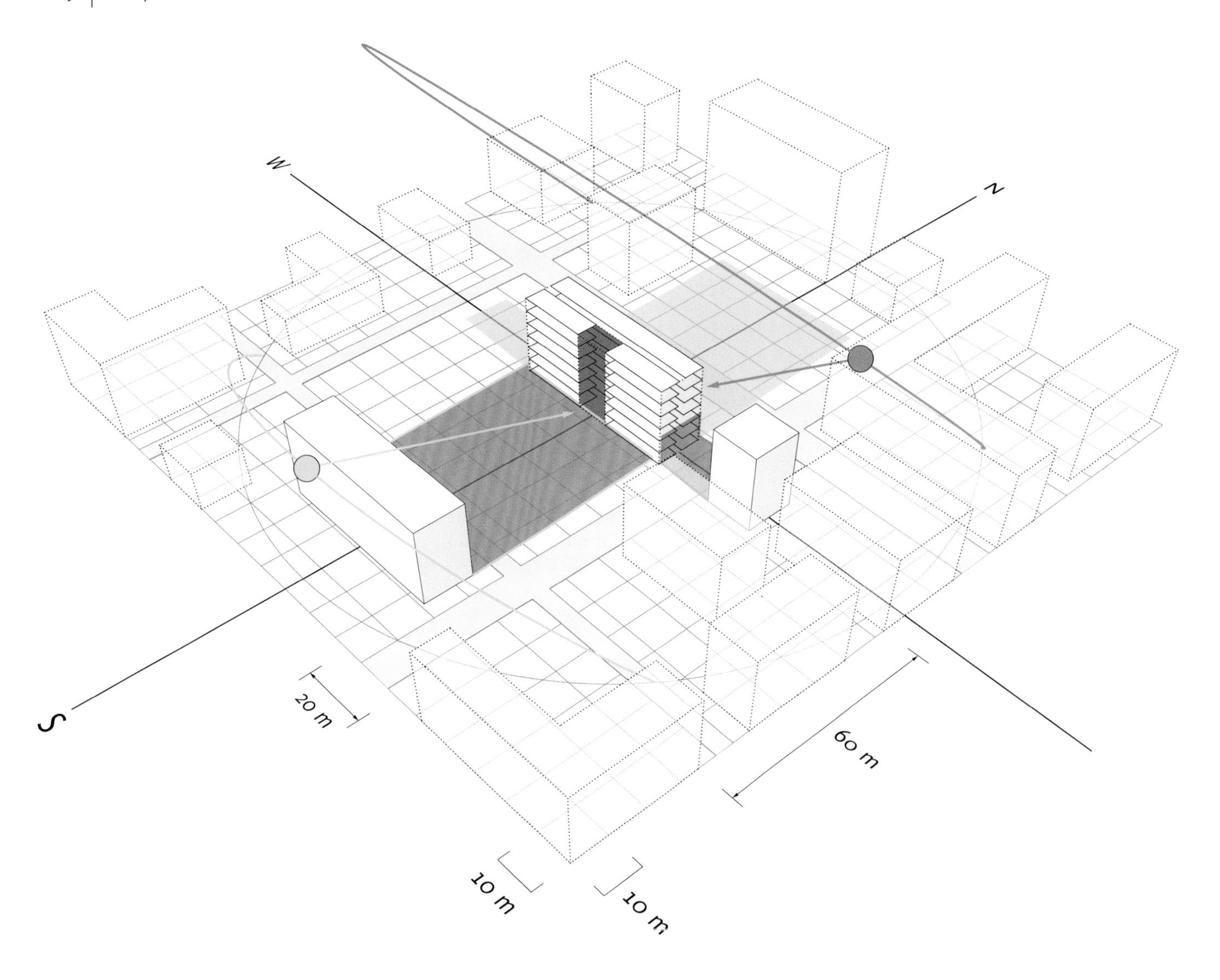

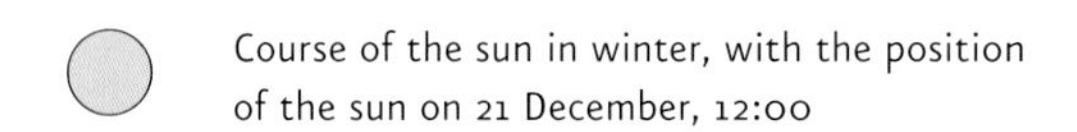
Course of the sun in winter, with the position of the sun on 21 December, 12:00

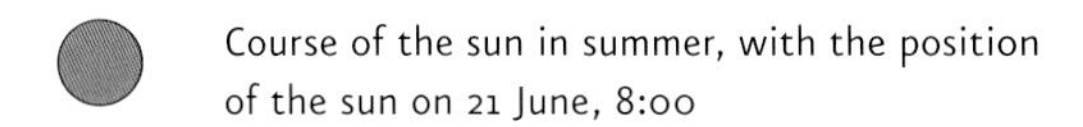
Course of the sun in summer, with the position of the sun on 21 June, 8:00

Shade at midday on 21 December. To keep the south facade clear of shade in the winter, a large clear area or area of low development is required to the south.

Shade in the morning on 21 June. With appropriate space left for daylight, east-to-west shading of the building in summer is only possible for the lower storeys. In summer, the sun shines at a low angle during the early morning and late afternoon, partially from a northerly direction.

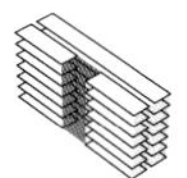
A compact building with a north-to-south orientation and an internal atrium. A low surface-to-volume ratio minimises heat losses. In this case, a triple-loaded floor plan arrangement represents a good compromise. Internalising the atrium reduces outer shell surface whilst creating a buffer climate zone. In some cases, the atrium can be incorporated into the ventilation concept. The south orientation enables solar gains in winter. If the facade is daylight-optimised, the south-facing rooms can be given a greater depth.

Fig. 3.6 Building structures for a temperate climate
In Munich, a compromise must be found that combines compactness with daylight and natural ventilation. The south facade should not be shaded by nearby buildings. Shading of the east and west facades by other buildings can be advantageous, but minimum distances should be maintained in order to ensure sufficient daylight provision.

Building Skin

A facade concept for a temperate climate zone must avoid heat input in summer and maximise passive ↙solar gain in winter. Good thermal protection is required. Ideally, external sun protection should be provided. Sun protection coatings are inefficient because they lower the daylight incidence and because of the need for solar gain in winter. Integrated photovoltaic systems can be deployed.

↙ **solar gains** p. 144

Glazing percentage

Transmission heat loss is dictated by ↙glazing percentage in winter and solar input in summer. It should lie somewhere between 50% and 70%, depending on the facade's orientation. Sufficient ↙daylight provision should be ensured by setting the window lintels high.

↙ **glazing percentage** p. 146

daylight provision p. 148

Sun protection

External ↙sun protection is required (except where the facade faces north, in which case internal systems can be used). The east and west facades receive the highest solar yields in summer, and their sun protection must be able to block a low sun. Where the percentage is relatively low, another possibility is to add projections to the south facade with dimensions based on half the windows' height, combined with an internal sun protection system.

↙ **sun protection** p. 146

Glazing

Thermal protection glass is significantly better than ↙sun protection glazing, because it allows passive solar gain in winter and does not further reduce the low daylight levels of winter. Triple thermal protection glazing with a low-e coating and gas filling can achieve a U-value as low as 0.7 W/m²K, significantly reducing heat loss in winter. If the glazing percentage is relatively small, double thermal protection glazing with a ↙U-value of 1.1 W/m²K can be used for a south facade.

↙ **glazing** p. 146

U-value p. 146

Insulation

Good thermal protection for the building skin is necessary to avoid transmission heat loss and to improve ↙comfort in the winter. An ↙insulation layer thickness of 20 cm or more is recommended.

↙ **comfort** p. 150

thermal insulation p. 146

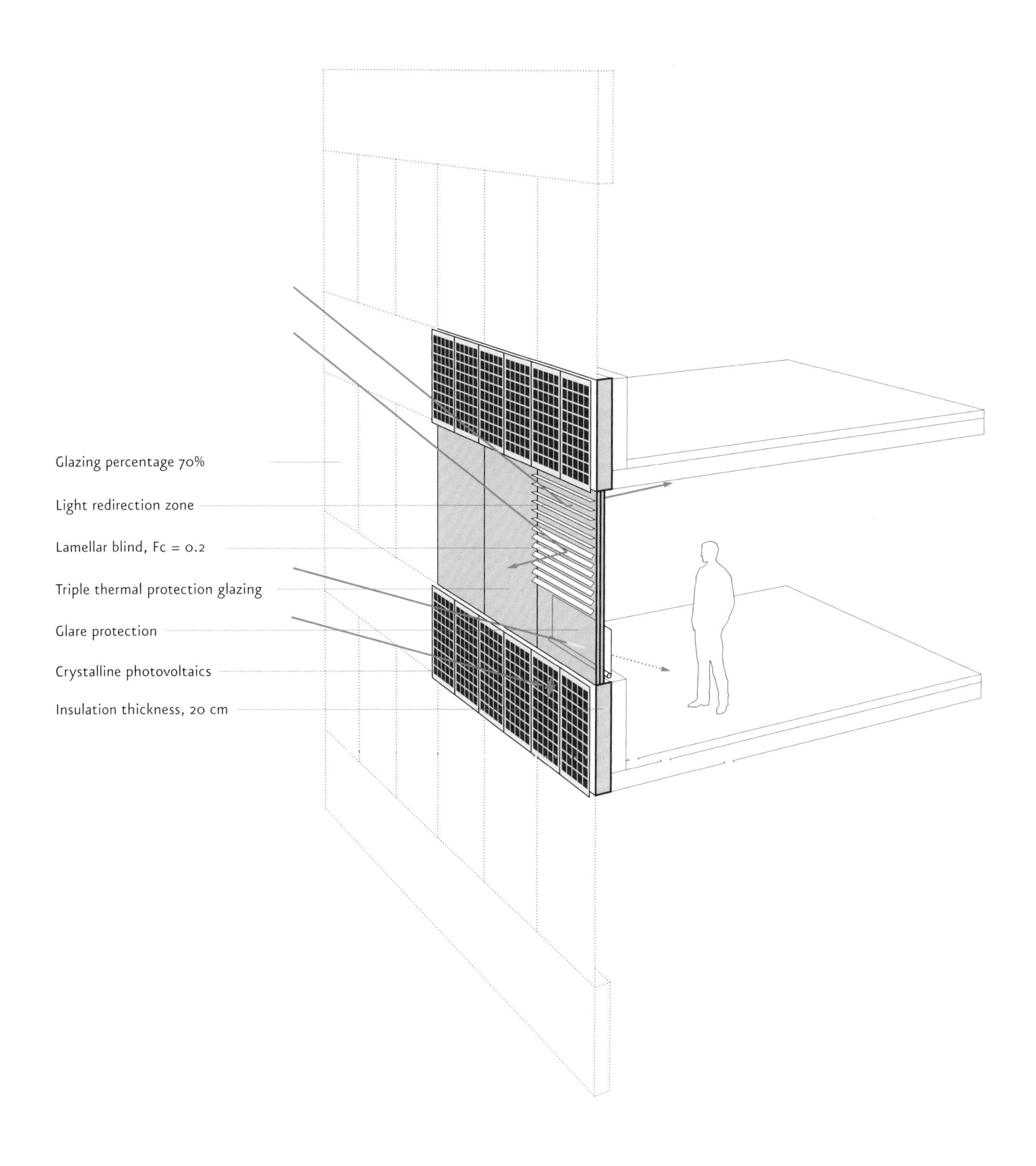

Fig. 3.7 Facade concept for the temperate climate zone

Showing strategies for a south facade with optimised energy, room climate and daylight features. One possible alternative would be a sheltering projection combined with internal sun protection. The glazing percentage for the east-facing and west-facing facades should be between 50% and 70%, and the sun protection should be able to block sunlight coming in at a shallow angle. The glazing percentage on the north-facing facade should be kept below 40%. Internal glare protection is sufficient for the north side.

Building Systems

In a temperate climate zone, the emphasis is on heating provision and renewable cooling. Where there is a high level of air exchange, mechanical ventilation with ↙heat recovery should be installed to conserve energy and improve comfort.

↙ **heat recovery** p. 144

Due to its low temperature, the soil can be used as a renewable cooling source via ↙earth piles or underground registers (Fig. 3.2). In combination with a ↙heat pump, this system can also be used for heating. Where hot water is needed, a solar thermal system should be provided. If it is sufficiently large, the ↙solar thermal system can also be used for auxiliary heating during transitional periods. The yield of a photovoltaic system in an optimal installation system is approximately 200 kWh/m²a (Fig. 3.3).

earth piles/ groundwater utilisation p. 154

refrigeration unit p. 154

solar thermal systmes p. 154

Radiator

If simple technology is required, natural ventilation with radiator heating is suitable. ↙Night ventilation openings and storage mass should be included to improve the room climate in summer. Mechanical ventilation can also be used to cool the indoor space.

↙ **night ventilation** p. 152

Concrete core activation

If renewable cooling sources such as groundwater, ground source heat pumps (earth piles) or ↙night recooling are to be used, then ↙concrete core activation is ideal. Moderate system temperatures ensure efficient operation.

↙ **cooling tower** p. 154

concrete core activation p. 152

Cooling ceilings

Where there is a great need for cooling, a cooling ceiling is a comfortable way of cooling a room. The low inflow temperatures required generally make a ↙refrigeration unit necessary. When the air is moist, the dew point regulator reduces cooling performance: in this case, a mechanical ventilation unit with an incoming air dehumidifying system is needed.

↙ **refrigeration unit** p. 154

Decentralised ventilation

If some of a building's rooms have an increased need for air, or a ventilation system has to be upgraded, facade-integrated ↙decentralised ventilation systems are ideal. These can be used for heat recovery, to condition incoming air or to provide a comfortable level of ventilation. These systems have relatively high maintenance costs. If all the rooms in a building require mechanical ventilation, centralised systems are generally more efficient and cost-effective.

↙ **decentralised ventilation system** p. 152

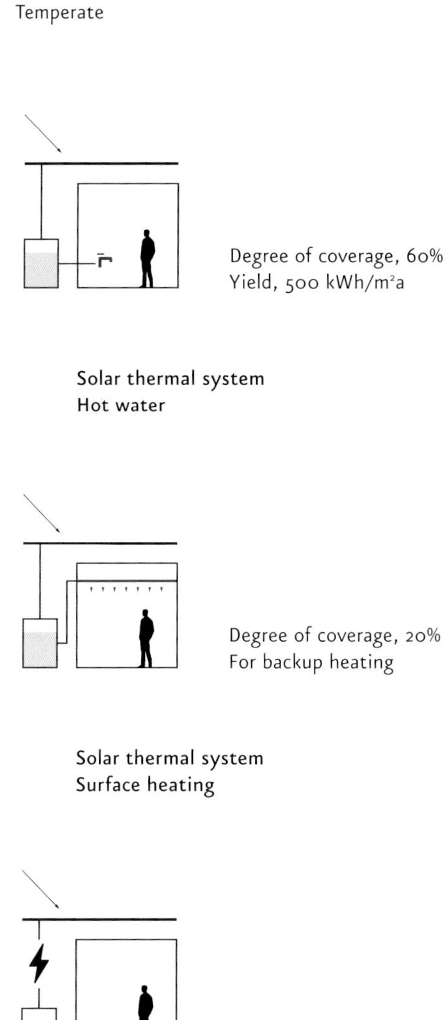

Degree of coverage, 60%
Yield, 500 kWh/m^2a

Solar thermal system
Hot water

Degree of coverage, 100%
Performance, 40–50 W/m^2
Work figure, 5

Earth piles / groundwater
Heat pump, surface heating

Degree of coverage, 20%
For backup heating

Solar thermal system
Surface heating

Degree of coverage, 100%
Performance, 35–60 W/m^2
Can also be used in a cooling ceiling

Earth piles/groundwater
Convection cooling

Yield, 200 kWh/m^2a

Photovoltaics
Feeding into mains grid

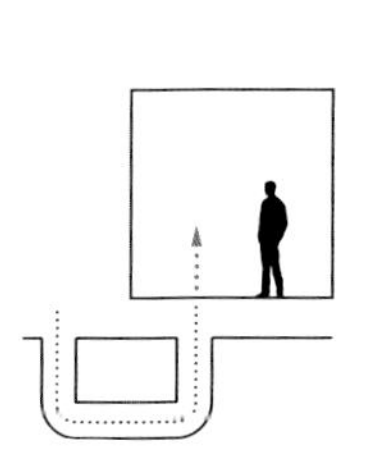

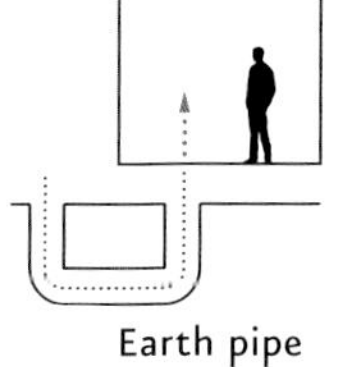

Degree of coverage, 50–100%
Performance, 20–60 W/m^2
Applies only where mechanical ventilation is in place

Earth pipe
Incoming air precooling

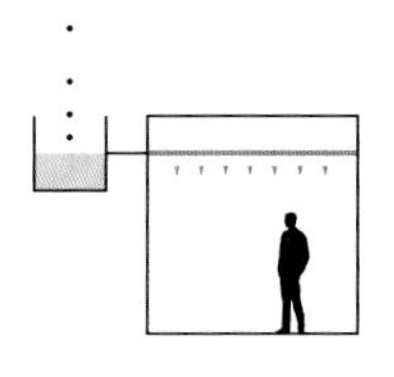

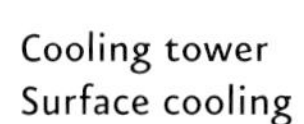

Degree of coverage, 70–100%
Performance, 35 W/m^2
Applies only where concrete core activation is in place

Cooling tower
Surface cooling

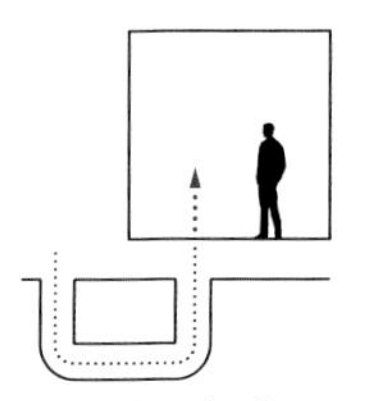

Degree of coverage, 50%
Applies only where mechanical ventilation is in place

Earth pipe
Incoming air prewarming

Fig. 3.8 Room conditioning concept combined with renewable energy generation systems for a temperate climate zone

Diagram showing suitable system combinations. The degree of coverage shows the proportion of renewable heat or cooling provided. The annual yield for a solar power system in an optimal installation position and the specific heating or cooling performance of the room conditioning systems are given.

Planning Rules for Munich

In the temperate climate zone, heating is required. Cooling energy is sometimes also required. There are virtually no humidifying or dehumidifying energy demands. These factors mean that the strategies below are effective for Munich.

Heating

↙ glazing p. 146

heating energy demand p. 144

glazing percentage p. 146

storage mass p. 144

heat recovery p. 144

glazing p. 146

Due to the long winters with low outdoor temperatures, the building skin must have good thermal insulation. Triple heat protection ↙glazing is ideal. In winter, extensive use of daylight for illumination is required and solar radiation is desirable. For this reason, sun protection glass should not be used.

The ↙heating energy demand is 20–40 kWh/m²a. The impact of a south facade's ↙glazing percentage is negligible if it is unshaded in the winter, whereas for other facades, the impact of glazing percentage may be as high as 25%. The orientation of rooms influences the heating energy demand by up to 50%. Good thermal protection for the outer wall saves 30% of energy. A thermally activated ↙storage mass can also save energy. Ventilation with a ↙heat recovery system cuts energy use by 30%.

Very good facade heat protection and triple thermal protection ↙glazing combined with internal heat loads make the heating energy demand almost non-existent, as long as a mechanical ventilation system with heat recovery is in place.

The results of the thermal simulation are accurate for a standard office space with typical internal loads. Unless stated otherwise, the space is a light construction facing south, with a glazing percentage of 50%. The glazing has a g-value of 0.6 with internal sun protection. The U-value of the outer wall is 0.3 W/m²K.

Cooling

If active cooling is not included in the plan, a good room climate can still be achieved using construction measures. During the summer, a moderated room climate can be achieved using external ↘sun protection, thermally activated ↘storage mass and intensive ↘night ventilation. A dehumidifying energy demand is not a factor.

An indoor space's orientation has a major impact on its climate, as does its glazing percentage. East and west facades have a higher cooling energy demand than south facades. Reducing the glazing percentage can reduce the cooling energy demand by 50%. Where internal ↘sun protection systems have to be used instead of external sun protection systems, the cooling energy demand is twice as high.

↘
sun protection
p. 146

storage mass
p. 144

night ventilation
p. 152

sun protection
p. 146

Potentials and strategies

In a temperate climate zone and with the right building and facade concept, a heating system can be dispensed with for most of the time. Active cooling is not required. A thermal insulation layer at least 20 cm thick, triple heat protection glazing and mechanical ventilation with heat recovery are necessary. In winter, the relatively high temperature of the soil can be used to warm the incoming air or to provide heating by means of a ↘heat pump that uses ↘earth piles or groundwater.

To create a good room climate in summer, external sun protection combined with passive cooling strategies such as a ↘concrete core activation system are advisable. Renewable cooling systems such as free night ↘recooling or groundwater and underground registers can also be used.

↘
refrigeration unit
p. 154

earth piles/ groundwater utilisation
p. 154

concrete core activation
p. 152

cooling tower
p. 154

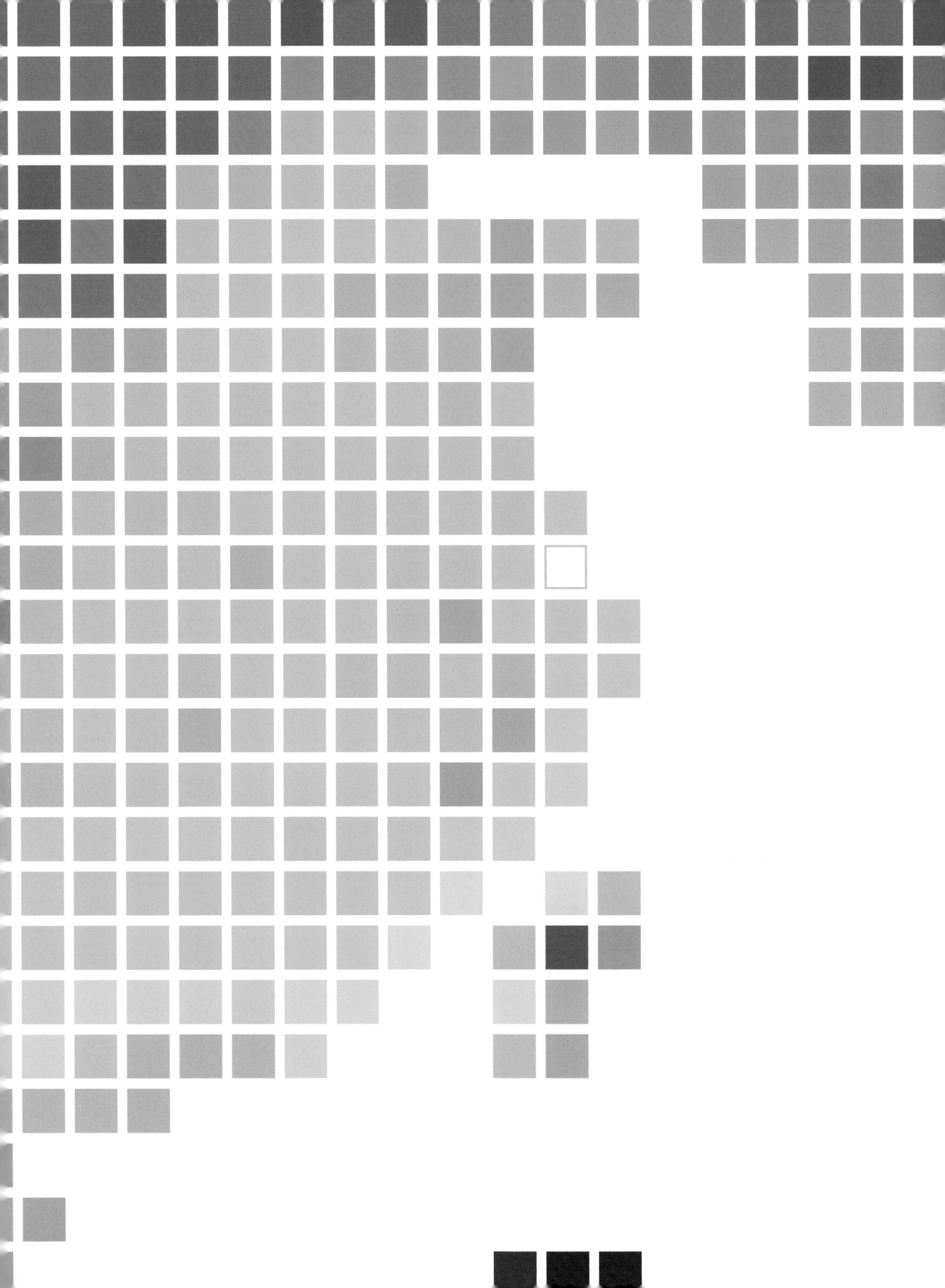

Subtropics

Shanghai, gateway to the world

Shanghai is a typical wet subtropical location. The climate is moderate and humid, with precipitation all year round and maximum temperatures exceeding 36 °C in the summer. There are four seasons in the year, with a fairly short spring and summer. It is damp and cold during the winter due to cool air blowing in from the interior of the continent and the northwest monsoon. The city's location on the sea mitigates the low temperatures; the lower limit is about -5 °C. Snow is almost unheard of. The Yangtze used to mark the "heating line"; winter heating was only permitted in buildings north of the river. From mid-May to September, there are three distinct rainy periods – the spring rains, the so-called plum rains and the autumn rains. In October, the first cold air masses blow in from the north.

100 75 50 25 0

Nights per year with an average temperature lower than 20 °C [%]

Climate in the Subtropics

The wet subtropical climate zone includes easterly continental areas at latitudes between 25° and 35° in the northern or southern hemisphere. The subtropical areas that are wet only in winter are farther away from the equator; these are widely dispersed areas on the west sides of continents, narrow coastal strips between the 30th and 40th parallel.

In the wet subtropics, summer is hot with a high degree of solar radiation, while it can freeze in winter. Precipitation is high all year round. These zones stretch from the equator to the tropics, which means that they include rainforest, savannah and desert areas. There is a west-east asymmetry of humidity and vegetation due to the monsoons, but no latitudinal succession.

The summer climate is created by warm and humid winds from the ocean. During the summer, the area of low pressure accompanied by high temperature over the continent's interior draws humid air inland from the ocean, resulting in heavy rainfall. As they move farther inland, the air masses become drier and the precipitation decreases. As a result, it may be dry here for months. In winter, cool, dry winds blow from the continent. In East Asia, these winds are known as monsoons: the southeast monsoon blows in summer and the northwest monsoon in winter.

Lush rainforests are the predominant natural vegetation along the coasts and on the windward side of mountains. As one moves inland and the precipitation level decreases, the vegetation changes to evergreen wet forests and laurel forests. Farther inland are deciduous monsoon forests or dry forests.

Range of outdoor air temperatures and absolute humidity over the 8,760 hours in a year

Jan Monthly average values for outdoor air temperature and absolute humidity

ASHRAE-55 comfort zone for winter and summer

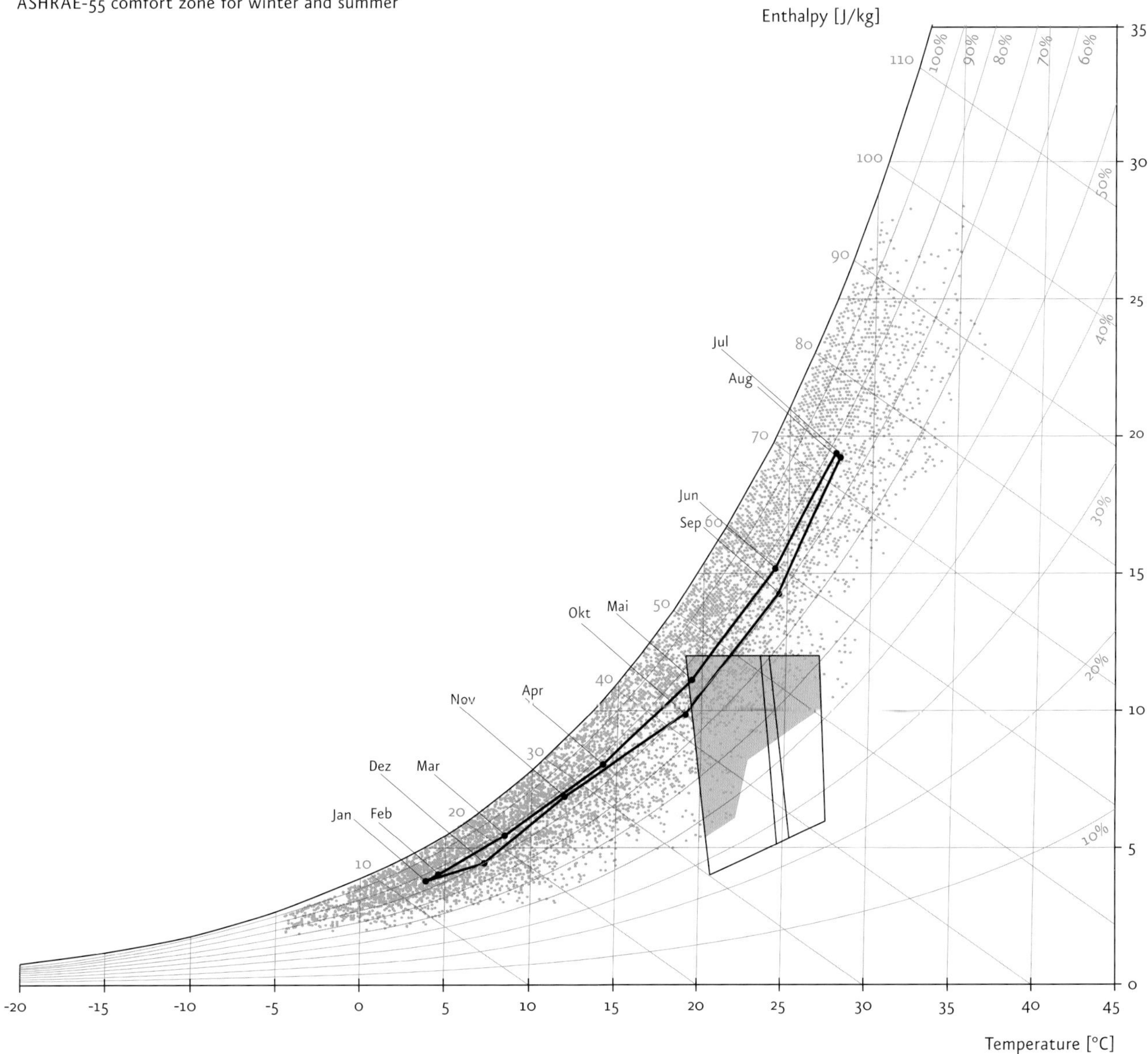

Fig. 4.1 Range of outdoor air temperatures and absolute humidity for Shanghai, with the ASHRAE-55 comfort zone superimposed

Shanghai's climate features low winter temperatures (around freezing point) and hot and humid summers with temperatures of over 30 °C. The main need is for cooling, with almost no heating energy demand. Because the absolute humidity is above 12 g/kg, air must be dehumidified from May to September to create a comfortable indoor humidity. Humidifying is unnecessary.

Climate and Construction

Shanghai has a typical wet subtropical climate. There are pronounced seasons with relatively short transitional periods. Temperature fluctuations are moderate. A very small degree of heating energy is needed, along with a very large degree of cooling and dehumidifying energy (Fig. 4.1). ↙ Natural ventilation is possible during the transitional period. A description of climatic conditions in Shanghai (Fig. 4.2) for the purpose of constructing buildings adapted to the climate is given below.

↙ **natural ventilation** p. 146

Temperature

Outdoor temperatures fluctuate between freezing point and over 30 °C. Heating is generally required in winter, and in summer a comfortable room climate is only possible with cooling. The ↙ soil temperature at a depth of 12 m is a potential source of heat in winter and of cooling source in summer; heat can also be sourced at greater depths. The differences between the maximum temperatures during the day and the minimum temperatures at night are relatively low – less than 10 K during the summer. This reduces the effectiveness of night cooling.

↙ **soil temperature** p. 142

Humidity

During the winter, absolute air humidity is rarely lower than 4 g/kg. There is no humidifying energy demand in winter. From May to September, air humidity is so high that dehumidifying is required. The high air humidity during the hot summer months can create ↙ dew point issues in surface cooling systems.

↙ **dew point temperature** p. 142

Global radiation

The ↙ global radiation rate is 1,282 kWh/m²a. The fact that rain falls all year round creates a high level of diffuse radiation, resulting in a reduced amount of radiation energy relative to other areas in the same latitude. Maximum values occur in July, and minimum values occur in December. Solar thermal energy systems produce very good yields in Shanghai, and this, combined with the low heating energy demand, means that solar heating is a possibility. ↙ Solar cooling systems are very cost-effective because the collectors can remain active all year round. Integrated ↙ photovoltaic systems are also suitable.

↙ **global radiation** p. 142

solar cooling p. 154

photovoltaics p. 154

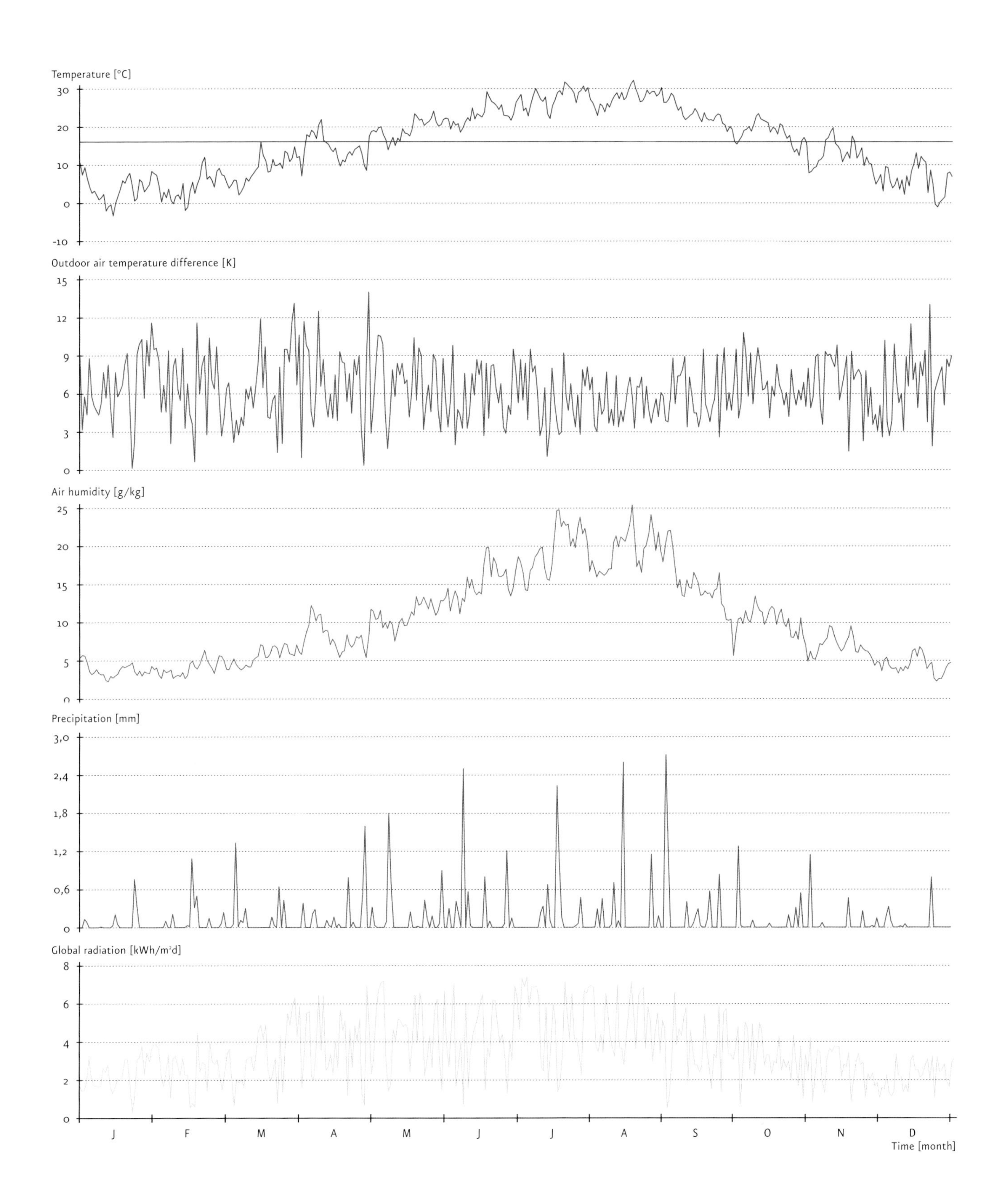

Fig. 4.2 The major climate elements for Shanghai over the course of a year

Average daily outdoor air temperatures (1st line), with soil temperatures at a depth of 10–12 m (red horizontal line), and the outdoor air temperature difference between the maximum temperature (during the day) and the minimum temperature (at night), (2nd line). Also included are the average daily absolute air humidity (3rd line) and precipitation (4th line) values, as well as the amount of energy relating to a horizontal surface received in a day (5th line).

Solar radiation

The city's position near the 30th parallel means that changes in day length and angle of daylight incidence throughout the year are moderate. There is only a small degree of change in the amount of radiation received by facades throughout the year – except in the case of south-facing facades (Fig. 4.4).

Due to the steep angle of incidence, horizontal surfaces receive the highest solar radiation values almost all year round – unlike facades. In summer, east and west facades are the most irradiated facade surfaces, whereas south facades, which are exposed almost exclusively to ↙ diffuse radiation, receive the highest degree of radiation energy in the winter. During the short transitional periods, the difference between these three facade orientations is low. The north facade receives only diffuse radiation all year round.

↙
global radiation
p. 142

Winter days are shorter than summer days, creating an illumination energy need. ↙ Sun protection glazing reduces the high indoor diffuse radiation input. Due to the high environmental ↙ illuminance, the reduction in ↙ daylight transmission this creates is not a significant consideration.

↙
glazing
p. 146

illuminance
p. 148

degree of daylight transmission
p. 148

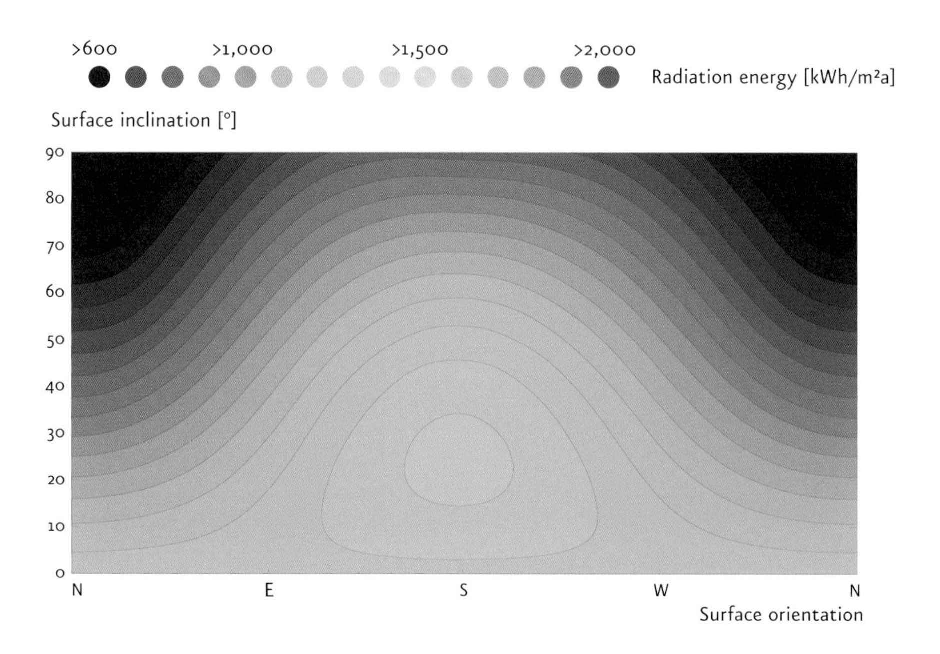

Fig. 4.3 Radiation energy in kWh/m²a correlated with orientation and angle of inclination, to be used for evaluating the alignment of solar power systems in Shanghai

Measured on the horizontal plane, the global radiation level is 1,282 kWh/m²a. At the optimal angle of inclination (24.5°) and with a south-facing orientation, the level of energy received is 1,363 kWh/m²a.

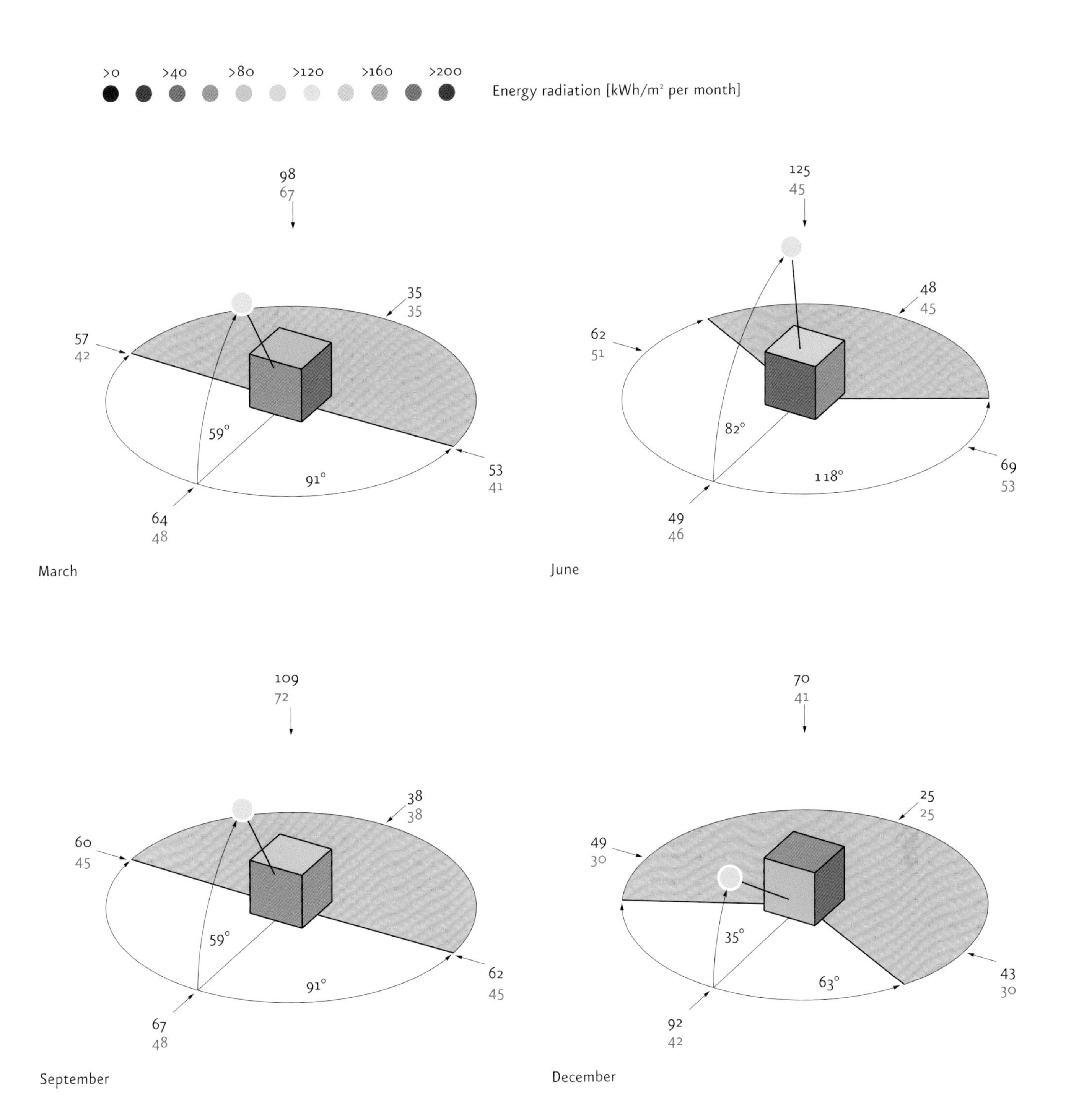

Fig. 4.4 Solar radiation and path of the sun for Shanghai

The sides of this cube show the amount of energy received in kWh/m² for a given month. The numbers in black quantify the overall radiation level, and those in grey the diffuse radiation level. Also included are the maximum elevation angle and azimuth angle of the sun for the 21st of the month.

Building Structure

In the subtropics, compactness is less important due to the low heating energy demand. A less compact structure improves daylight provision and opportunities for ↙natural ventilation. The building depth should therefore generally be low.

↙ **natural ventilation** p. 146

A north-south ↙orientation is the most favourable in solar radiation terms, in summer as well as in winter. Due to the relatively low difference between the amounts of radiation received by differently oriented facades and the low heating energy demand, however, this is not the primary or decisive factor. As the major problem is how to avoid solar yield, being shaded by other buildings is an advantage (Fig. 4.6).

As much of the radiation the city receives is diffuse, the radiation energy level is not very high in spite of the low latitude. The impact of orientation and of angle of obstruction is less than in locations with more direct radiation (Fig. 4.5). Distance between buildings should be great enough to protect ↙daylight provision.

↙ **daylight provision** p. 148

Clear space around building 20 m

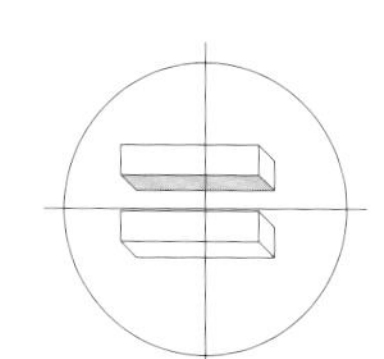

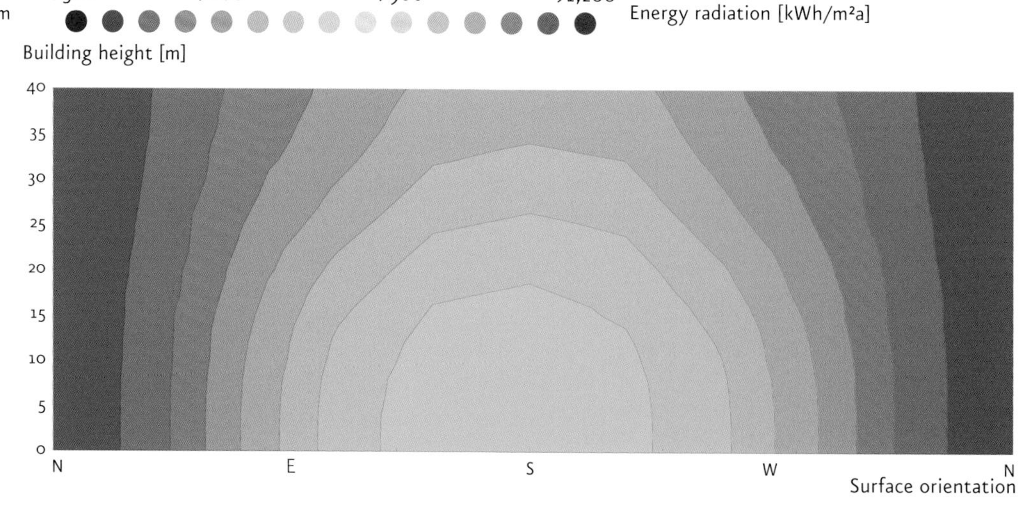

Fig. 4.5 Radiation energy [kWh/m²a], as an average value, received by the facade, correlated with its orientation and the height of a building 20 m away in Shanghai

This simulation is based on a typical office block, 70 m x 15 m x 20 m (l x w x h). The height of the shading block 20 m away is variable. In Shanghai, the solar radiation received by a south-facing facade, even where the neighbouring development is as low as 10 m high, is about half as high again as that received by a north facade.

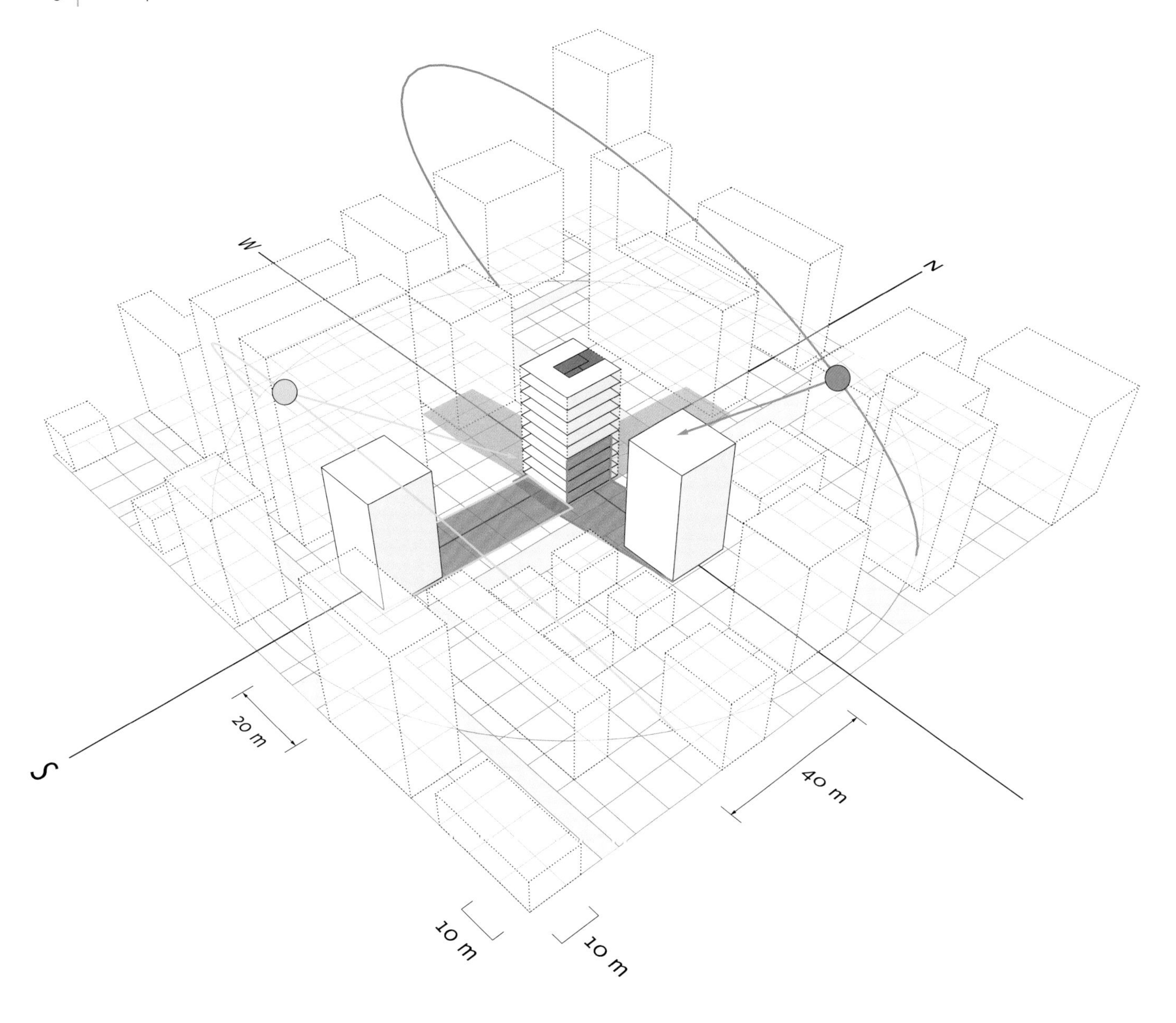

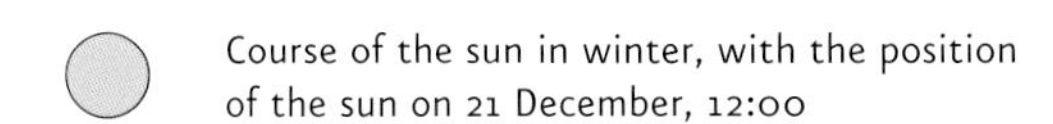
Course of the sun in winter, with the position of the sun on 21 December, 12:00

Course of the sun in summer, with the position of the sun on 21 June, 8:00

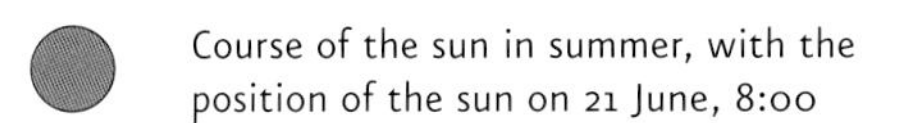
Shade at midday on 21 December. To keep the south facade free of shade in the winter, the nearest building on the south side should not be closer than about 1.3 times the building's height.

Shade in the morning on 21 June. With appropriate space left for daylight, a maximum of half the facade can be shaded by buildings to the east and west during the morning and evening.

A point (rather than linear) building with a north-facing access zone. The surface-to-volume ratio and the orientation play only a minor role. Daylight use can be optimised by grouping rooms with low depth around a centre. The open, north-facing area houses the access area and a combined-use area. This reduces the solar loads on the north facade. Where the location is favourable, all zones can easily be naturally ventilated.

Fig. 4.6 Building structures for the subtropics
In Shanghai, compactness and orientation are of minor significance. Cubature can be planned with the daylight incidence in mind. Solar gains are desirable in winter, whilst east-west shading reduces the cooling energy demand in summer.

Building Skin

The high level of diffuse radiation in the subtropics, particularly on east, south and west facades, means that sun protection concepts must include glazing that reduces this radiation yield. The cooling energy demand is much higher than the heating energy demand. Solar energy generation on the building skin is an option.

Glazing percentage

↙ glazing percentage p. 146

The ↙ glazing percentage must be chosen with solar input and daylight illumination in mind. It should not be greater than 60%. Full-length skylights improve the lighting depth.

Sun protection

↙ sun protection p. 146

External ↙ sun protection is recommended. Room temperature-responsive systems are more efficient because they also block diffuse radiation input. For a south facade, projections are an efficient alternative if they are used in combination with sun protection glass or internal sun protection. They are unaffected by weather.

Glazing

↙ glazing p. 146
g-value p. 146
U-value p. 146

Sun protection ↙ glass with additional low-e coating, a ↙ g-value of lower than 0.4 and a maximum ↙ U-value of 1.4 W/m²K should be used. In terms of cooling energy energy demand, sun protection glazing with a g-value of 0.3 combined with internal sun protection is as efficient as glazing with a g-value of 0.6 combined with external, radiation-responsive sun protection. For skylights, it may be sensible to dispense with sun protection coating.

Insulation

↙ transmission heat loss p. 144
thermal insultaion p. 146

A thermal protection layer at least 5 cm thick is recommended, as it reduces ↙ transmission heat loss. ↙ Insulation has no significant impact on the cooling energy demand.

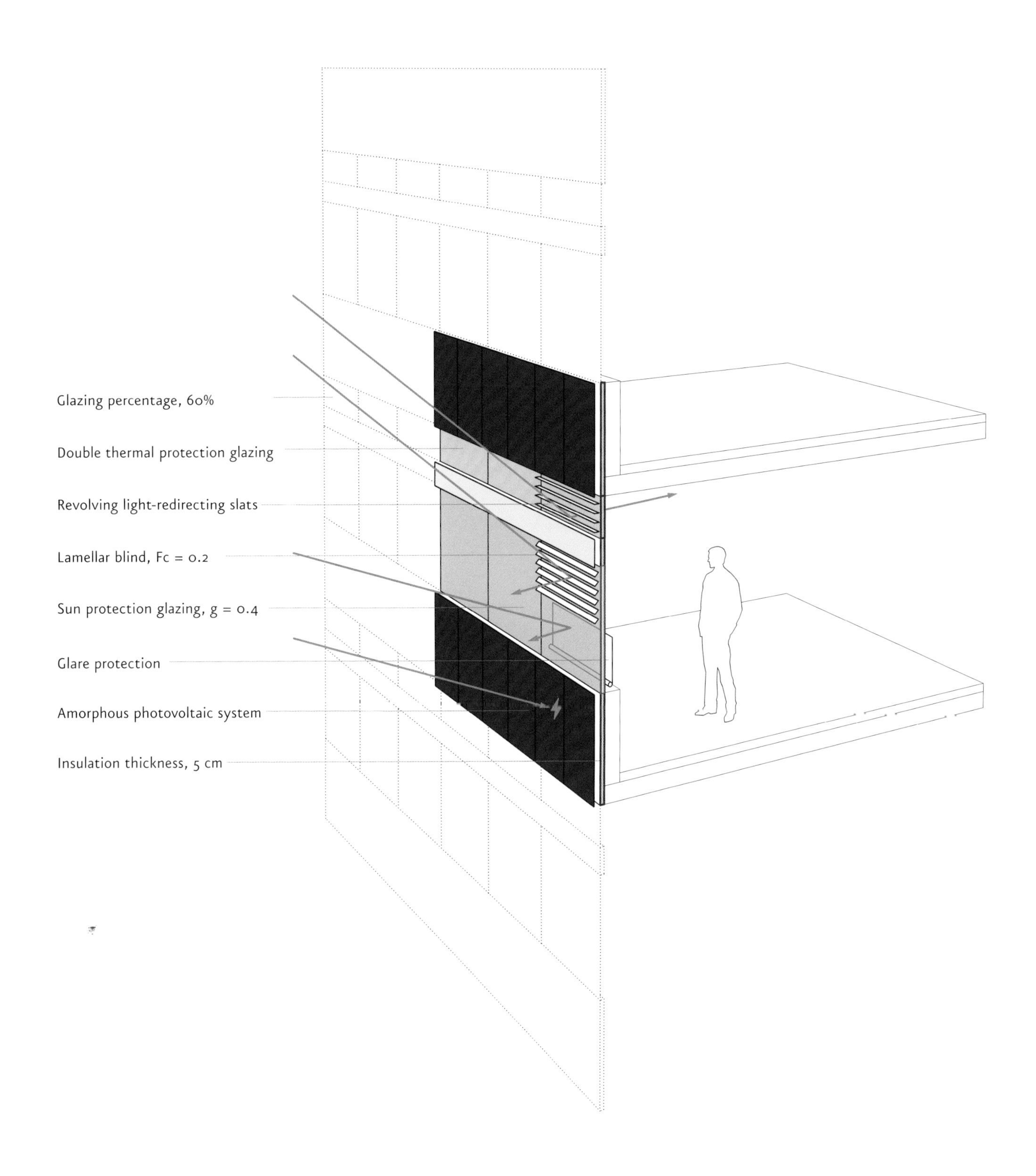

Fig. 4.7 Facade concept for the subtropics

Strategies for a south facade optimised in terms of energy, room climate and daylight. Alternatively, a more efficient sun protection glass with an internal system could be used. The glazing percentage should also be around 50% for the east and west facades. The sun protection must be able to block daylight coming in at a shallow angle. For the north facade, a glazing percentage of 50% is also recommended. Here, sun protection glass is sufficient without any other sun protection measures.

Building Systems

In the subtropics, a low degree of heating and a high degree of cooling and dehumidifying are needed. In winter and during the transitional period, natural ventilation is a possibility. In summer, mechanical ventilation is advantageous due to the humidity and the high outdoor air temperatures.

↙ **refrigeration unit** p. 154
solar thermal system p. 154
solar cooling p. 154

Renewable heat sources provide effective heating measures – e.g. ground source ↙ heat pumps. ↙ Solar collectors can also contribute to heat provision. The soil can also be used as a cooling source for base load cooling (Fig. 4.2). ↙ Solar cooling concepts are also practical, and the collector surfaces required for this can be used for heating in winter. Where there is a hot water energy demand, thermal collectors are a very effective solution. Where the installation situation is optimal, a photovoltaic system's yield is around 200 kWh/m^2a (Fig. 4.3).

Heating/cooling convector

↙ **convector** p. 152

Where the ventilation requirement is low and the cooling loads are moderate, natural ventilation with a heating/cooling convector is sufficient. As this is used for both heating and cooling, a ventilator is necessary. The convector can be effectively regulated. Condensate drainage is generally required. Where there are moderate to high cooling loads and an increased need for fresh air, a ↙ convector can also be combined with mechanical ventilation. Another advantage of this system is that it dehumidifies the incoming air centrally.

Concrete core activation

↙ **concrete core activation** p. 152
dew point temperature p. 142

If renewable energy sources are needed for heating and cooling, a ↙ concrete core activation system can be used as a heat and cooling transfer system. The inflow temperatures required for a concrete core activation system are moderate. Because of ↙ dew point issues, a mechanical ventilation system with inflow air dehumidifying is required. This setup can handle moderate loads.

Split units

↙ **split units** p. 152

Where a system is being renovated or upgraded, or where the internal heat loads have changed, ↙ split units may be a cost-effective targeted room conditioning measure. They can be combined with natural ventilation. In reverse operation, they can also be used for heating.

Decentralised ventilation

↙ **Decentralised ventilation system** p. 152
heat recovery p. 144

↙ Decentralised facade-integrated ↙ ventilation apparatus is a way of providing ventilation plus ↙ heat recovery and heating and cooling services within a building. Maintenance is more demanding, but this system is also easier to upgrade.

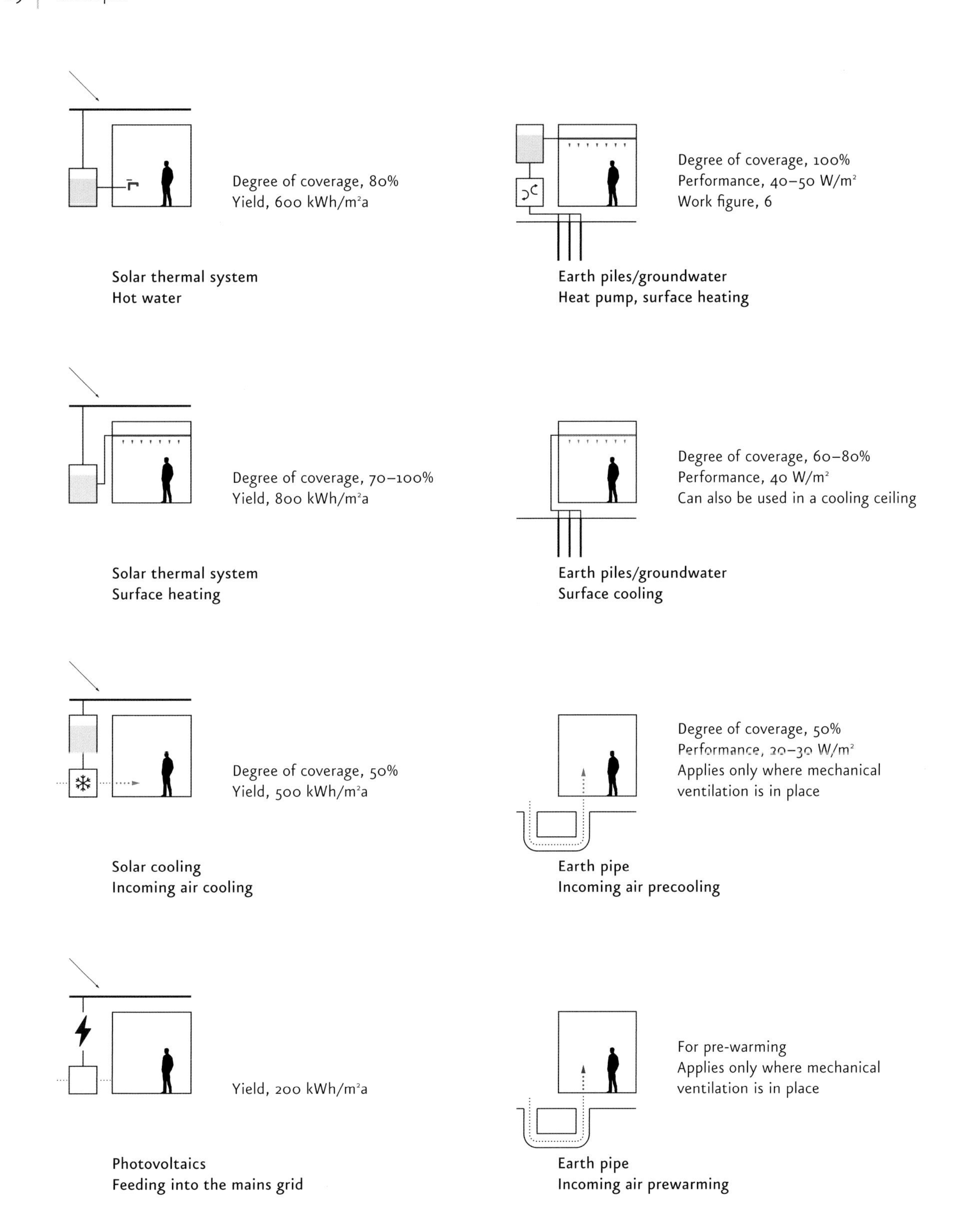

Fig. 4.8 Room conditioning concepts combined with renewable energy generation systems for the subtropics

Suitable system combinations. The degree of coverage shows the proportion of renewable heat or cooling provided. The annual yield for a solar power system in an optimal installation position and the specific heating or cooling performance of the room conditioning systems are given.

Planning Rules for Shanghai

In the subtropics, a very low amount of heating energy and a very high amount of cooling and dehumidifying energy are required. The levels of diffuse radiation in summer are a major factor in planning. The following planning strategies are effective for Shanghai:

Cooling and dehumidifying

↙
night ventilation p. 152
storage masses p. 144
sun protection p. 146
glazing percentage p. 146
cooling energy demand p. 144

Conditions during a Shanghai summer without cooling can be seriously uncomfortable. Acceptable conditions cannot be achieved without cooling, even with a reduced glazing percentage, intensive ↙night ventilation and extensive ↙storage masses combined with a radiation-responsive, external ↙sun protection system. Air inflow dehumidifying is required. The temperature level created by renewable cooling sources such as groundwater or the soil may be sufficient to dehumidify the inflow in some cases.

For an office building, the cooling energy demand is between 70 and 100 kWh/m^2a. Approximately 70–80% of this is for cooling, and the rest for dehumidifying. The ↙glazing percentage affects the ↙cooling energy demand by 25%, as does orientation. External sun protection is better than an internal system – allowing for the fact that an additional sun protection coating is generally used, the potential reduction is approximately 15%, and room temperature-responsive controlled sun protection increases this value. Night cooling is advantageous in energy terms, cutting energy use by as much as 30% when combined with a heavy construction.

A combination of passive measures – a heavy construction with night ventilation combined with efficient sun protection – can reduce cooling energy expenditure by up to 40%. In a space with no external sun protection and a low glazing percentage, night ventilation reduces the cooling energy demand by about 40%.

The results of the thermal simulation are accurate for a standard office space with typical internal loads. Unless stated otherwise, the space is a light construction facing south, with a glazing percentage of 50%. The glazing has a g-value of 0.3 with internal sun protection. The U-value of the outer wall is 0.6 W/m^2K.

Heating

A low-level ↘heating energy demand exists in Shanghai due to the low winter temperatures. For office buildings with a medium glazing percentage and no outer wall insulation, this is generally lower than 20 kWh/m²a. A 5 cm heat insulation layer can reduce the heating energy demand by 50%. Reducing the wall's ↘U-value has no significant effect.

The influence of the glazing percentage on the heating energy demand is relatively small, but orientation does have some impact. Because the heating energy demand is so low, the savings generated by heat recovery and increased storage mass are negligible.

A heavy-duty sun protection coating is slightly more efficient than external sun protection in terms of the cooling energy demand, but it reduces indoor daylight and the passive ↘solar gain in winter.

Potentials and strategies

If a cooling source – such as ↘groundwater or the soil – is reliably available, it makes sense to utilise ↘concrete core activation. Because of ↘dew point issues, incoming air must be dehumidified, particularly in months with a high environmental air humidity level. In combination with precooling of the incoming air – which is, in practice, necessary in any case due to the dehumidifying energy demand – and efficient sun protection, this system can, under the right conditions, obviate the need for machine cooling.

With the right combination of construction and technical measures, no heat generation or heating system is required. To achieve this, the U-value of the walls should be at least 0.3 W/m²K, and double heat protection glazing is also necessary. Large glazing percentages can have a positive impact on the heating energy demand, particularly in a south facade.

↘
heating energy demand
p. 144

↘
solar gains
p. 144

↘
earth piles/ groundwater utilisation
p. 154

concrete core activation
p. 152

dew point temperature
p. 142

Tropics

Bangalore: India's Silicon Valley

Bangalore, a tropical location that is wet in summer, is fortunate enough to have the most pleasant climate in India – it was once the summer resort of the British colonial classes. It has comparatively mild temperatures due to its high altitude. Bangalore's climate is dictated by India's monsoon cycle. Due to the nearness of the equator, variations in temperature throughout the year are low, and the sun remains in a similar position, high in the sky. Temperatures are highest immediately before the rainy season, reaching 36 °C. The rainy season brings a degree of coolness. In the dry season, temperatures sink as low as 14 °C. Higher radiation levels during the day and a higher degree of reflection at night make the temperature differences during the dry season significantly greater than the temperature differences during the rainy season.

100 75 50 25 0

Nights per year with an average temperature lower than 20 °C [%]

Climate in the Tropics

Tropical areas that are alternately dry and humid, or wet in summer, which are also known as the savannahs, exist in both the northern and southern hemisphere, stretching from tropical rainforests at the equator to the dry areas on the tropics.

The rainy season falls in the summer half-year due to the influence of the inner tropical convergence zone, while the near-total absence of precipitation in winter is created by the dry trade winds. The length of the rainy season decreases as one moves towards the tropic line. Towards the equator, the rainy season lasts longer, with more rain falling.

The wet savannahs of the dry-humid tropics have two precipitation maxima per year. Dry savannahs have a single maximum precipitation period.

Temperatures are high all year round, with the highest values occurring immediately prior to the rainy season. The lowest temperatures occur in the middle of the dry period. There may be frost in high areas at a distance from the equator during the dry period.

The cooling, moderating effect of the summer rainy season means that the temperature is relatively well balanced over the year.

The vegetation is predominantly continuous grassland with scattered trees and bushes.

Range of outdoor air temperatures and absolute humidity over the 8,760 hours in a year

Jan Monthly average values for outdoor air temperature and absolute humidity

ASHRAE-55 comfort zone for winter and summer

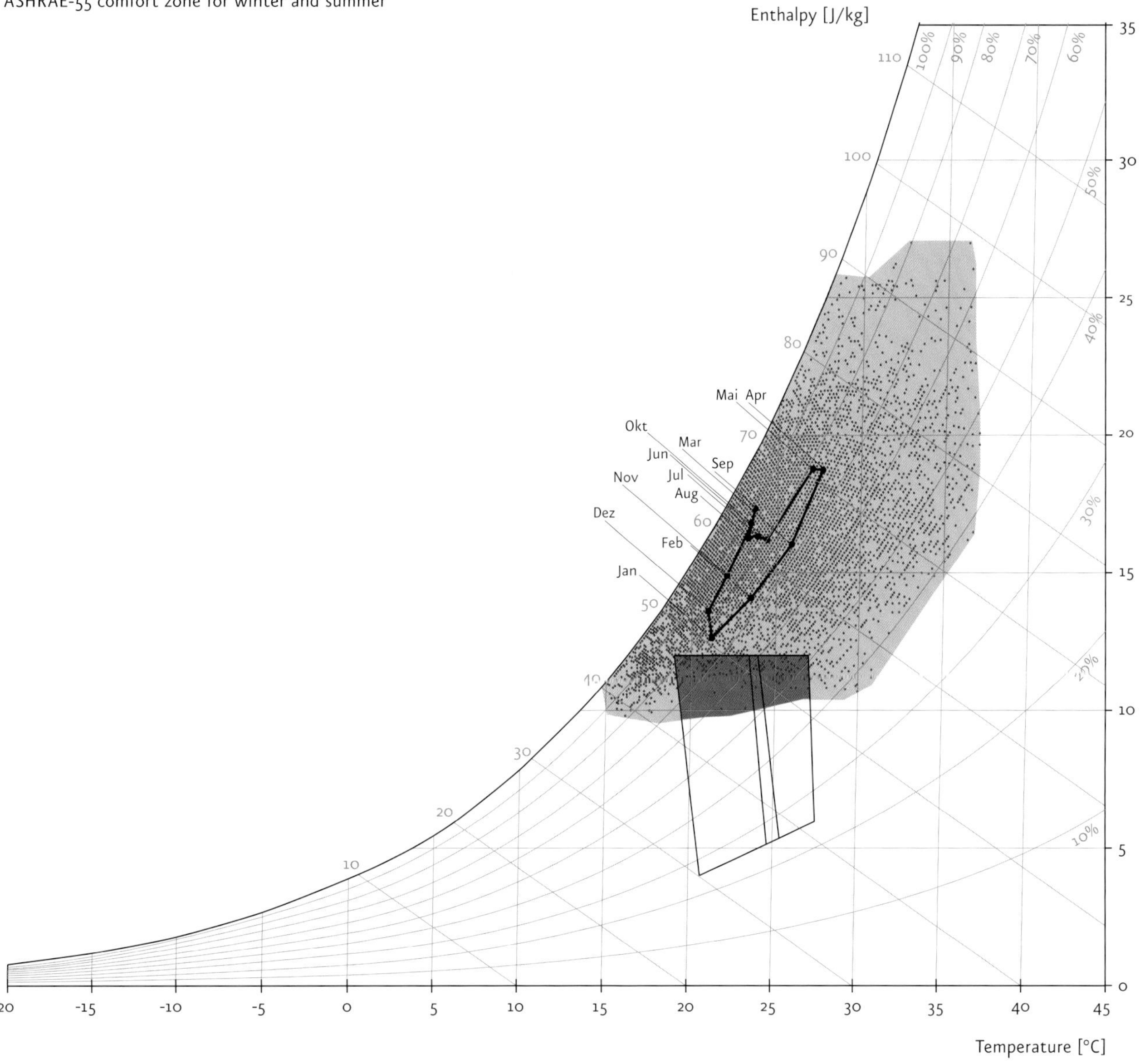

Fig. 5.1 Range of outdoor air temperature and absolute humidity for Bangalore, with the ASHRAE-55 comfort zone superimposed

Bangalore's climate features high temperatures all year round, with maximum values of over 35 °C. Cooling is needed to create a comfortable room climate. The focus is on dehumidifying – because the absolute humidity level is above 12 g/kg almost all the time, the incoming air has to be dehumidified all year round. A heating system is not required.

Climate and Construction

Bangalore is a typical dry/humid tropics location. Heating systems are not required in the tropics unless the altitude is very high. Otherwise, only hot water provision is required. Cooling is required almost all year round. Absolute humidity is so high all year round that an incoming air dehumidifying system should be provided if at all possible (Fig. 5.1). ↙ Natural ventilation is possible all year round, but the area's high absolute humidity should be borne in mind. A description of climatic conditions in Bangalore for the purpose of constructing buildings adapted to the climate is given below (Fig. 5.2).

↙ **natural ventilation** p. 146

Temperature

Bangalore's low latitude means that the temperature remains at the same relatively high level all year round, with little fluctuation. Heat loss is not a factor in Bangalore; cooling, on the other hand, is required all year round. The outdoor air temperatures are invariably higher than 14 °C, with maximum values of over 35 °C. The fact that there is no real cooling during the night means that ↙ night cooling is only possible in the winter months, in combination with cooling. Because the average annual temperature is approximately 24 °C, the soil's usefulness as a renewable cooling source is limited; even at greater depths, it can only provide incoming air cooling.

↙ **night ventilation** p. 152

Humidity

The absolute humidity value is always above the comfortable level of 12 g/kg; sometimes it is as high as 26 g/kg. This makes it impossible to deploy ↙ surface cooling systems without dehumidifying the incoming air.

↙ **heat/cold transfer** p. 150

Global radiation

The sum of the ↙ global radiation is 2,030 kWh/m²a. The high position of the sun all year round leads to high solar radiation all year round, with lower values only occurring during the monsoon period, which is also the period with the highest level of diffuse radiation. For this reason, solar energy systems such as ↙ photovoltaics and ↙ solar cooling can be used. Desiccant cooling is particularly suitable.

↙ **global radiation** p. 142
photovoltaics p. 154
solar cooling p. 154

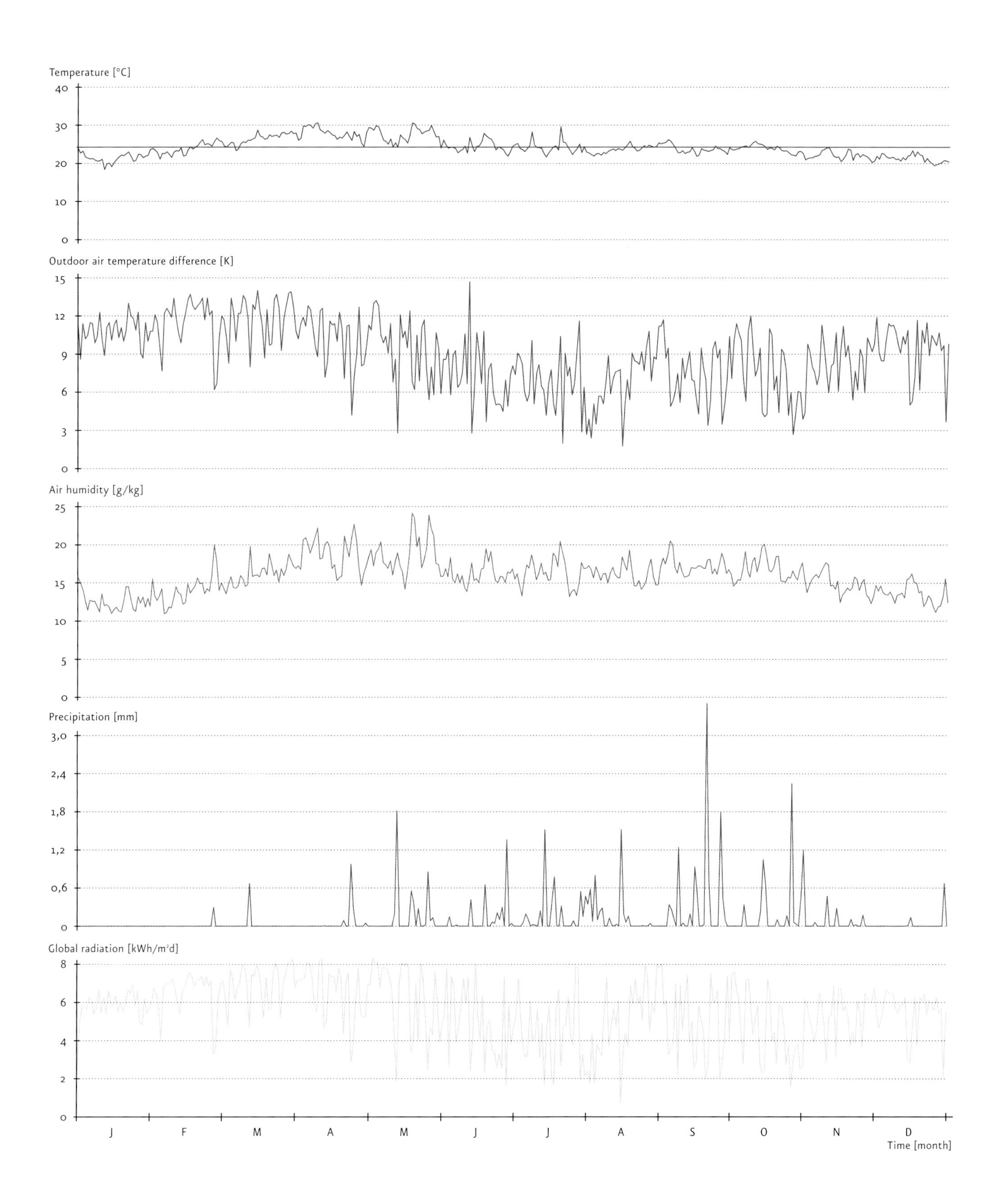

Fig. 5.2 The major climate elements for Bangalore over the course of a year

Average daily outdoor air temperatures (1st line), with soil temperatures at a depth of 10–12 m (red horizontal line), and the outdoor air temperature difference between the maximum temperature (during the day) and the minimum temperature (at night), (2nd line). Also included are the average daily absolute air humidity (3rd line) and precipitation (4th line) values, as well as the amount of energy relating to a horizontal surface received in a day (5th line).

Solar radiation

Bangalore's low latitude and position close to the equator mean that the day length barely changes over the year. The angle of radiation incidence is very high. In March and September, the sun stands almost at the zenith at noon. In summer, it passes the zenith, with the result that the solar radiation comes from a northerly direction all day.

Horizontal surfaces consistently receive the highest amount of radiation energy due to the steep angle of radiation incidence all year round. The radiation level facades receive generally changes only slightly throughout the year, with the only significant fluctuations occurring on south facades. South facades receive the highest amount of radiation during the winter months; in the summer months, north facades receive more radiation than south facades. The radiation received by north facades is almost exclusively ↙ diffuse radiation (Fig. 5.4).

↙
global radiation
p. 142

glazing percentage
p. 146

During the monsoon period (May to September), this value decreases significantly. The ↙ glazing percentage can safely be reduced to restrict radiation input due to the high daylight intensity.

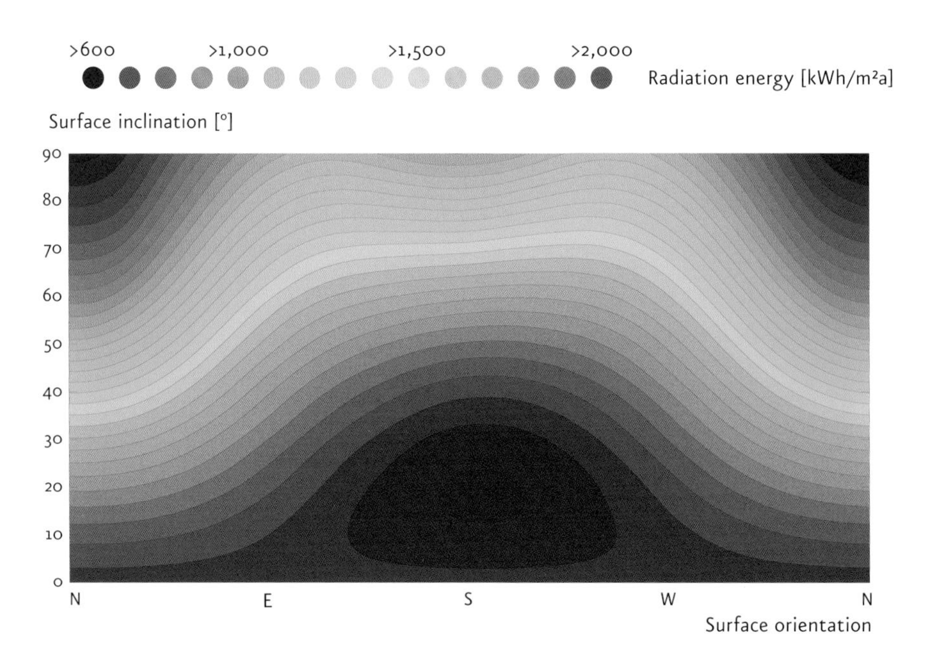

Fig. 5.3 Amount of energy received in the form of radiation in kWh/m²a correlated with orientation and angle of inclination, to be used for evaluating the alignment of solar power systems in Bangalore

Measured on the horizontal plane, the global radiation level is 2,030 kWh/m²a. At the optimal angle of inclination (18°) and with a south-facing orientation, the level of energy received is 2,107 kWh/m²a.

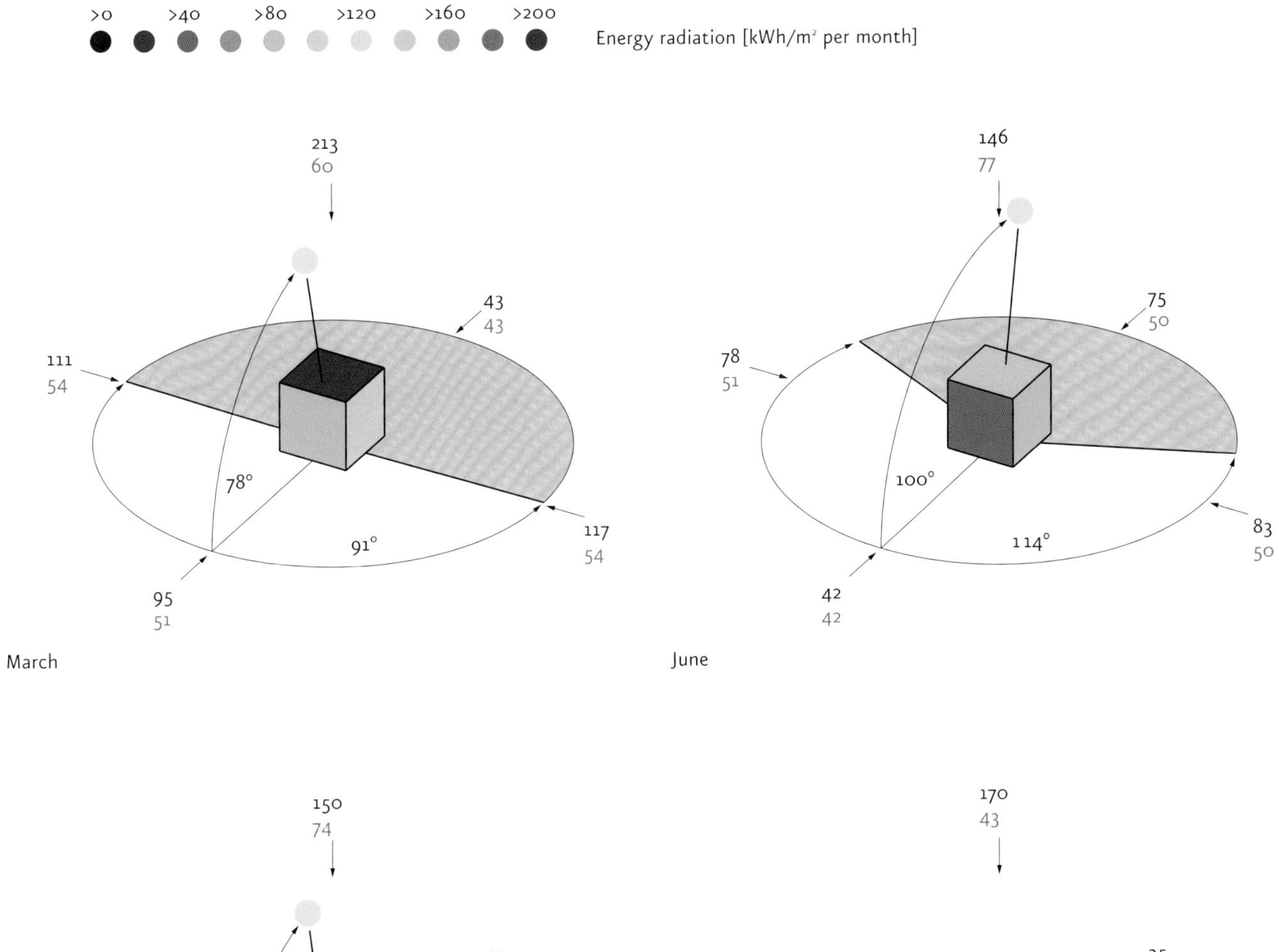

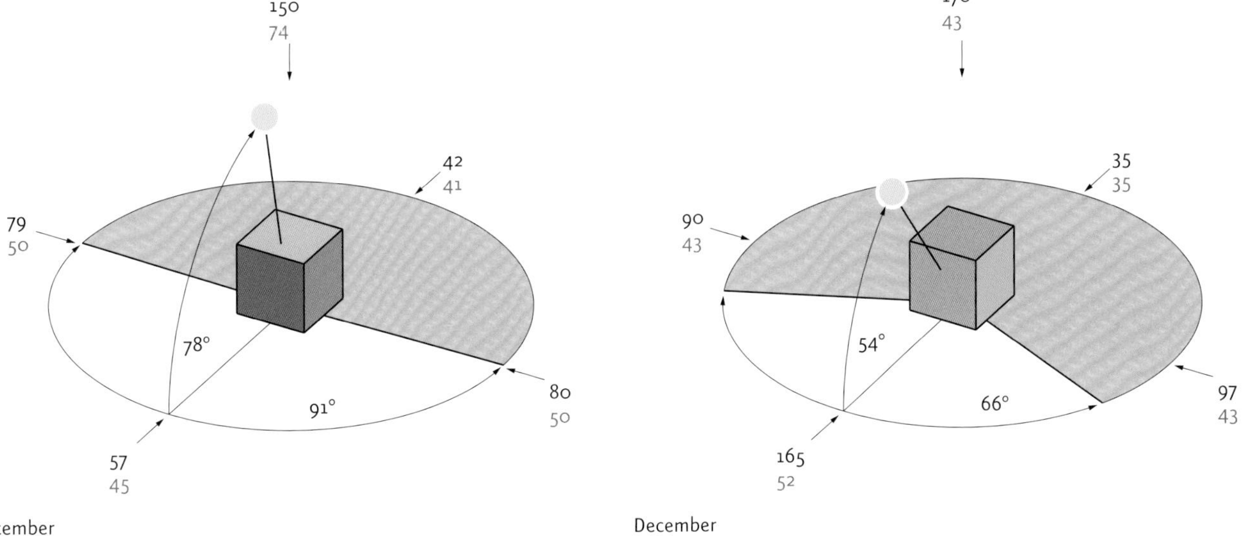

Fig. 5.4 Solar radiation and path of the sun for Bangalore
The sides of this cube show the amount of energy received in kWh/m² for a given month. The numbers in black quantify the overall radiation level, and those in grey the diffuse radiation level. Also included are the maximum elevation angle and azimuth angle of the sun for the 21st of the month.

Building Structure

To reduce undesirable radiation input, structures should be arranged so that they shade each other (Fig. 5.6). Corridors aligned with the wind direction should be provided to remove heat and pollutants and to keep the community well ventilated. Arranging structures in a stepped pattern also helps ventilation.

Naturally ventilated buildings should have an open rather than a compact plan to ensure maximum air movement. For air-conditioned buildings, ↙ compactness has a positive impact on the cooling energy demand.

↙ **cubature** p. 144

A north-south alignment is advantageous because it lowers radiation input and makes effective shading simpler. The north side of a building receives the least radiation, whereas east and west facades of an unshaded building receive the most radiation. Placing two buildings close together on the east-west axis limits radiation input. Due to the high position of the sun, it takes a very high angle of obstruction to reduce the high radiation levels received by the facade (Fig. 5.5).

Clear space around building 20 m

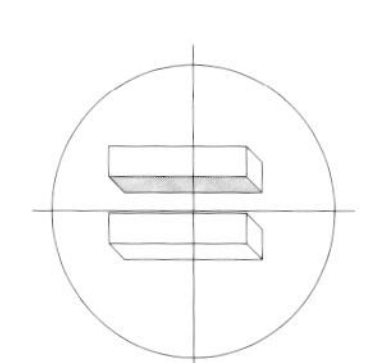

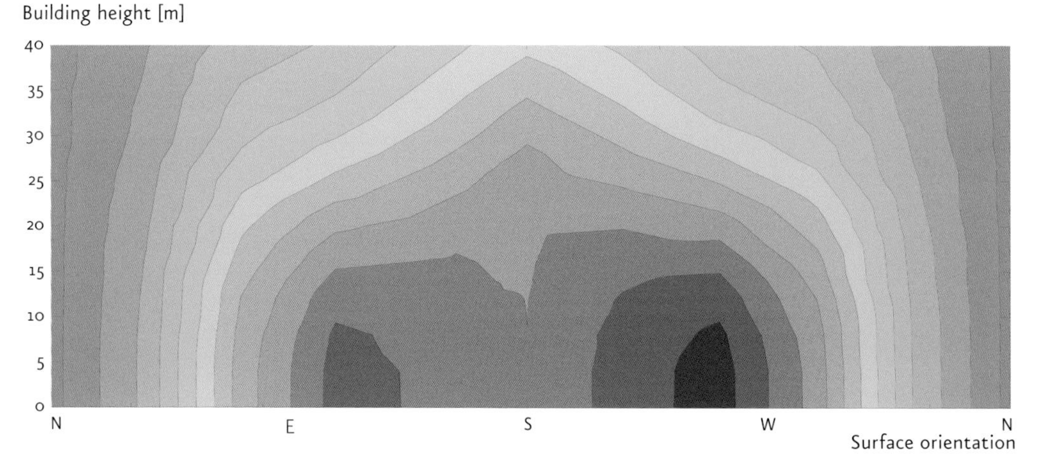

Fig. 5.5 Radiation energy [kWh/m²a], as an average value, received by the facade, correlated with its orientation and the height of a building 20 m away in the Bangalore area

This simulation is based on a typical office block, 70 m x 15 m x 20 m (l x w x h). The height of the shading block 20 m away is variable. In Bangalore, as the development's height increases, the differences between the levels of radiation received by the east, south and west sides of a building become significantly less.

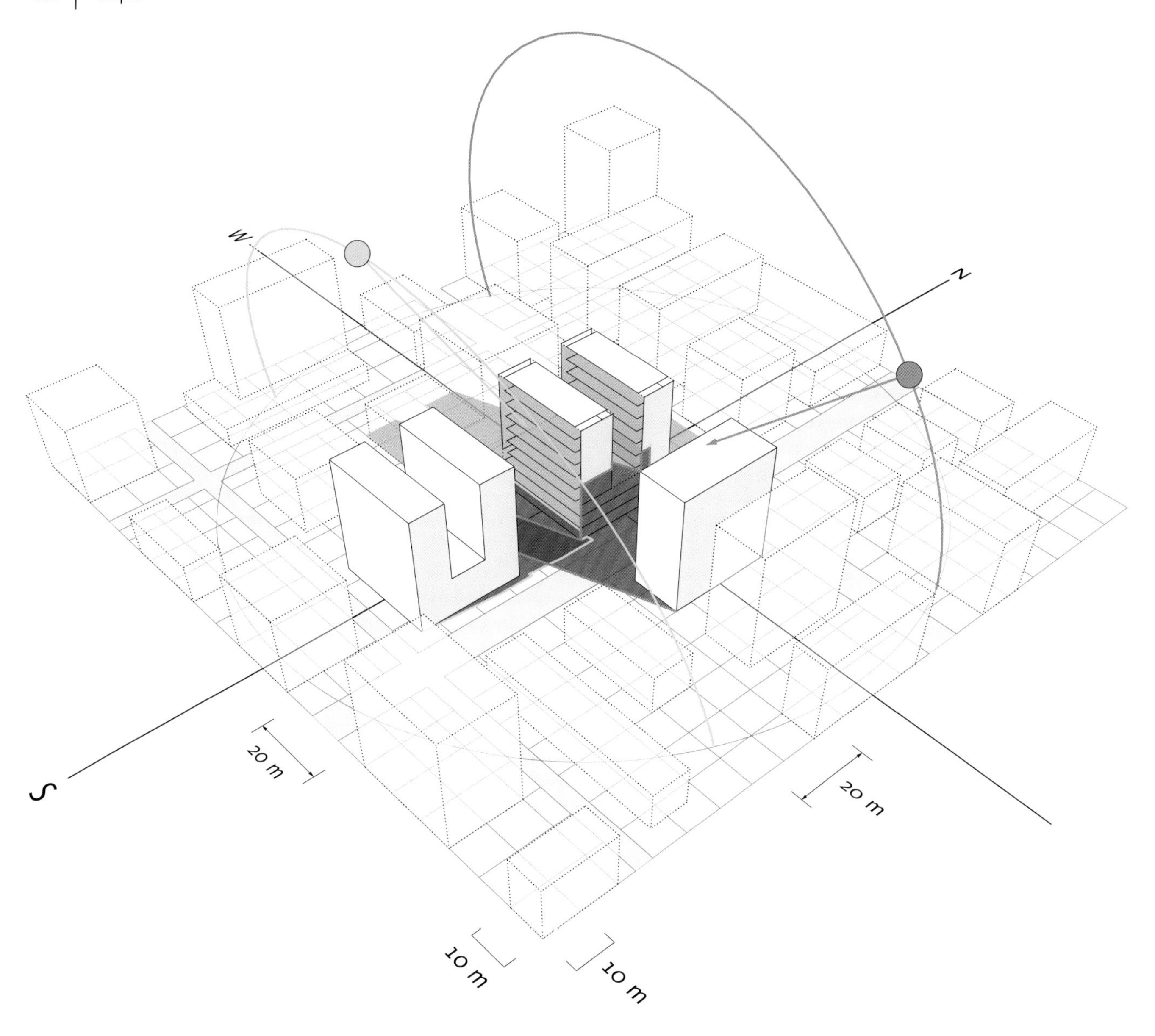

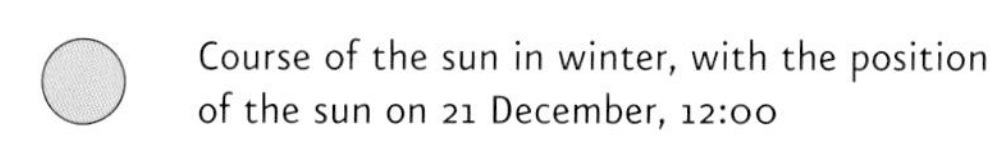
Course of the sun in winter, with the position of the sun on 21 December, 12:00

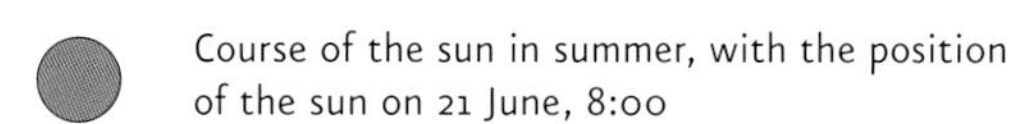
Course of the sun in summer, with the position of the sun on 21 June, 8:00

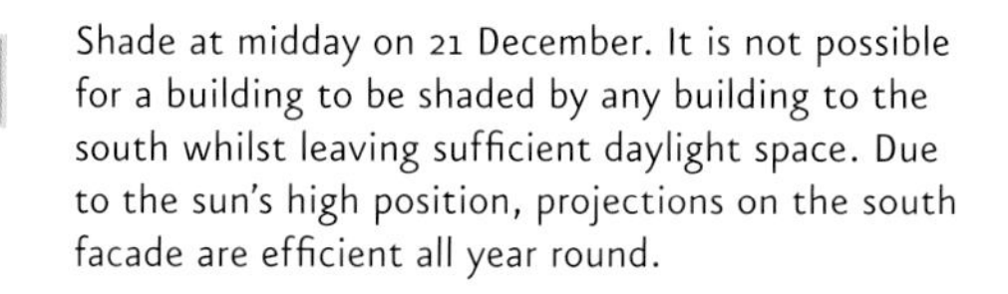
Shade at midday on 21 December. It is not possible for a building to be shaded by any building to the south whilst leaving sufficient daylight space. Due to the sun's high position, projections on the south facade are efficient all year round.

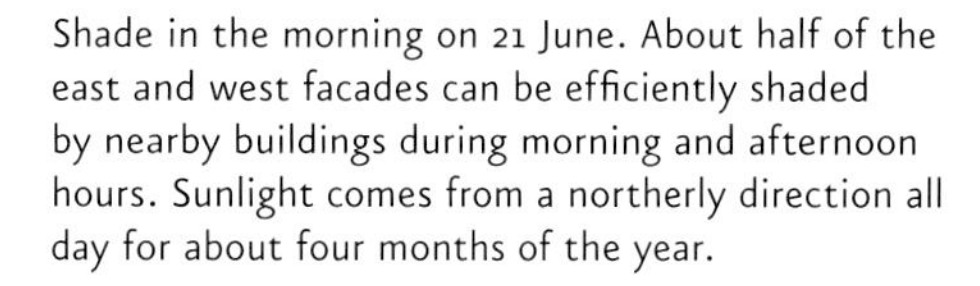
Shade in the morning on 21 June. About half of the east and west facades can be efficiently shaded by nearby buildings during morning and afternoon hours. Sunlight comes from a northerly direction all day for about four months of the year.

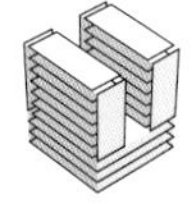
A non-compact construction with a north-south orientation. Linear building sections help to optimise daylight provision and natural ventilation. The room climate is improved if the unshaded areas of the east and west facades have no openings; in some cases, the access area can be placed in this zone. Because of the high outdoor luminance, room depth can be increased where rooms have light entering on two sides.

Fig. 5.6 Building structures for the tropics
In Bangalore, the main priority is to reduce radiation inputs. For this reason, north-to-south orientation of used space and arranging buildings to shade each other are advantageous strategies.

Building Skin

In the tropics, the primary function of a facade concept is to prevent solar input. Sun protection coating is advisable because the low latitude means that light availability is good all year round and no passive solar gain is required in winter. Solar energy generation works well on the east, south and west facades. Some thermal protection should be added to the facade to prevent transmission heat gain; the outer wall should be allowed to absorb only a small degree of radiation.

Glazing percentage

↙ **glazing percentage** p. 146

The ↙ glazing percentage is dictated by solar input. It should be as low as possible on all sides, around 30% to 40%.

Sun protection

↙ **sun protection** p. 146

Horizontal slats and projections can be used to ↙ protect against solar radiation, particularly on the north and south facades. Measures should also be taken to protect the south facade, which receives significant radiation levels throughout the whole utilisation period during the winter months, against the low morning and evening sun. A solution that is effective all year round must also be found to protect the east and west facades from direct and diffuse radiation.

Glazing

↙ **glazing** p. 146

g-value p. 146

Sun protection ↙ glazing is recommended in the tropics, as without a sun protection coating the heat inputs are too high regardless of the orientation. The glazing's ↙ g-value should be lower than 0.4.

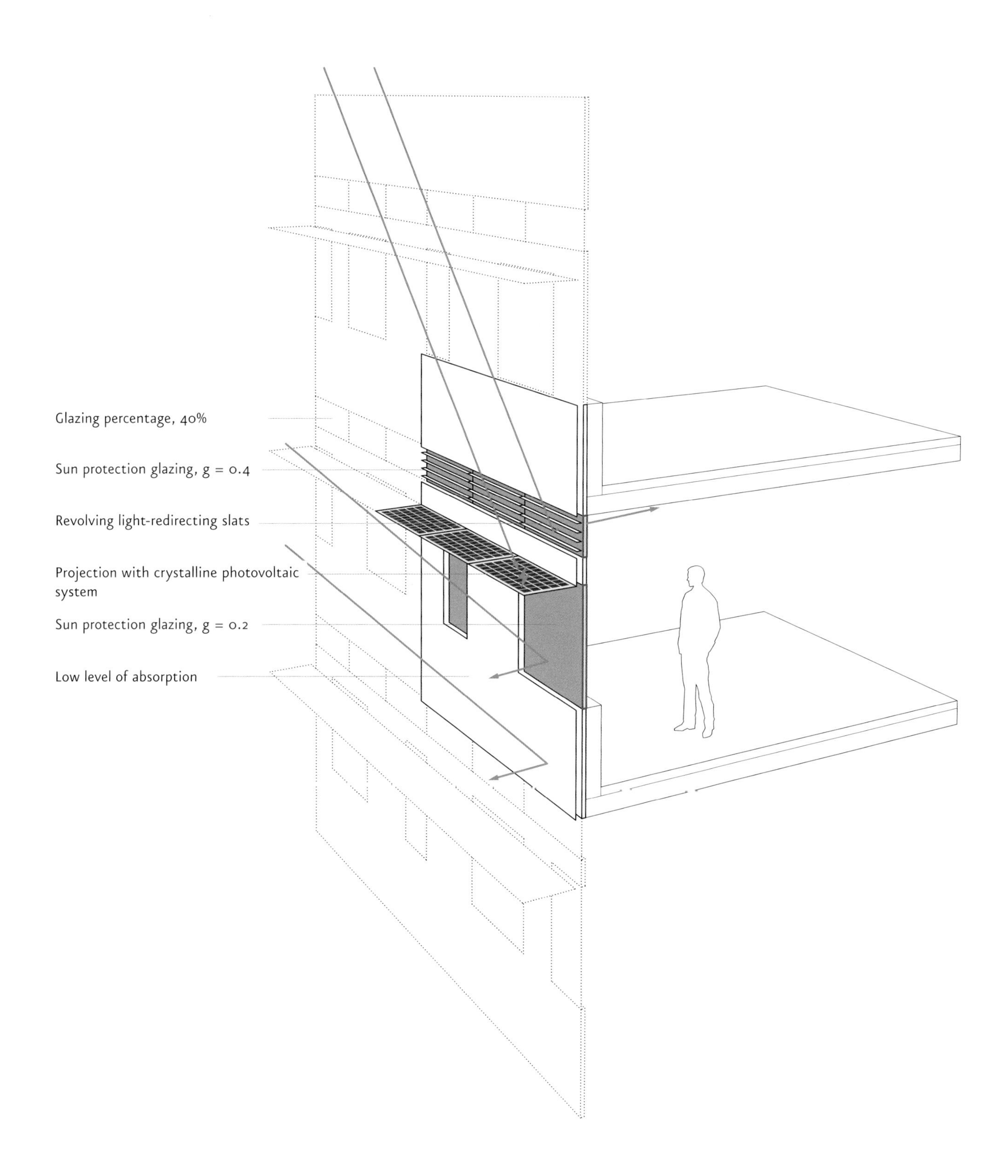

Fig. 5.7 Facade concept for the tropics

Strategies for a south facade optimised in terms of energy, room climate and daylight. Alternatively, external slats could be used. The glazing percentage should also be around 30–40% for the east and west facades, and the sun protection should be able to block rays from the sun at a shallower angle. For the north facade, an average glazing percentage of 50% combined with sun protection glass is a possibility.

Building Systems

↙ dew point temperature p. 142

heat/cold transfer p. 150

solar thermal system p. 154

solar cooling p. 154

photovoltaics p. 154

In the tropics, the main need is for cooling and humidifying. Because of ↙dew point issues, ↙surface cooling systems can only be used when combined with mechanical ventilation and dehumidifying of incoming air.

Heating is required only to provide hot water. In some cases, it can be provided by ↙solar collectors. Due to the high average annual temperature, the soil temperature is so high that it can only be used for precooling (Fig. 5.2). ↙Solar cooling strategies are practical in the summer. Desiccant cooling systems are recommended, primarily because of their dehumidifying performance. ↙Photovoltaic systems can be utilised due to the high radiation yields. Ideally, they should be installed on the roof at a flat angle (Fig. 5.3). The yield will be approximately 300 kWh/m^{2}a.

Cooling convectors

↙ convector p. 152

Where the ventilation requirement is low and the cooling loads are moderate, natural ventilation can be combined with a cooling ↙convector. This kind of system is easy to regulate, and the cooling convector also dehumidifies the air to some degree. For moderate to high cooling loads, combining this system with mechanical cooling is ideal. This apparatus treats air centrally, dehumidifying it and introducing it into the room in a precooled state.

Cooling ceilings

↙ cooling ceiling p. 152

If the cooling loads are very high, a ↙cooling ceiling mechanical ventilation system can ensure a comfortable room temperature. A reliable system for dehumidifying the incoming air must be ensured, because otherwise the dew point regulation will cancel out the cooling performance.

Split units

↙ split units p. 152

Where a system is being upgraded or where the internal loads have changed, a ↙split unit can be installed. This is also an option for rooms with natural ventilation. This arrangement enables good regulation.

Decentralised ventilation

↙ decentralised ventilation system p. 152

A ↙decentralised, facade-integrated ventilation apparatus allows incoming air to be cooled and dehumidified without the need for shafts and channels that take up additional space. This system's energy efficiency is lower and its maintenance demands are higher, but it is easy to upgrade or expand. During planning and installation, surface level effects on the facade should be borne in mind, as these can significantly increase the suction temperature.

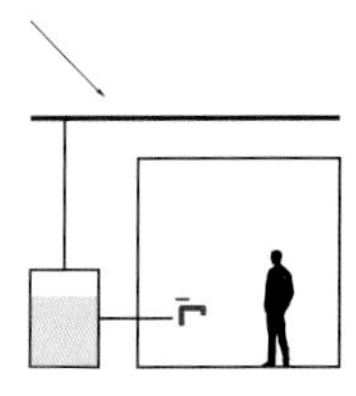

Degree of coverage, 100%
Yield, 1,200 kWh/m^2a

Solar thermal system
Hot water

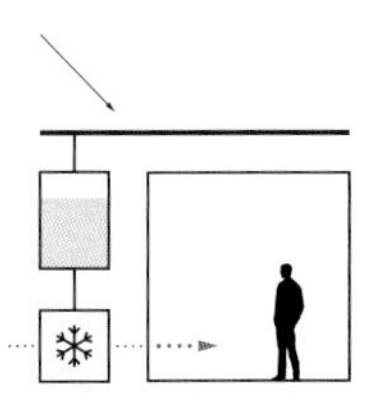

Degree of coverage, 50–80%
Yield, 1,000 kWh/m^2a

Solar cooling
Incoming air cooling

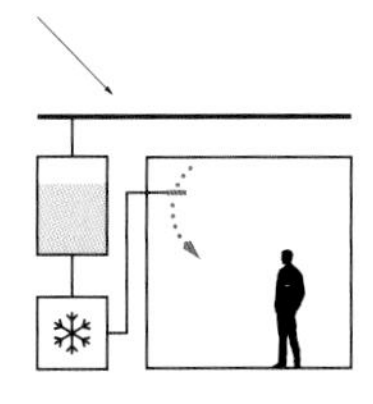

Degree of coverage, 50%
Yield, 1,000 kWh/m^2a

Solar cooling unit
Water-based cooling system

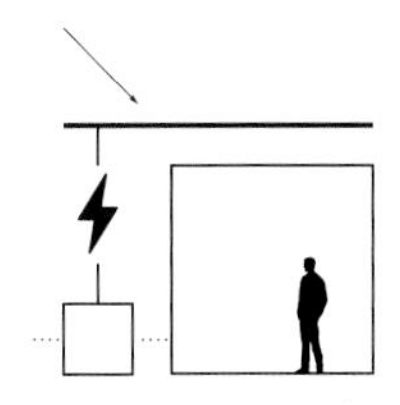

Yield, 300 kWh/m^2a

Photovoltaics
Feeding into the mains grid

Fig. 5.8 Room conditioning concept combined with renewable energy generation systems for the tropics

Suitable system combinations. The degree of coverage shows the proportion of renewable heat or cooling provided. The annual yield for a solar power system in an optimal installation position is given.

Planning Rules for Bangalore

A heating system is not required in the tropics. Cooling is required almost all year round. Absolute air humidity is high enough all year round that it is desirable to dehumidify incoming air. The following planning strategies are suitable for Bangalore:

Cooling and dehumidifying

The climate situation in Bangalore invariably requires an active cooling system. It is impossible to achieve a comfortable room climate without an active cooling system, even if all possible construction measures are utilised – reduced glazing percentage, external sun protection and intensive night ventilation.

↙
heating energy demand p. 144

glazing percentage p. 146

orientation p. 144

sun protection p. 146

glazing p. 146

night ventilation p. 152

storage mass p. 144

The ↙ cooling energy demand is high, at 120–150 kWh/m²a, and is accompanied by a dehumidifying energy demand of approximately 30–50 kWh/m²a, giving an overall cooling energy demand of 150–200 kWh/m²a.

Minimising the ↙ glazing percentage can cut cooling energy expenditure by about 25%. ↙ Orientation affects energy use by about 30%, with the heat yield on the west facade being particularly significant.

External ↙ sun protection combined with sun protection ↙ glass is 15% more efficient than an internal system. A porch on a south or north facade is 20% more efficient. For a lightly constructed facade, a certain amount of thermal protection is required to reduce transmission heat gain. The outer wall's degree of absorption influences the cooling energy demand, and should therefore be as low as possible.

Intensive ↙ night ventilation cuts energy use by up to 20%. The influence of the construction type (heavy, light) is generally low. A night ventilation strategy, however, requires ↙ storage mass. A combination of passive measures – a reduced glazing percentage of 30% combined with a very efficient sun protection system and intensive night ventilation – can reduce the cooling energy demand by 40%.

The results of the thermal simulation are accurate for a standard office space with typical internal loads. Unless stated otherwise, the space is a light construction facing south, with a glazing percentage of 50%. The glazing has a g-value of 0.3 with internal sun protection. The U-value of the outer wall is 0.6 W/m²K.

Potentials and strategies

The high average temperature throughout the year limits the usefulness of the soil and ↘groundwater as cooling sources, and the high air humidity means that the same is true of free ↘recooling, although the soil can be used to precool the incoming air as part of a practical room conditioning strategy. The temperature level of the renewable cooling source can sometimes be used to assist in dehumidifying the incoming air. Any additional cooling required should be delivered to the room by water-based systems; this saves operating energy and improves system regulation. ↘Surface cooling systems require dehumidifying of incoming air all year round due to ↘dew point issues. Passive measures do achieve a significant reduction of the cooling energy demand when combined with this setup.

Because the outdoor climate and the soil offer only limited cooling possibilities in the tropics, the focus is on reducing the internal heat loads. Another possibility is to optimise the energy systems and apparatus by adding cold recovery, ↘desiccant cooling and solar cooling with cold recovery.

↘
earth piles/ groundwater utilisation
p. 154

cooling tower
p. 154

heat/cold transfer
p. 150

dew point temperature
p. 142

solar cooling
p. 154

Deserts

Dubai, the commercial metropolis of the Orient

Dubai is located in a subtropical dry area close to the Tropic of Cancer. Temperatures are high all year round, with maximum temperatures of above 43 °C. From November to March, temperatures are somewhere between 18 °C and 28 °C. The difference between minimum and maximum temperatures during the summer is slightly higher than during the warm winter. Dubai receives very little precipitation: less than 130 mm per year. Rainfall is irregular, occurring mainly on a few days between December and March. Brief, heavy downpours may occur early in the year. Air humidity is very high in Dubai due to the city's proximity to the sea. Sandstorms occur during the winter months.

100 75 50 25 0

Nights per year with an average temperature lower than 20 °C [%]

Climate in the Desert

↙ **condensation** p. 142

The subtropical drylands are located on the northern and southern tropics between the 15th and 30th parallel. This zone has a characteristic belt of high pressure that creates clear skies, a high proportion of direct radiation and very low precipitation levels. Because rainfall is low and irregular, the ↙ evaporation rate is always greater than the precipitation rate.

The annual rate of global radiation in Dubai is higher than that of areas nearer the equator. In dry areas like Dubai, a proportion of the incoming radiation is immediately reflected back. Temperatures in the arid subtropics are high all year round, reaching their maximum value when the sun reaches the tropic line.

Desert climate varies depending on coastal position, continentality and proximity to the mountains. There are major differences in summers and winters, in temperature amplitudes over the course of a day, in the air's moisture content and the precipitation rate. Inland, summer temperatures are higher and air humidity is significantly lower. Due to a lack of cloud cover and air with a low water content, continental areas receive a high level of radiation, but also emit much of this radiation by reflection; this means that the temperature fluctuates to a considerable degree over the course of 24 hours.

Deserts have little vegetation, limited to patches of grass and bushes. More extensive vegetation is found only close to rivers or where there is groundwater.

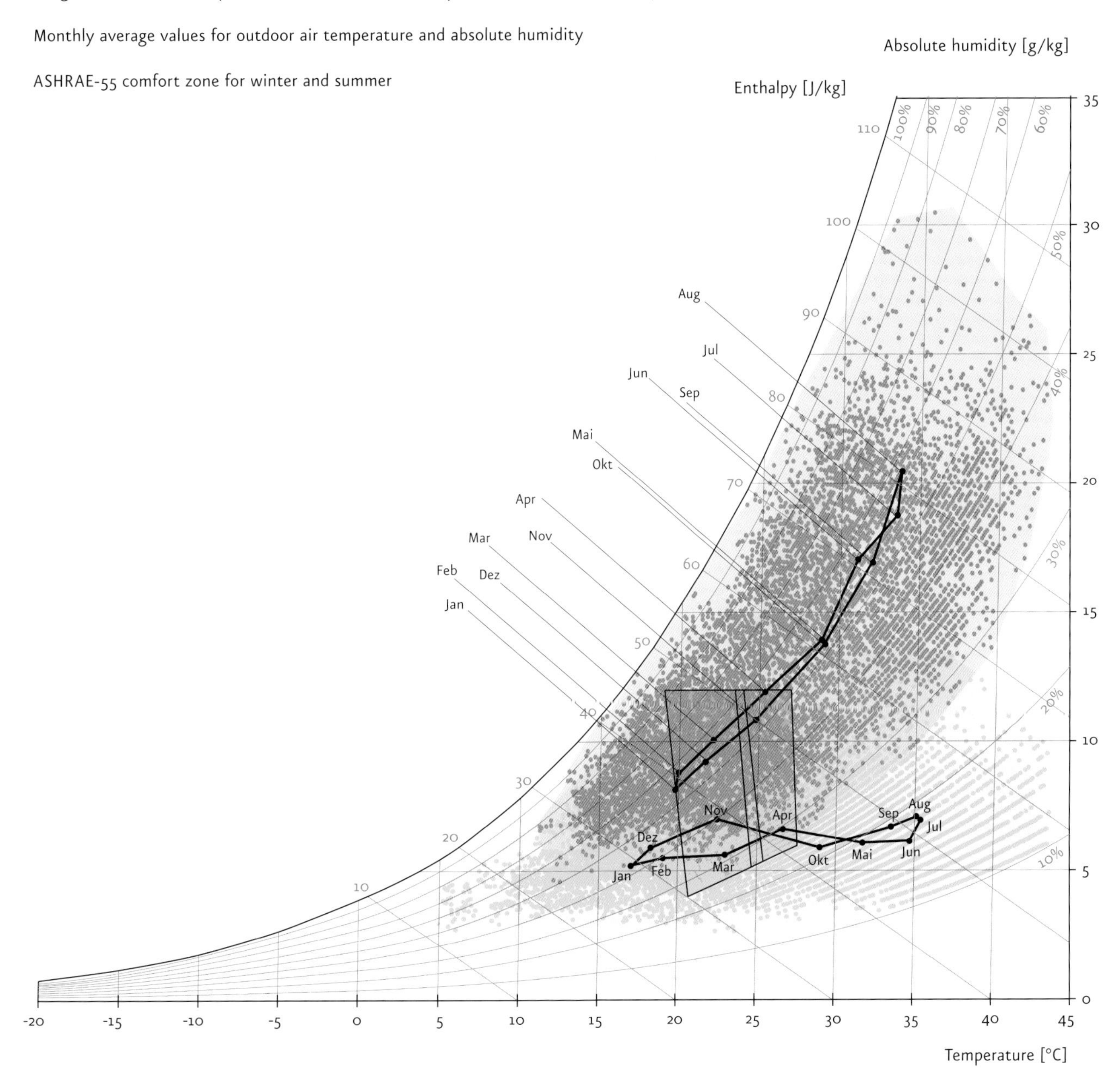

Fig. 6.1 Range of outdoor air temperatures and absolute humidity for Dubai and Riyadh, with ASHRAE-55 comfort zone superimposed

Dubai's climate features high temperatures all year round, with highs of above 40 °C. The focus is therefore on cooling and dehumidifying. From April to October, absolute air humidity is greater than 12 g/kg, meaning that incoming air must be dehumidified to achieve a comfortable air humidity level in an indoor space. A heating system is not required. In Riyadh, it is also very hot during the summer months, with temperatures above 40 °C; winters are more temperate, with temperatures of around 15 °C. The main need is for cooling. As humidity is low – 6 g/kg – there is no dehumidifying energy demand. Humidifying the incoming air results in adiabatic cooling.

Climate and Construction

Dubai has a typical coastal desert climate, while Riyadh has a typical continental desert climate. High levels of cooling energy are required in the desert. In locations close to the sea, air humidity is so high during most of the year that incoming air has to be dehumidified (Fig. 6.1). In the months when the temperature is lower, natural ventilation is possible, as during these times the air humidity is moderate even in areas where it is high at other times. In some cases, natural ventilation may be restricted by the air's dust load. A description of climatic conditions in Dubai and Riyadh for the purpose of constructing buildings adapted to the climate is given below (Fig. 6.2).

Temperature

↙
night ventilation
p. 152

cooling tower
p. 154

refrigeration unit
p. 154

Over the course of a year, there are two high-temperature periods in Dubai. The day-night temperature difference is greater during the hot summer months than during the cooler winter months. Night temperatures, however, can reach high absolute values, meaning that ↙ night cooling is possible only during the winter, if at all. A heating system is not required. It is possible to precool incoming air using the soil. Seawater can be used directly for cooling during the winter months, and it can also be used for ↙ recooling in ↙ refrigeration units in order to increase their efficiency.

In Riyadh, summers are very hot and winters more temperate. The temperature difference is rather higher in summer than in the winter. The high night temperatures during the summer allow the additional use of night ventilation. A heating system is not required. Due to its high temperature, the soil can be used only to precool the incoming air.

Humidity

↙
heat/cold transfer
p. 150

dew point temperature
p. 142

condensation
p. 142

wet bulb temperature
p. 142

Close to the sea, the air humidity is very high, with peaks of 25 g/kg. For most of the year, it is necessary to dehumidify the incoming air. The high air humidity is also problematic for ↙ surface cooling systems. In winter, free recooling can be used to reduce the cooling energy demand.

In Riyadh, the air humidity is so low – 6 g/kg on average Circumstances are favourable for deploying surface cooling systems, as there are no ↙ dew point issues. ↙ Condensation cooling systems such as recooling plants also work well due to the low ↙ cooling limit temperatures. However, this may be problematic during the hot summer months.

Global radiation

Because Dubai and Riyadh are on almost the same latitude, their year lengths and levels of radiation energy are almost the same. The total global radiation is 2,026 kWh/m²a in Dubai and 2,189 kWh/m²a in Riyadh. In both locations, the solar radiation level is very high all year round. In summer, it exceeds that of equatorial areas at lower latitudes; this is due to a lack of cloud cover and low levels of precipitation. The overall high level of radiation only decreases (somewhat) between October and February.

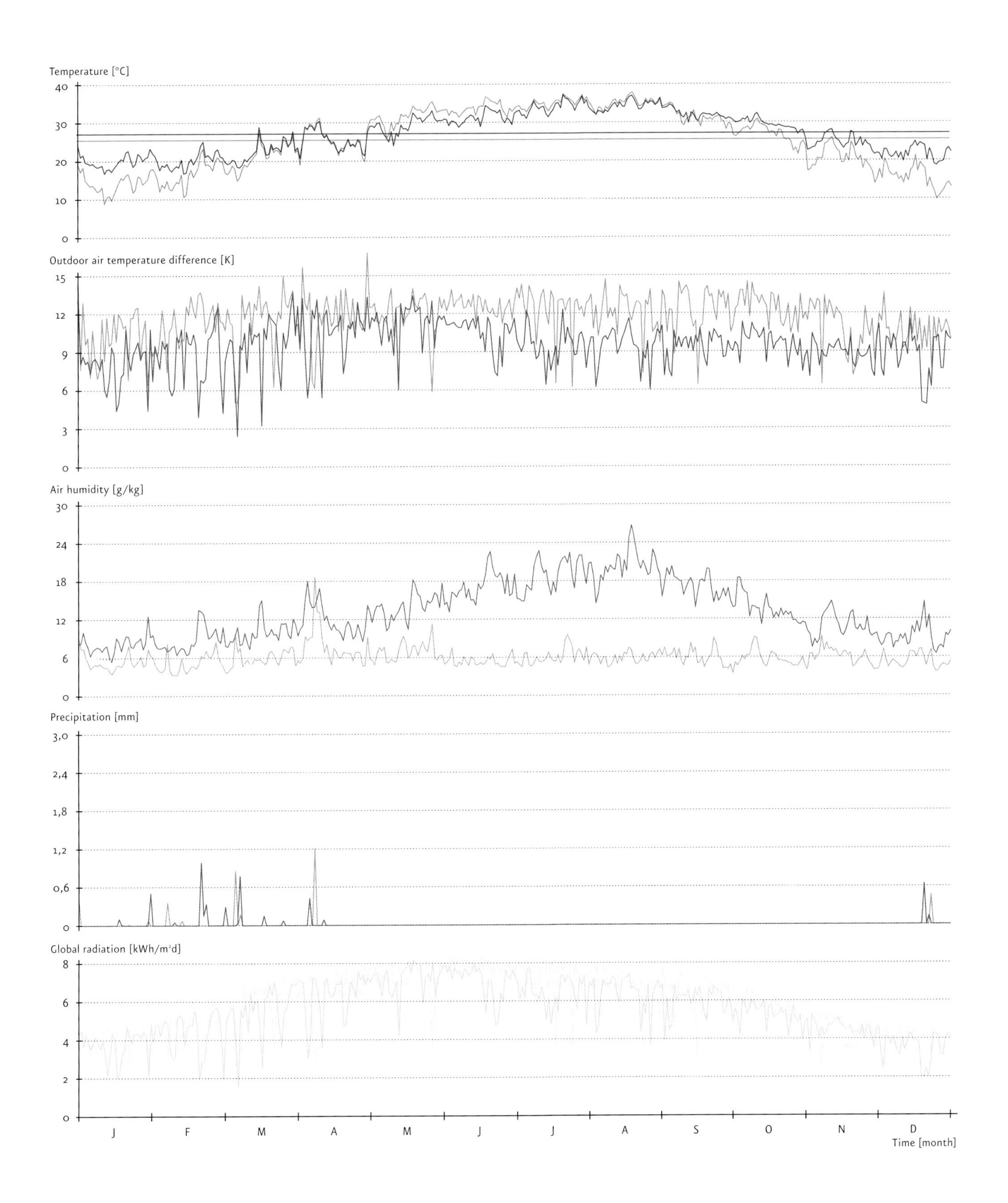

Fig. 6.2 The major climate elements for the Dubai and Riyadh (light coloured curves) areas over the course of a year
Average daily outdoor air temperatures (1st line), with soil temperatures at a depth of 10–12 m (red horizontal line), and the outdoor air temperature difference between the maximum temperature (during the day) and the minimum temperature (at night), (2nd line). Also included are the average daily absolute air humidity (3rd line) and precipitation (4th line) values, as well as the amount of energy relating to a horizontal surface received in a day (5th line).

Solar radiation

Due to both cities' proximity to the equator, the sun is at zenithal position in Dubai and Riyadh during the summer. Their day lengths vary only slightly. The angle of radiation incidence is relatively steep all year round.

The only time when the high overall level of solar radiation decreases somewhat is in the winter. During this period, south facades receive the most radiation, but for most of the year, horizontal surfaces receive the highest amounts of radiation energy. The zenithal position of the sun on 21 June means that this month has the highest monthly overall radiation value of the year. South sides of buildings receive the least radiation at this time of the year, receiving only diffuse radiation. During the summer months, east-facing and west-facing facades receive the most radiation. In the transitional periods (around March and September), the amount of energy radiation received by east, south and west facades is almost the same, ↙ direct radiation is significantly higher than diffuse radiation. North facades receive the lowest levels of radiation all year round except in summer (Fig. 6.4).

The ↙ illuminance is generally very high. Due to the high daylight intensity, the ↙ glazing percentages can be reduced to limit radiation yields and ↙ glazing with sun protection qualities can be used.

↙
global radiation p. 142

illuminance p. 148

glazing percentage p. 146

glazing p. 146

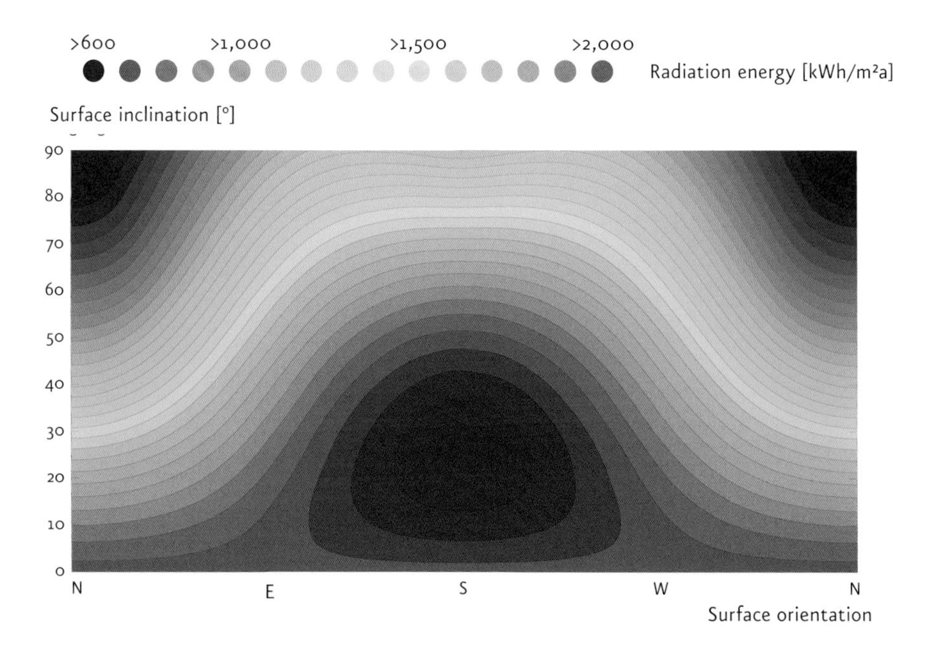

Fig. 6.3 Radiation energy in kWh/m²a correlated with orientation and angle of inclination, to be used for evaluating the alignment of solar power systems in the Dubai area

Measured on the horizontal plane, the global radiation level is 2,026 kWh/m²a. At the optimal angle of inclination (23°) and with a south-facing orientation, the level of energy received is 2,185 kWh/m²a.

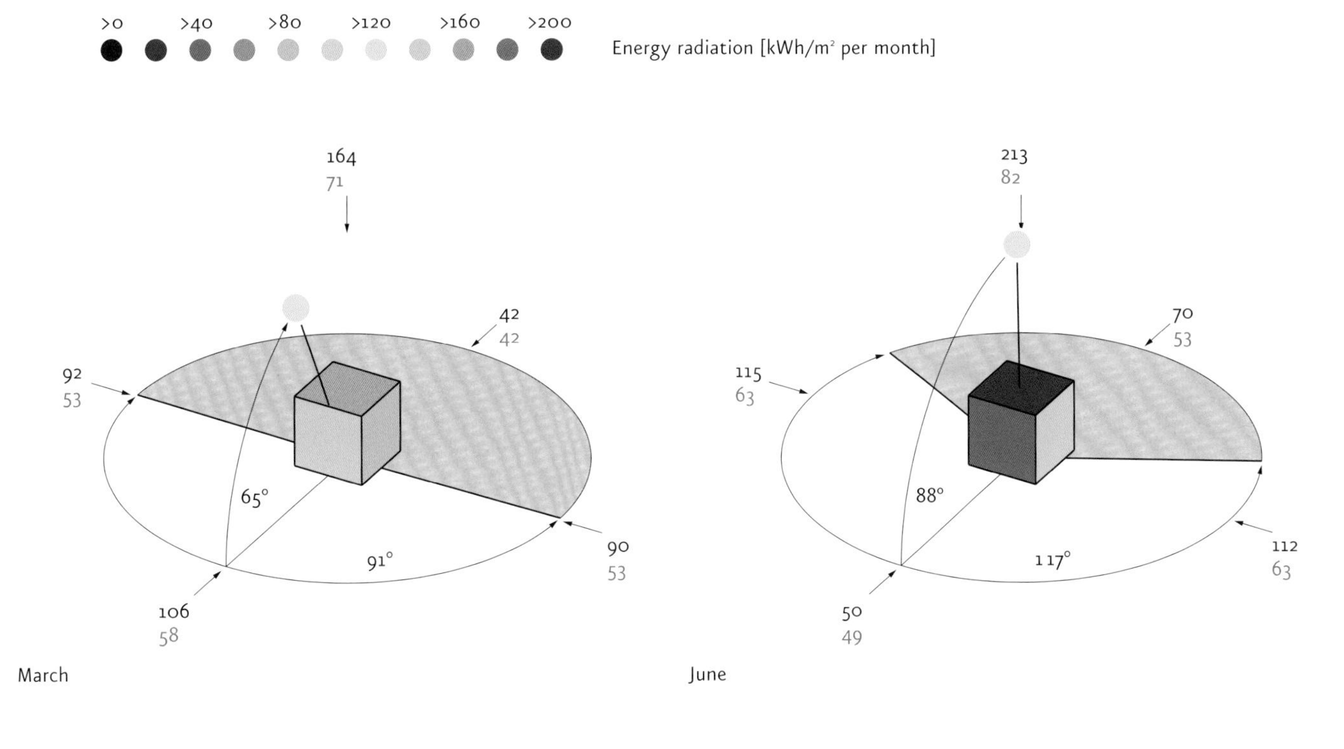

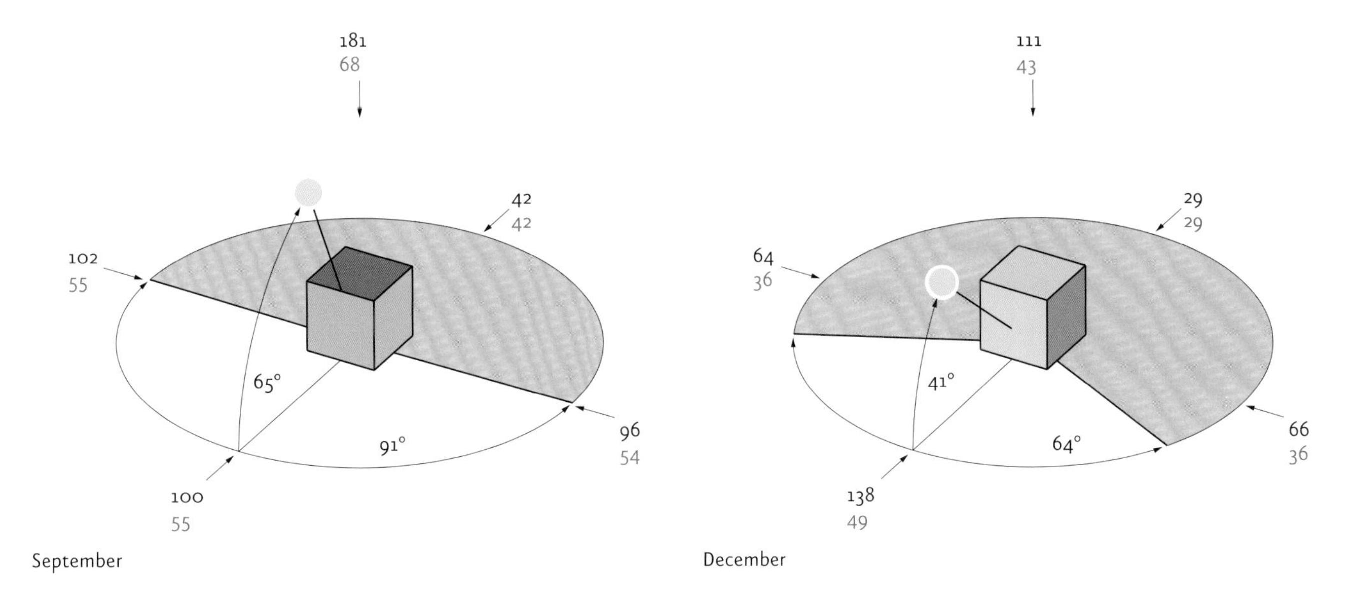

Fig. 6.4 Solar radiation and path of the sun for Dubai

The sides of this cube show the amount of energy received in kWh/m² for a given month. The numbers in black quantify the overall radiation level, and those in grey the diffuse radiation level. Also included are the maximum elevation angle and azimuth angle of the sun for the 21st of the month.

Building Structure

In coastal deserts, a heating energy demand is not a factor, but in continental deserts or in deserts with high altitudes, a heating system may be required. A highly compact building structure has a positive impact on the cooling energy demand. In par- ticular, a high degree of building depth helps to achieve a low ↙ surface-to-volume ratio. Placing buildings close together on an east-west axis is a good idea, as the buildings can then shade each other (Fig. 6.6). ↙ Daylight provision is of secondary importance due to the high environmental ↙ illuminance and the high degree of reflection from surrounding facades. Complexes with inner courtyards have a positive impact, because they permit high-density urban plans, which, in turn, allow the buildings to shade each other.

↙
cubatur
p. 144

daylight provision
p. 148

illuminance
p. 148

orientation
p. 144

↙ Orientation, the heights of neighbouring buildings and their proximity all have a major impact on the amount of radiation energy received by a facade (Fig. 6.5). South-facing facades receive the highest level of solar radiation, but they can easily be shaded by the use of projections. The greater the distance between the buildings, the greater the difference between the south facade and the east and west facades in terms of radiation energy. The building's distance from the neighbouring structures must be very low in order to ensure shading on the east-west axis. Good localised ventilation should be ensured.

Clear space around building 20 m

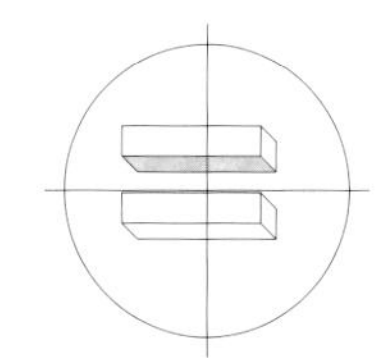

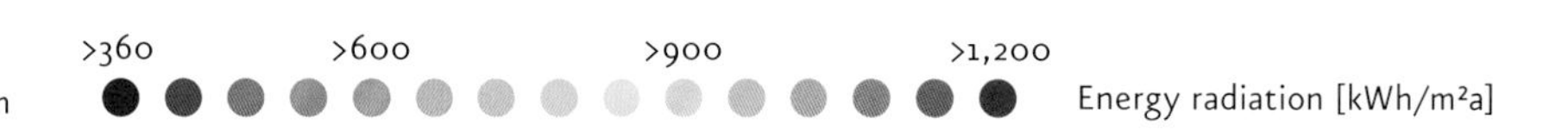

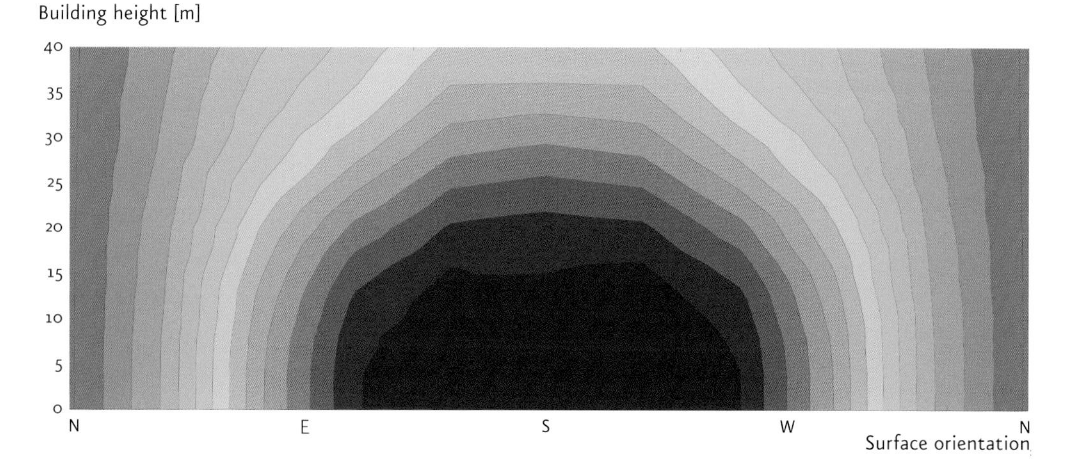

Fig. 6.5 Radiation energy [kWh/m²a], as an average value, received by the facade, correlated with orientation and the height of a building 20 m away in Dubai
This simulation is based on a typical office block, 70 m x 15 m x 20 m (l x w x h). The height of the shading block 20 m away is variable. The solar radiation received by a south-facing facade where the neighbouring development is 40 m high is about 800 kWh/m²a. If the neighbouring development is only 20 m high, the radiation energy will be just over 1,200 kWh/m²a.

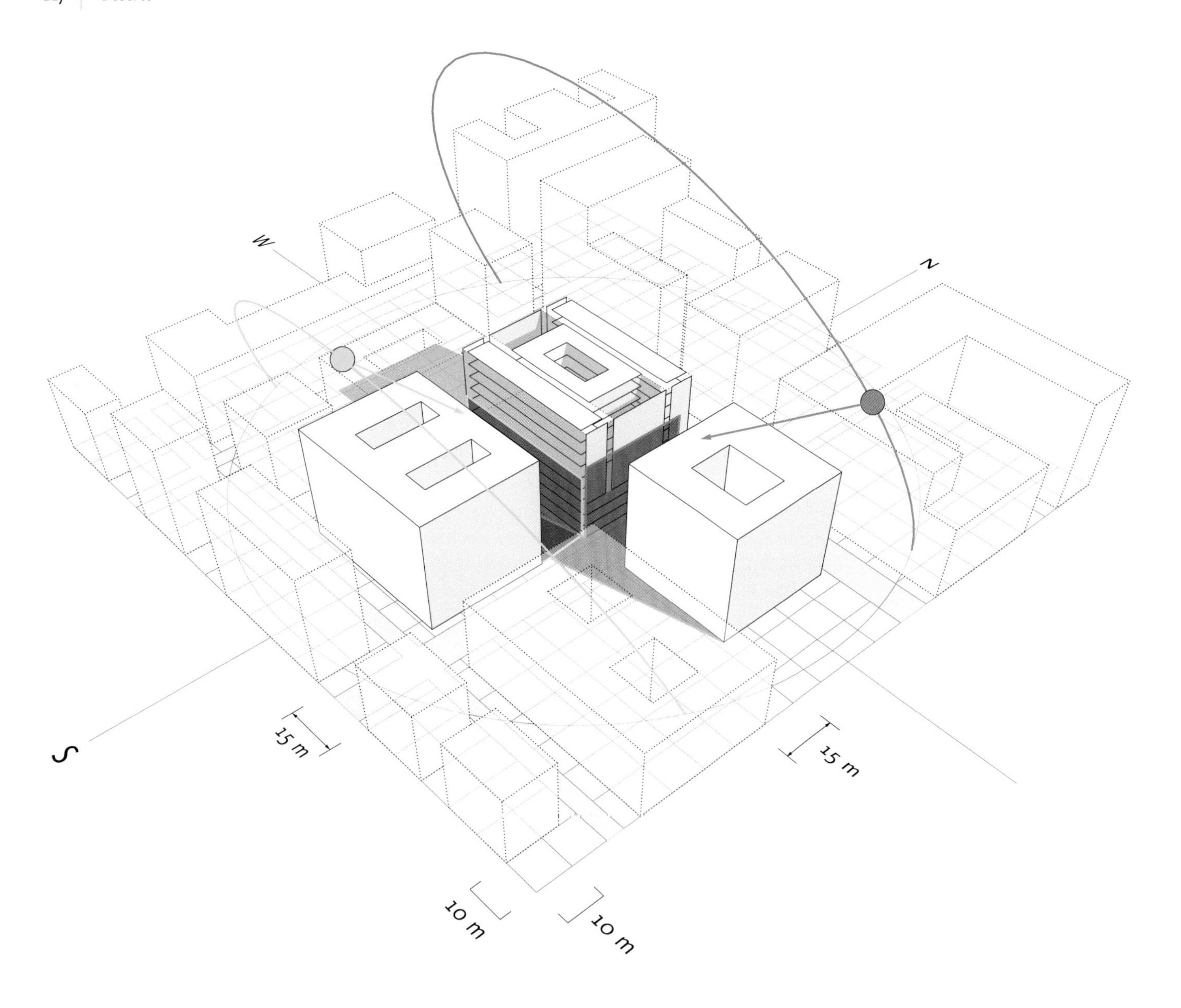

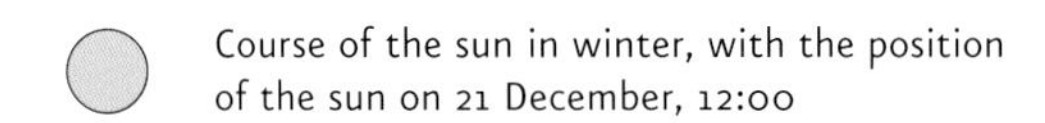
Course of the sun in winter, with the position of the sun on 21 December, 12:00

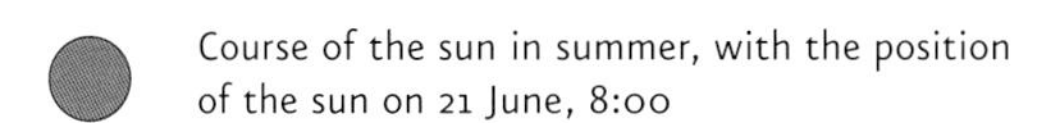
Course of the sun in summer, with the position of the sun on 21 June, 8:00

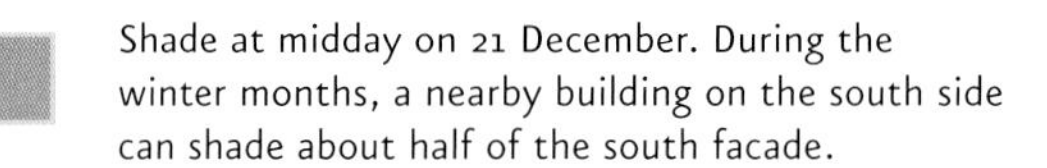
Shade at midday on 21 December. During the winter months, a nearby building on the south side can shade about half of the south facade.

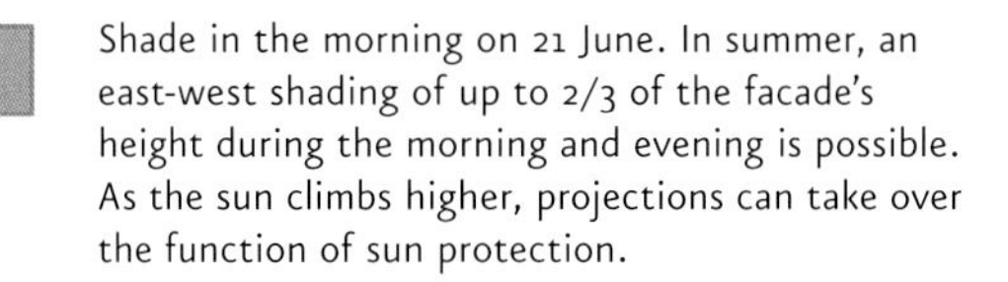
Shade in the morning on 21 June. In summer, an east-west shading of up to 2/3 of the facade's height during the morning and evening is possible. As the sun climbs higher, projections can take over the function of sun protection.

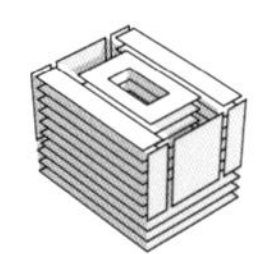
A building in a north-south orientation with courtyards. In conditions of high outer illuminance, an inner courtyard can be used for lighting and ventilation. Courtyard facades have the advantage of being shaded on all sides by the building itself. Neighbouring buildings can also be placed in close proximity, and east and west facades – particularly their upper sections – should be largely without openings. It may be a good idea to add additional surfaces to these facades. Due to the high position of the sun all year round, the south facade can easily be shaded using projections.

Fig. 6.6 Building structures for the desert
In Dubai, the main priority is to reduce radiation yields. A compact building with a courtyard has reduced facade surfaces and also provides its own shading.

Building Skin

Due to the high levels of radiation all year round, a desert facade concept must avoid solar input. Ideally, it should include external sun protection. The glazing should have a sun protection coating. Minimal thermal protection for the facade is advisable in order to avoid transmission heat gain. Due to the high level of direct radiation, the outer wall should have a low degree of absorption.

Glazing percentage

For all facades, the glazing percentage is dictated by solar input and should not be greater than 30%. Due to the high environmental ↙ illuminance, there will be sufficient ↙ daylight provision even with a reduced glazing percentage.

↙ illuminance p. 148
daylight provision p. 148

Sun protection

A projection can be an effective addition to the ↙ sun protection strategy for a south facade. Measures should also be taken against the low morning and evening sun in winter. The sun protection concept must also combat radiation striking the east and west facades at a shallow angle, with moveable slats being the best solution.

↙ sun protection p. 146

Glazing

Sun protection ↙ glass is recommended, as without it the diffuse radiation yields are too high regardless of orientation. The glazing's ↙ g-value should be lower than 0.3.

↙ glazing p. 146
g-value p. 146

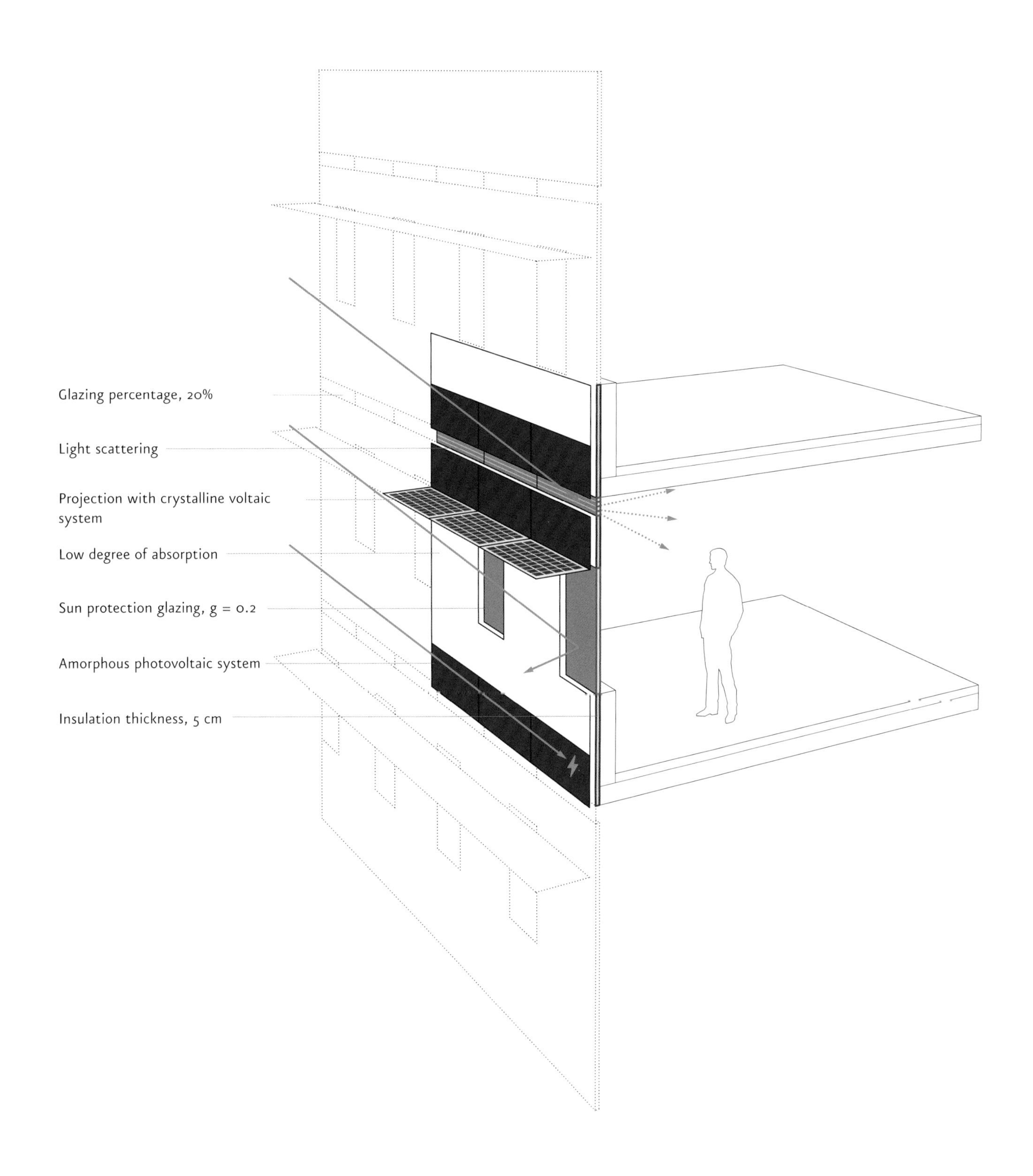

Fig. 6.7 Facade concept for the desert

Strategies for a south facade with optimised energy, room climate and daylight features. The glazing percentage should also be around 30% for the east and west facades. Sun protection must be chosen with the sun's shallow arc and the steep angle of radiation incidence in mind. In some cases, the glazing percentage can be slightly increased for a north facade. Sun protection glass is effective as a sun protection measure.

Building Systems

In the desert, natural ventilation is problematic for most of the year due to the high outdoor air temperatures. Depending on the location's distance from the sea, there may also be a significant dehumidifying energy demand. In continental locations, there will be a humidifying energy demand. For these reasons, a mechanical ventilation concept with incoming air conditioning makes the most sense. In the right circumstances, natural ventilation can be used for some months of the year without compromising comfort, but there may be difficulties due to the air's high dust content.

In the desert, a high degree of cooling energy is required. The soil has some potential as a cooling source, as long as the average temperature for a year is lower than 20 °C. When the night temperatures are low, night ventilation or night recooling can be used as a renewable cooling source. Where the humidity of the outdoor air is low, ↙ adiabatic cooling is a good solution. Solar thermal collectors can meet the need for hot water and the heating energy demand all year round. ↙ Solar cooling is an efficient way of producing lower temperatures all year round, and desiccant cooling systems are also suitable. Due to the high levels of radiation, photovoltaic systems can produce a yield of up to 350 kWh/m^2a (Fig. 6.3), but the impact of dust on the units should be considered.

↙ cooling tower p. 154

solar cooling p. 154

Cooling convector

Where the cooling loads are moderate, mechanical ventilation can be combined with a cooling ↙ convector. This system can be easily regulated. Where outdoor air temperatures are moderate, the cooling convector can also be combined with natural ventilation.

↙ convector p. 152

Concrete core activation

Where the outdoor air humidity is low and there is a potential for free recooling, ↙ concrete core activation is a suitable cooling system because the ↙ inflow temperatures it requires are moderate. Combined with a mechanical ventilation system, it can handle moderate loads. If there is also a heating energy demand, the concrete core activation can also function optimally as a heating system. The soil or solar thermal energy can be used as renewable heating sources.

↙ concrete core activation p. 152

system temperature p. 152

Cooling ceiling

Where there is a high cooling energy demand, ↙ comfort is improved by additionally introducing coolness to a room via radiation. Where there are ↙ dew point issues, efficient dehumidifying of the incoming air is required.

↙ comfort p. 150

dew point temperature p. 142

Split units

Where a system is being upgraded or where the internal loads have changed, ↙ split units can easily be installed. Energy efficiency is not optimal, but the system can be regulated easily.

↙ split units p. 152

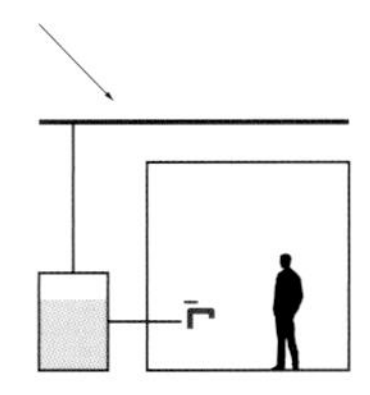

Degree of coverage, 100%
Yield, 1,400 kWh/m^2a

Solar thermal system
Hot water

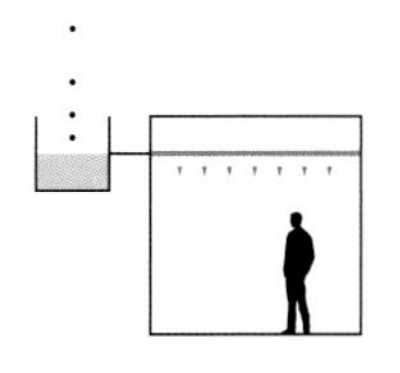

Degree of coverage, 50–70%
Performance, 35 W/m^2
Applies only where building system activation is in place
Only with low exterior air humidity

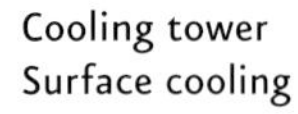

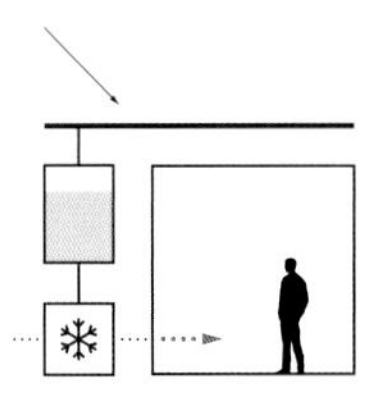

Degree of coverage, 50–80%
Yield, 1,100 kWh/m^2a

Solar cooling
Incoming air cooling

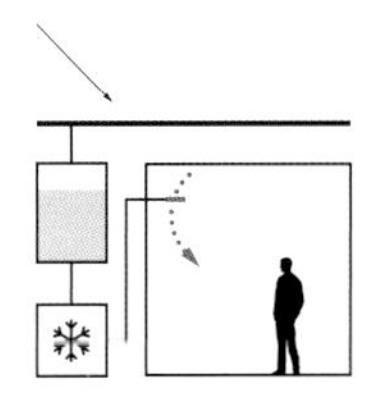

Degree of coverage, 50%
Yield, 1,000 kWh/m^2a

Solar cooling
Water-based cooling system

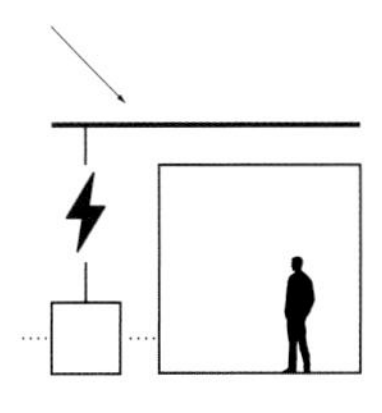

Yield, 350 kWh/m^2a

Photovoltaics
Grid supply

Fig. 6.8 Room conditioning concept combined with renewable energy generation systems for the desert. The concept displayed on the right is only possible in continental locations with a low outdoor air humidity.

Suitable system combinations. The degree of coverage shows the proportion of renewable heat or cooling provided. The annual yield for a solar power system in an optimal installation position and the specific cooling performance of the room conditioning systems are given.

Planning Rules for Dubai

A high degree of cooling energy is required in the desert. In locations close to the sea, the air must also be dehumidified during most of the year. In continental locations, on the other hand, adiabatic air humidifying can be used as a cooling strategy. It is particularly important to reduce radiation yields. The following planning strategies are effective for Dubai and Riyadh:

Cooling and humidifying/dehumidifying

↙ **heating energy demand** p. 144

Even where there is no ↙heating energy demand, it makes sense to provide facades exposed to the sun with minimal thermal insulation to prevent transmission heat gain through the outer wall. The outer wall's degree of absorption also influences the solar heat gain, and should therefore be kept very low. In any case, the climate situation in both Dubai and Riyadh requires an active cooling system during the summer months. Even if all construction measures are exhausted – a reduced glazing percentage combined with efficient sun protection, extensive storage masses and intensive ↙night ventilation – the room climate will still only be acceptable for short periods during the winter, and for most of the year conditions would be severely uncomfortable.

↙ **night ventilation** p. 152

In Dubai and Riyadh, there is a cooling energy demand of 150–200 kWh/m²a. The dehumidifying energy demand in Dubai is 20–40 kWh/m²a, resulting in an overall cooling energy demand of 170–240 kWh/m²a. In both locations, the glazing percentage and the orientation can influence the cooling energy demand by up to 30%.

↙ **sun protection** p. 146

g-value p. 146

storage mass p. 144

External ↙sun protection reduces the cooling energy demand by 20%. Reducing the ↙g-value of the glazing from 0.3 to 0.2 creates a saving of 10%. A 5 cm insulation layer and a reduced glazing percentage reduce the cooling energy demand by around 10% compared to a non-insulated outer wall. Because the temperature at night may be high, night ventilation does not always reduce the cooling energy demand, and the potential dust input should also be considered. Without night ventilation, the influence of ↙storage mass is very low.

A combination of passive measures – a reduced glazing percentage combined with a very efficient sun protection system and intensive night ventilation – can cut the cooling energy demand by almost 30%.

The results of the thermal simulation are accurate for a standard office space with typical internal loads. Unless stated otherwise, the space is a light construction facing south, with a glazing percentage of 50%. The glazing has a g-value of 0.3 with internal sun protection. The U-value of the outer wall is 0.6 W/m²K.

Potentials and strategies

The soil offers no significant cooling potential in Dubai or Riyadh, because the average temperature over the year is very high. The seawater at Dubai also retains a relatively high temperature all year round; this means that both the soil and the seawater can be used as the main precooling medium. Free ↘recooling is only possible in Dubai during the winter months. In Riyadh, ↘condensation cooling systems may work well because of the low environmental air humidity. During the hot summer months, however, this can be problematic.

In Dubai, additional cooling can be provided by a ↘concrete core activation system, together with recooling. Introducing precooled air into a room is an effective room conditioning strategy. It may be possible to use renewable cooling sources such as ↘groundwater or the soil to support the dehumidifying of incoming air. Any further cooling that is required should be supplied to the room via a water-based system; this saves operating energy and improves regulation.

In Riyadh, ↘surface cooling systems work well because there are no ↘dew point issues. Concrete core activation is particularly suitable because the outdoor air's low humidity can be used for recooling. Potential ground-based renewable cooling sources can be used to precool incoming air.

Priority should be given to reducing internal heating loads, since the outdoor climate offers few opportunities for cooling, particularly in Dubai. For instance, data processing systems should be designed not to release heat into inhabited rooms. Optimised layouts and energy technologies can be used. ↘Solar cooling is efficient all year round, and desiccant cooling systems are also suitable due to their high performance. In Dubai, they can also be used to dehumidify incoming air.

↘
refrigeration unit
p. 154

condensation
p. 142

concrete core activation
p. 152

**earth piles/
groundwater utilisation**
p. 154

↘
heat/cold transfer
p. 150

dew point temperature
p. 142

↘
solar cooling
p. 154

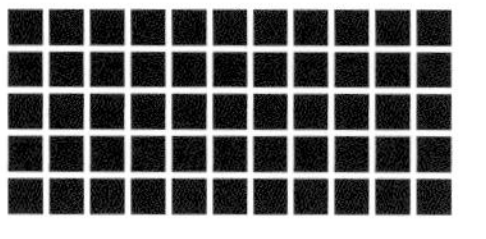

Economics

Getting ahead through planning optimisation

The sooner a Climatedesigner is included in the planning process, the better he or she can influence the project. Savings can be made even at the stage of formulating the work to be done if the requirements are defined precisely. Matters relating to energy and the room climate of the building can be dealt with when conceiving the shape of the building and the nature of the facade. As a rule, technical demands and susceptibility to error are reduced in simple room climate and energy concepts. If too many components are built into a system, unintended interactions may cancel out savings, or even increase consumption. Simple concepts are also more easily understood by users, which makes them more readily accepted.

Energy saving potential in the planning phases

Preliminary studies · Design · Energy concept · Realisation planning · Realisation

Costs and Energy

Three principal cost categories emerge during the life-cycle of a building: investment costs, running costs and costs for maintenance and change of use. Energy-relevant investment costs include planning costs, expenses for the building concept, the building skin, and for the technology inside the building. These include heat and sun protection, and also systems for energy generation and room conditioning. Secondary investment also has to be made for building measures required by the technical systems, such as the space needed for technical hubs and for shafts and pipelines. On the other hand, increased building investment can reduce the cost for building services and energy, and this has a positive effect overall on economic viability. Running costs are made up of energy, maintenance and cleaning costs. Maintenance costs can make a considerable impact on the economic viability of energy-efficient systems. This is why ↙combined heat and power plants, for example, have to run for a long time each year in order to be economically viable. Maintenance and conversion costs include costs for renewing, altering and demolishing a building. The operating life of energy and room conditioning systems leads to different reserve expenses for replacement investment. Other indirect costs can emerge through servicing loans, write-offs and reserves.

↙ **combined heat and power plant** p. 154

Investment costs are of secondary importance in relation to overall life cycle. This effect increases the longer it is under consideration. Investment costs tie up capital and then attract interest payments, which reduces financial flexibility. This has an effect on the required economic viability of energy and room climate concepts. Some of this impact can be shifted by using leasing and contracting models. Future developments such as increased energy costs, legal conditions and interest payments should be built into the running costs in particular. This can influence conceptual decisions in relation to investment. Systems requiring high investment levels be run efficiently only with high utilisation levels.

Planning and building process costs

Holistic planning can make a considerable contribution to reducing investment costs and later the running costs for a building. Increased planning costs, for energy and room climate simulations, for example, are usually recouped through reduced investment. Synergy effects can be activated to reduce costs. Specifying trade intersection points is very important, as it optimises the building process and reduces susceptibility to errors. Simple control systems reduce costs for commissioning the building and optimising operations.

Building concept

Efficient configuration of the building structure can considerably reduce expenditure on technology and thus the investment and running costs. For example, arranging the building so that it faces away from the road can make noise-free ↙natural ventilation possible and thus obviate the need for a ventilation plant. The best possible ↙orientation for the main facade usually means savings on sun protection. If the building has thermal storage, a more comfortable room climate can be created with lower system performance. Optimised integration of technology reduces pipe and cable runs and the space needed for shafts and switchboards.

↙ **natural ventilation** p. 146

orientation p. 144

Building skin

The skin of the building generates costs for ↘thermal insulation and highly energy-efficient glass, and for elements to avoid ↘thermal bridges. Reducing transmission heat losses saves energy costs for heating. Thermal insulation produces costs for insulating materials and secondary construction. Reduced floor space resulting from greater insulation material thicknesses must also be considered here. Using better quality glass reduces ↘problems arising from cold air, leading to greater comfort with simpler room conditioning concepts. Additional investment is needed to acquire systems for reducing unwanted solar radiation by means of sun protection meas-ures and coated glass. Lighting energy demands can be reduced by optimising the window geometry for daylight and good daylight transmission by the glazing. Reduced g-values for the glazing also reduce daylight transmission. Fixed sun protection systems mean lower investment costs, and do not generate maintenance costs. Flexible systems placed on the outside mean high investment costs and are expensive to maintain. There is a significant interaction between sun protection concepts, room climate and investment costs for room conditioning systems and for cooling energy costs.

↘
thermal insulation
p. 146

thermal bridges
p. 146

cold air decline
p. 146

Room conditioning

There are considerable differences in room conditioning systems in relation to investment costs. Generally speaking, heating and cooling systems using water are associated with lower investment and energy costs. Systems with ↘concrete core activation are considerably less expensive than ↘cooling ceilings and are more flexible if there is to be a change of use. ↘Decentralised ventilation systems are more expensive in terms of technology and maintenance than central devices, but can offer overall price advantages through savings on switchboards, shafts and channels.

↘
concrete core activation
p. 152

cooling ceiling
p. 152

decentralised ventilation system
p. 152

Energy generation

Conventional systems such as gas boilers are considerably more economically viable for energy generation than innovative heat generators. ↘Heat pumps require heavy investment for access to the soil for soil temperature monitors, ↘soil sensors or for groundwater wells. Heat and power coupling plants generate high investment and servicing costs, and are viable only if usage is very heavy. Costs for ↘solar generation systems are very high, but pay themselves off in the medium to short term according to the amount of radiation available. Passive cooling systems relate closely to the soil conditions and the climatic conditions at the location. Photovoltaics demand high investment levels. The ideal solution is integration into the skin of the building, which produces economical synergy effects. Where payments are made for feeding into the electricity grid, the investment generally amortises more quickly than if the electricity is consumed.

↘
refrigeration unit
p. 154

earth piles/ groundwater utilisation
p. 154

solar thermal system
p. 154

Energy costs

Energy costs can be incurred in the form of fuel costs for gas, oil or biomass, or as purchasing costs for district heating. Considerable price differences occur according to the amount of energy used (Fig. 7.1). Biomass is half as expensive as gas or oil; electricity is three times as expensive. Electricity prices differ according to the time of day, and a service cost has to be built in. Fuels without a service charge incur storage costs. Coupled plants produce a high yield through combined heat and power production. Generating heat via heat pumps is economically viable only when the ↙degree of efficiency is greater than 3, which balances out the higher electricity price. Concepts should be developed and implemented for building and room climate and energy that do not bring about major load fluctuations. Peak loads can be smoothed out by short-term heat or cold storage in buffers or thermo-active building components, or by load-shedding. Intelligent power networks, so-called smart grids, make it possible to shift peak loads and thus run energy components as efficiently and cheaply as possible.

↙
degree of efficiency
p. 154

Maintenance costs

Maintenance expenses for technical systems vary considerably. This influences the choice of system and the economic viability of the system as a whole. To an extent, systems with low energy costs can be relativised financially by high maintenance costs; examples of this are ↙combined heat and power plants and wood-chip heating systems. Centralised ventilation systems have high costs for duct-cleaning and inspection of the fire dampers. ↙Decentralised ventilation devices have high maintenance costs for filter replacement at large numbers of points in the building, which is also inconvenient for users. Complex regulation systems need a great deal of work on programming and software maintenance, and for error detection and operational optimisation in running the building.

↙
combined heat and power plant
p. 154

Decentralised ventilation systems
p. 152

Contracting

In larger buildings or building complexes, or housing estates with local heating provision, it can make sense to outsource energy services by contracting. This saves investment costs and reduces tied-up capital. Contractors can usually offer energy at more reasonable prices through synergy effects. Contracts have a particular role to play in combined heat and power and biomass use.

Economic interaction

The cost of equipment has to be taken into account for technical systems, but so have secondary construction costs generated by the space needed for switchboards, spaces for devices or storage, and the areas required for shafts. In addition to this, greater building height may be needed for installation zones in false ceilings or raised floors. Secondary building requirements can be kept in check by optimal integration of the building services equipment and appropriate arrangement of switchboards and intermediate switchboards. As a rule, moderate investment in thermal and sun protection can lead to considerable savings in investment in technology, and also reduce energy costs.

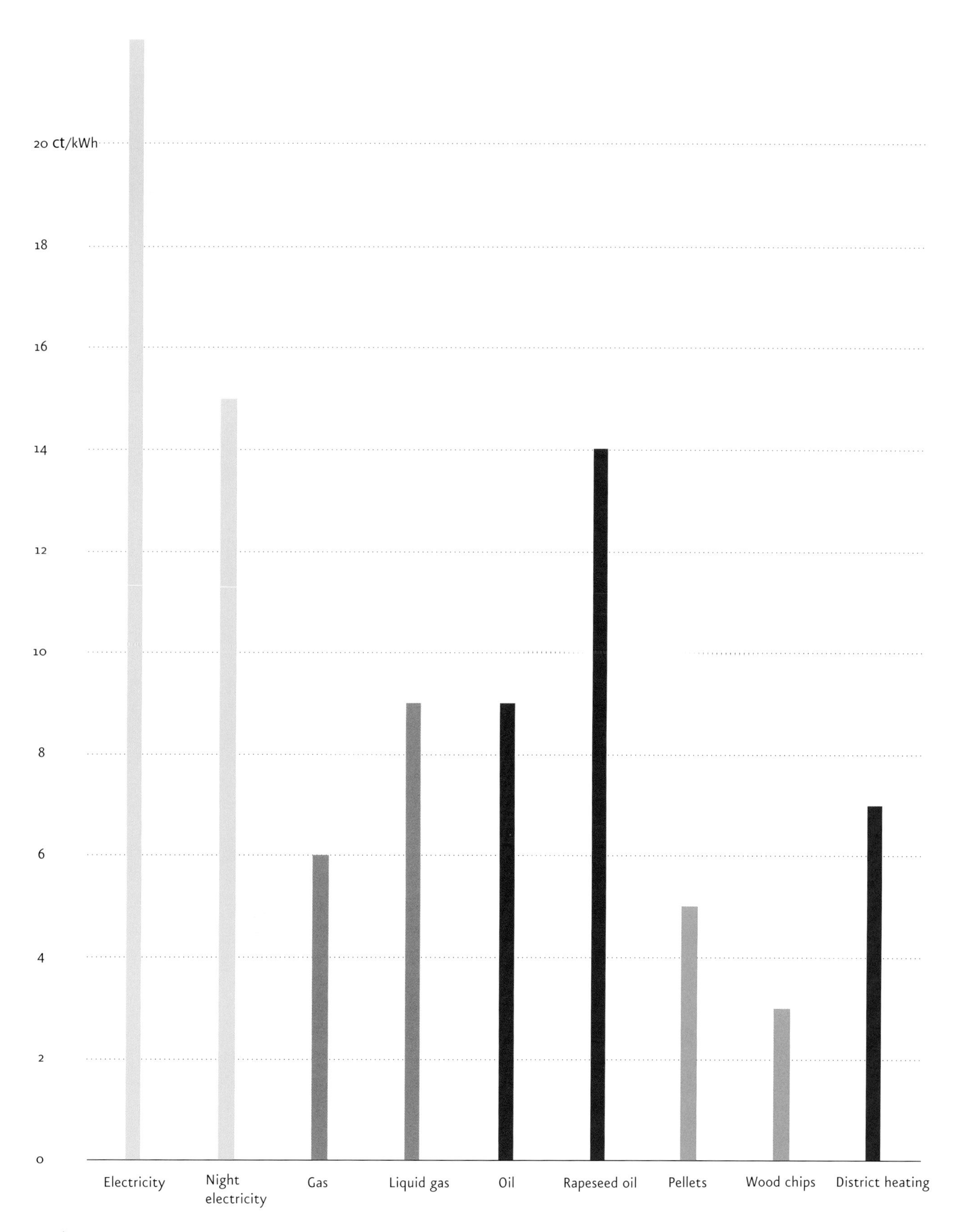

Fig. 7.1 Energy costs

Representation of the specific costs in ct/kWh for each energy source, including value-added tax and transport costs. For electricity and town gas costs, performance-linked costs may have to be taken into account. For fuels which are not grid-bound, the price is proportionate to the purchase volume. Position costs should also be taken into account.

Thermal Insulation

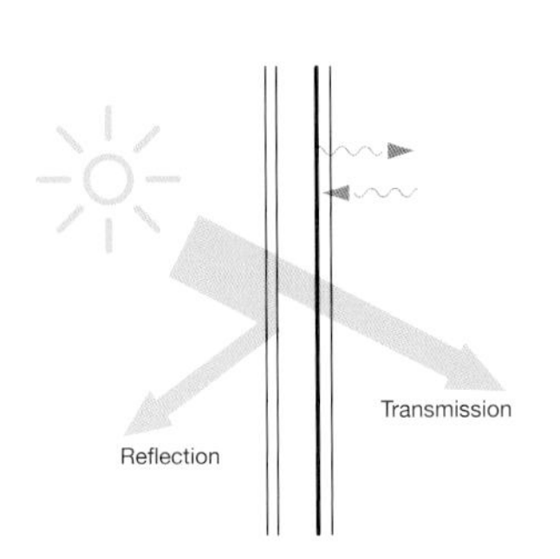

Thermal insulation glass

A choice has to be made between double glazing with U-values of 1.1 W/m²K and triple glazing with U-values of up to 0.7 W/m²K. Triple glazing costs twice as much for the ↙glass (Fig. 7.2) and a certain amount more for frames and fittings. However, triple glazing can reduce thermal transmission loss through the glass by up to 40%. Better glazing usually reduces costs for air-conditioning systems and can make it possible to use energy sources at low temperatures. As triple glazing has such a low ↙g-value it can sometimes replace sun protection glass, but costs rise after a certain pane size because the material has to be increasingly thick.

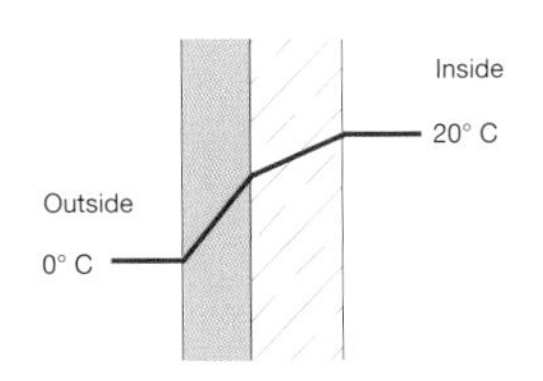

Insulation materials

The various insulating materials available include organic and mineral fibres, mats, sheets or fillers, and plastic foam sheets. ↙Thermal conductivity determines the thickness of the insulation required, producing values from 0.01 to 0.1 W/mK. The thickness of the sheeting can be greatly reduced by selecting an insulation material with lower conductivity. The heat insulation effect, expressed via the ↙U-value, does not stand in a linear relation to the thickness of the layer of insulating material, and thus the first 150 mm produce the greatest savings. The relationship between price and insulation thickness is as good as proportional for all insulating materials. The nature of the insulating material can generate considerable expense for secondary structures such as mounting devices and ventilated cladding.

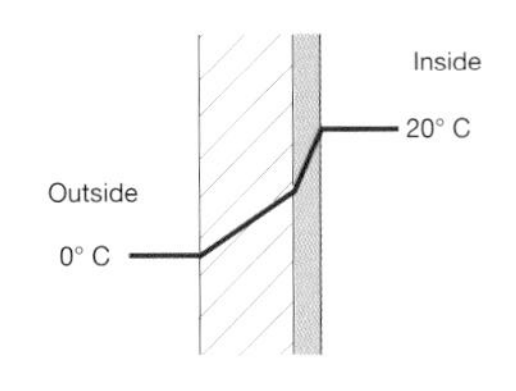

Vacuum insulation

Vacuum ventilation offers a very high insulation potential at very low thicknesses with thermal conductivity of less than 0.01 W/mK. In comparison with conventional insulation material, costs are increased by a factor of 10 (Fig. 7.2). In addition to this, more expenditure is needed for planning and processing, as vacuum insulation cannot be fitted retrospectively. The vacuum can be lost if it is damaged, which considerably reduces the insulation effect.

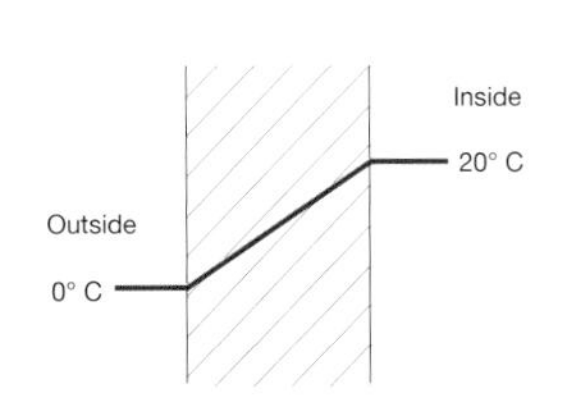

Bricks

Highly insulated bricks with thermal conductivity of up to 0.08 W/mK can produce U-values of less than 0.2 W/m²K with wall thicknesses of approx. 40 cm, which offers an interesting alternative to multi-layer outside wall constructions in moderate climates. The advantage of monolithic structures is their enormous durability. For a 40 cm wall, costs of 80–100 €/m², according to the statical and thermal conservation requirements, should be allowed for the insulating bricks.

↙
building skin
p. 146

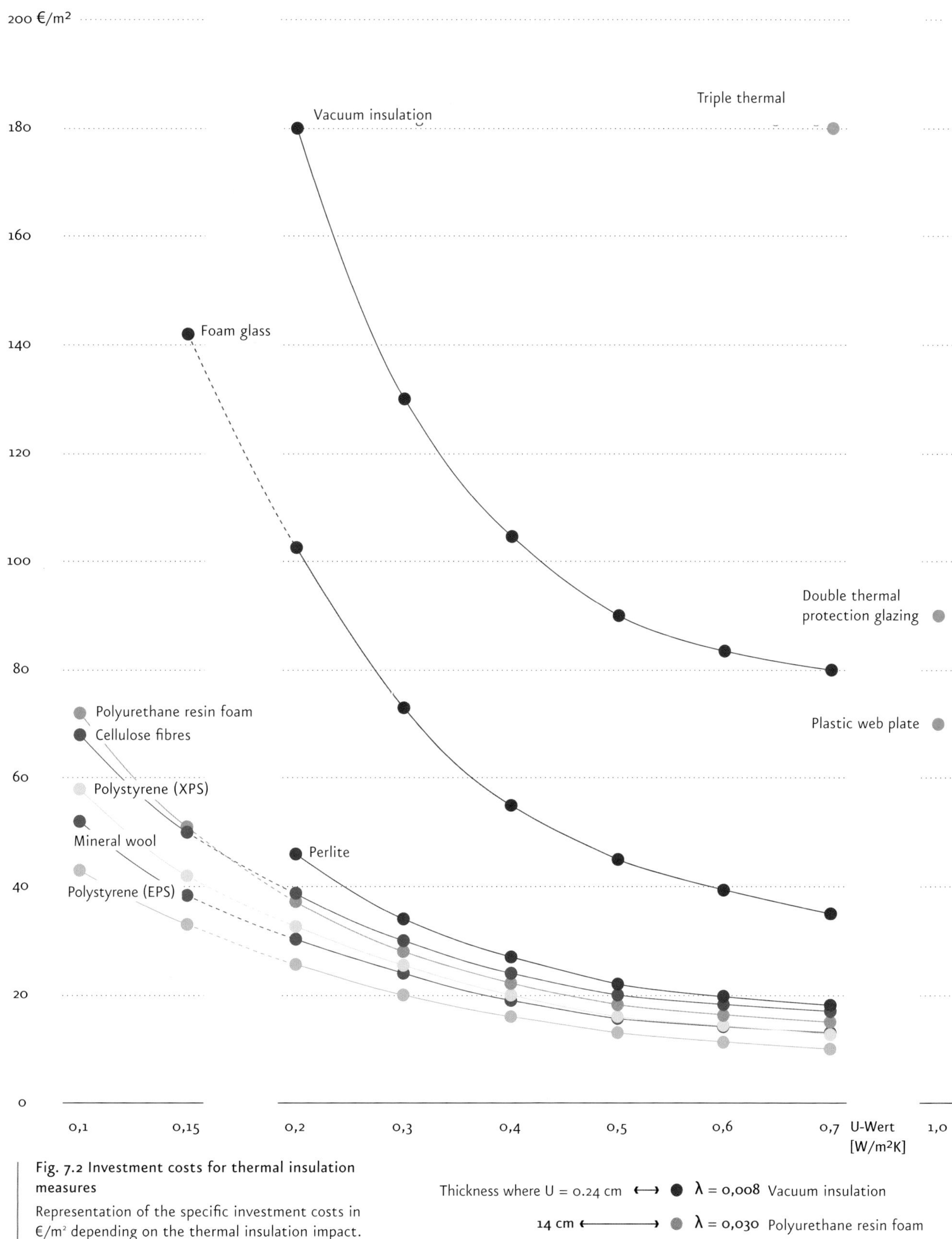

Fig. 7.2 Investment costs for thermal insulation measures

Representation of the specific investment costs in €/m² depending on the thermal insulation impact. The costs given take into account delivery and installation, but not any subconstruction or casing materials that might be required. With translucent thermal insulation, U-values of approximately 0.8 W/m²K can be achieved. The costs total approximately 200–300 €/m². In the small graph under the graph, the insulating materials are arranged according to their thermal conductivity, expressed in terms of the lambda value.

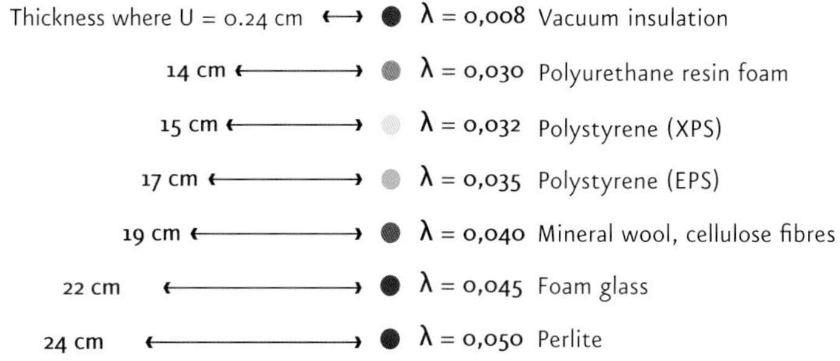

Sun Protection

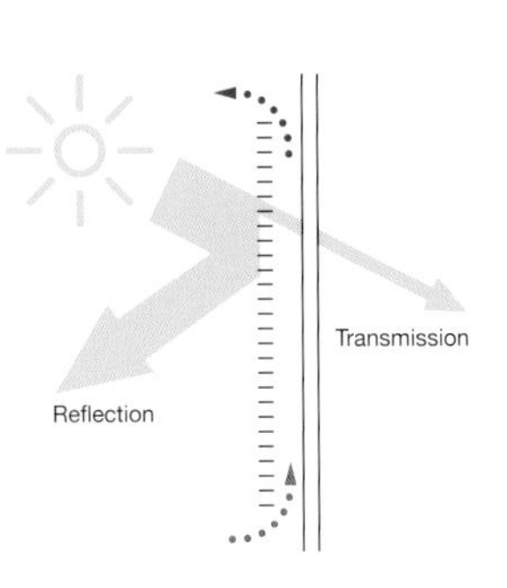

External sun protection

Exterior ↙ sun protection systems are the most efficient. The Fc-value is between 0.1 and 0.5 according to configuration. Moving systems generate higher investment and maintenance costs, especially if they are motorised (Fig. 7.3). Building automation and wind monitoring costs are relevant here. Venetian blinds can be configured so that an individually adjustable ↙ light deflection zone is created in the upper section. Adjustable vertical slats are usually custom-built and generate high investment costs. Awnings are prone to high maintenance costs because they are susceptible to wind and do not last for long (Fig. 7.3).

Sun protection between the panes

Systems fitted in the space between the window panes can be rigid, rotatable, or rotatable and movable. The g_{tot}-values lie between 0.15 and 0.4. Sometimes a light deflection function also ensues, and light scattering is also possible. If the systems have moving parts, there is a risk of failure, especially if they can be moved outwards. This can generate significant maintenance costs, as the whole pane often has to be replaced. Rigid systems reduce transparency.

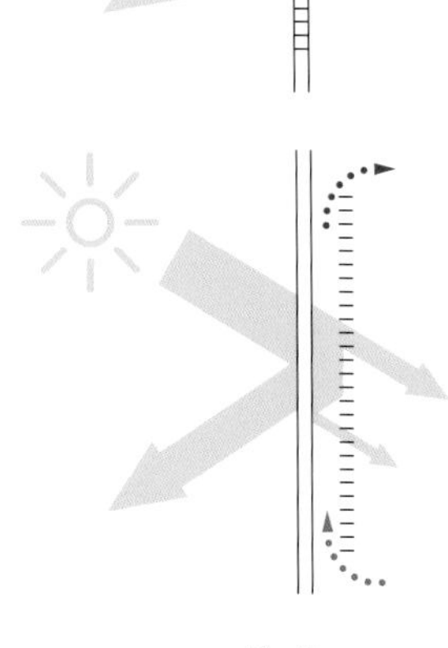

Interior sun protection systems

Interior sun protection systems can produce Fc-values of 0.3 to 0.6. Interior systems are protected against the weather and can be individually adjusted manually. They take the form of blinds, roller blinds or even screens. Reduced efficiency is compensated for by lower investment and maintenance costs. In the case of reflecting systems, efficiency is considerably reduced by dirt.

Sun protection glass

Transparent ↙ sun protection glass can produce ↙ g-values of 0.4 to 0.15. Costs are up to 50% higher than for conventional double thermal insulation glazing (Fig. 7.3). The g-value for sun protection coating has little effect on the price. Secondary financial effects can ensue because of lower ↙ daylight transmission. On the other hand, savings can be made in terms of cooling. If complete transparency is not required, g-values can be reduced by printing.

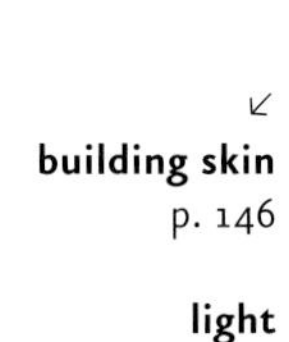

↙
building skin
p. 146

light
p. 148

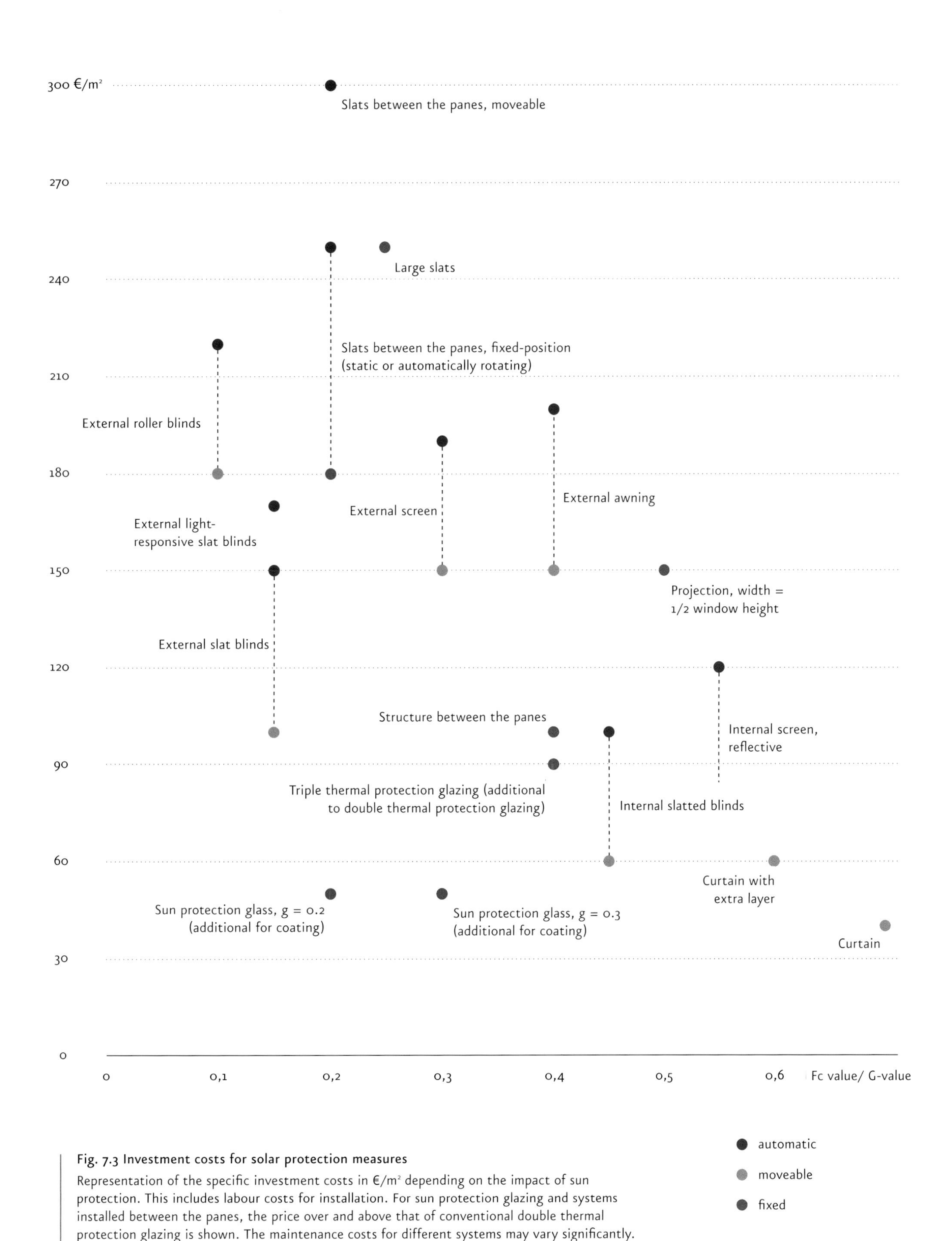

Fig. 7.3 Investment costs for solar protection measures

Representation of the specific investment costs in €/m² depending on the impact of sun protection. This includes labour costs for installation. For sun protection glazing and systems installed between the panes, the price over and above that of conventional double thermal protection glazing is shown. The maintenance costs for different systems may vary significantly. External systems are exposed to the weather all year round, and require more maintenance.

Room Conditioning

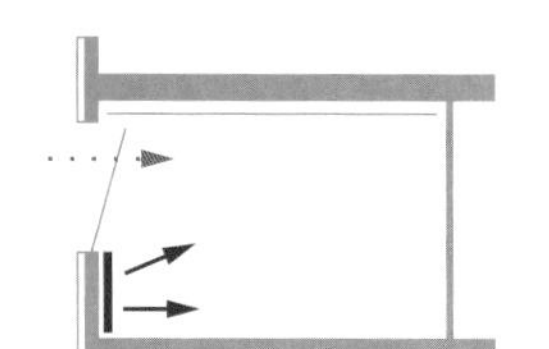

Radiator and convector

If natural ventilation is available, it is possible to use a radiator or a ↙ convector for heating. If a blower convector is to be used, it can also be used for cooling. This will produce a very reasonably priced system with high performance potential. The heating system must be able to generate high temperatures, and refrigeration equipment is required for cooling. Air conditioning costs rise by a factor of two or three if mechanical ventilation or heat recovery are required (Fig. 7.4). Comfort is enhanced, and an earth duct can be used for passive cooling and preheating incoming air.

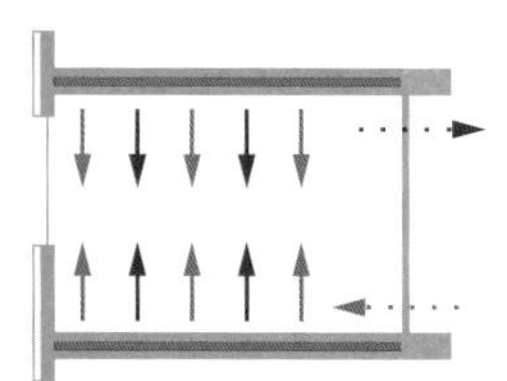

Concrete core activation

↙ Concrete core activation can be seen as a very reasonably priced room conditioning system that usually offers price advantages for energy use. Cooling performance and adjustability are limited, however, and it is not possible to calculate costs storey by storey. Measures also have to be taken in relation to room acoustics. It is possible to reconstruct a building very simply using concrete core activation. Mechanical ventilation with incoming air dehumidification is required in humid climates. There is next to no delay in the building phase if such systems are well planned.

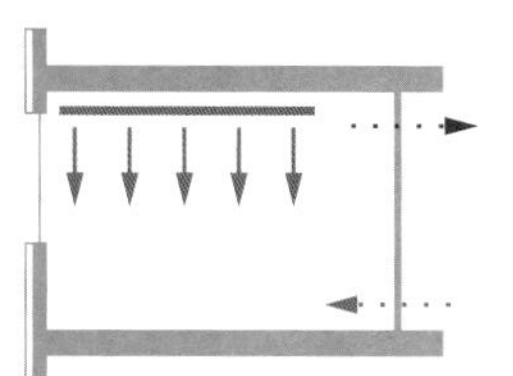

Cooing ceiling

A ↙ cooling ceiling can achieve very high performance. If the exterior humidity is very high, mechanical ventilation with incoming air dehumidification is essential. It is also possible to use a cooling ceiling for heating to a limited extent. Cooling ceilings can also provide space for fittings under the ceiling, and be used to optimise room acoustics. Dew point regulation requires a more costly regulation system. Mechanical ventilation with dehumidification of incoming air may be required. Costs will be higher if rooms are being remodelled. Renewable cooling sources can be used provided the temperatures are sufficiently low.

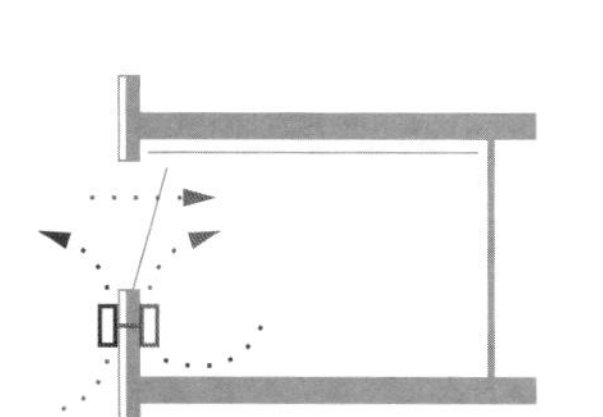

Split units

↙ Split units generate no installation costs inside the building. However, there must be sufficient space for the external elements on the facade or roof. They can be used for cooling and heating, and to a certain extent for dehumidification. They are comparatively less efficient than central systems. This is partially compensated for by the fact that they offer a very high level of adjustability. They generate no dew point problems, so can be combined with natural ventilation even if humidity is high. Split units offer the possibility of direct control in individual rooms.

↙
room conditioning
p. 152

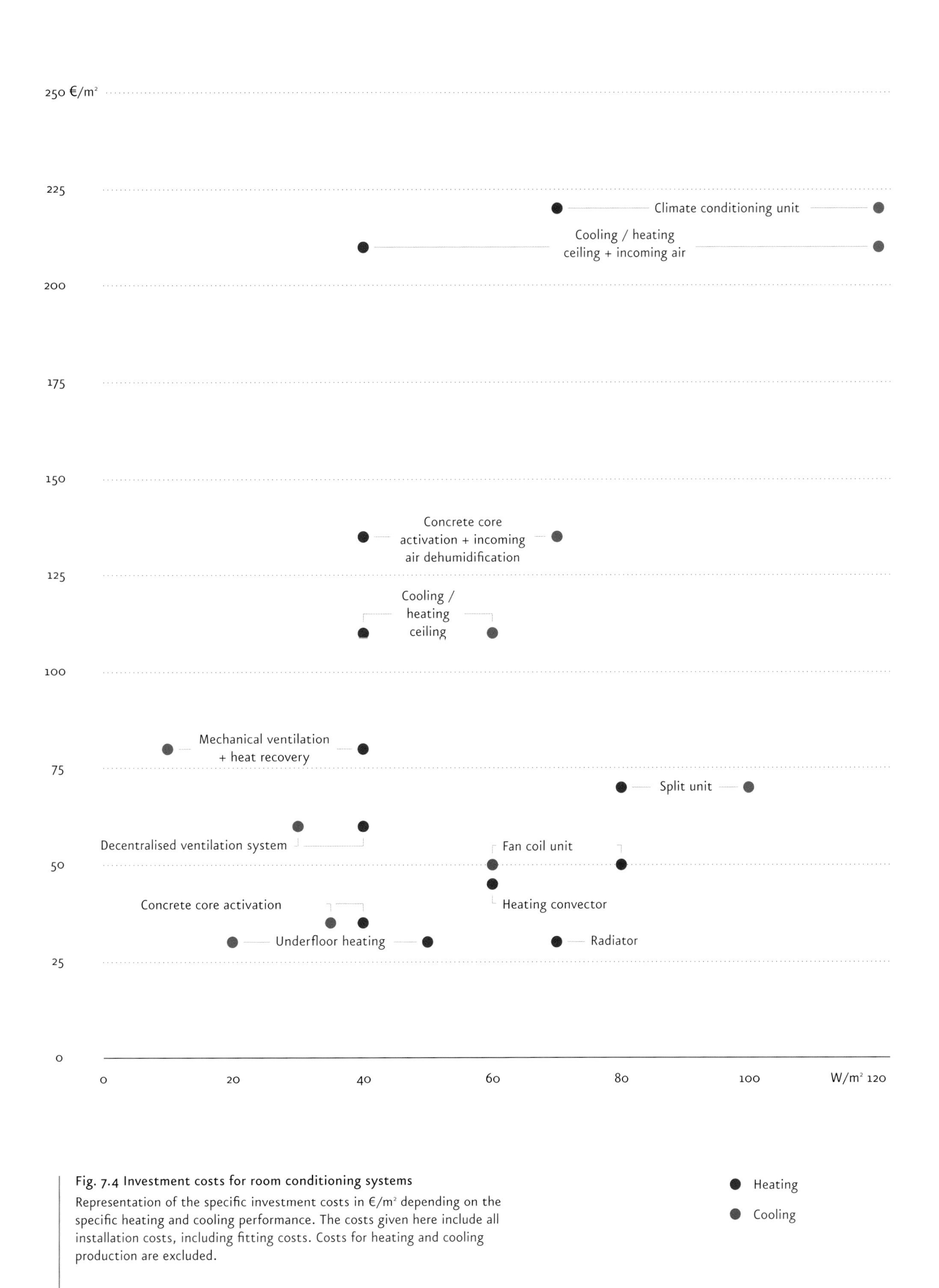

Fig. 7.4 Investment costs for room conditioning systems

Representation of the specific investment costs in €/m² depending on the specific heating and cooling performance. The costs given here include all installation costs, including fitting costs. Costs for heating and cooling production are excluded.

Energy Generation

Solar energy

↙ Solar collectors with up to 60% efficiency generate heat to a temperature level of up to 90 °C. This can be used to heat water, to support heating or to provide cooling. With some types of collector, efficiency may drop when outside temperatures are low. Solar cooling is particularly advantageous in locations where the array of panels can boost winter heating. This requires a very high cooling capacity. ↙ Photovoltaics can be used to convert solar radiation directly into electricity. The efficiency level is approx. 15%. Here, care must be taken to avoid loss of performance at high temperatures and as a result of dust. The high investment costs can be kept under control by installation in the facade.

Geothermal energy with heat pump

A ↙ heat pump can be used to raise the temperature of energy from the soil or from groundwater. As the coefficient of performance is linked directly with the difference in temperature between source and flow temperature, heat pumps with surface heating systems should be used. Soil also offers passive cooling potential in summer. A heat pump can be operated in reverse, and thus also function as a ↙ refrigeration unit. The energy potential of the soil can be accessed via ↙ earth piles, soil probes, soil collectors or groundwater wells.

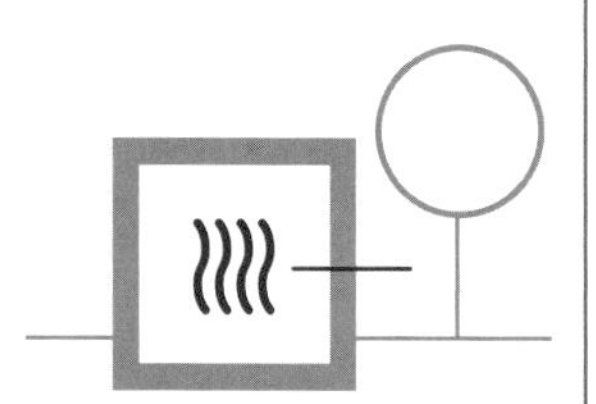

Biomass

Using wood as fuel sets a lower fuel price against greater maintenance costs. For this reason it is especially economical in the case of greater system capacities, for large buildings, for example, or combined with local heating concepts. Fuel storage expenses must also be taken into consideration. Wood should be bought locally to minimise transport costs.

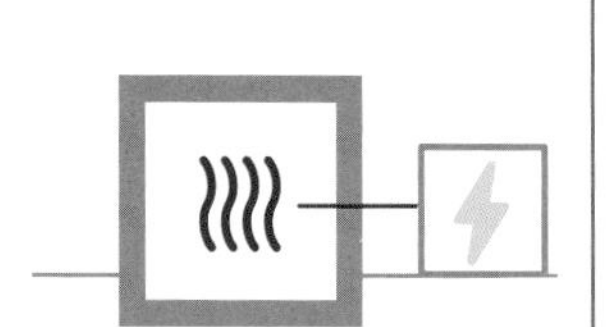

Combined heat and power plant

A ↙ combined heat and power plant (CHP) uses the waste heat created when generating electricity, which leads to very high efficiency levels. But very high investment and maintenance costs mean that a combined heat and power plant is economically viable only if it has an annual running time of over 5,000 hours. This is the case if heat is needed all the year round, in swimming baths, for example. For financial reasons, combined heat and power plants are usually designed to cover the base load, and combined with a conventional peak load boiler. Oil, natural gas, rapeseed oil or biogas are possible fuels.

↙
energy generation
p. 154

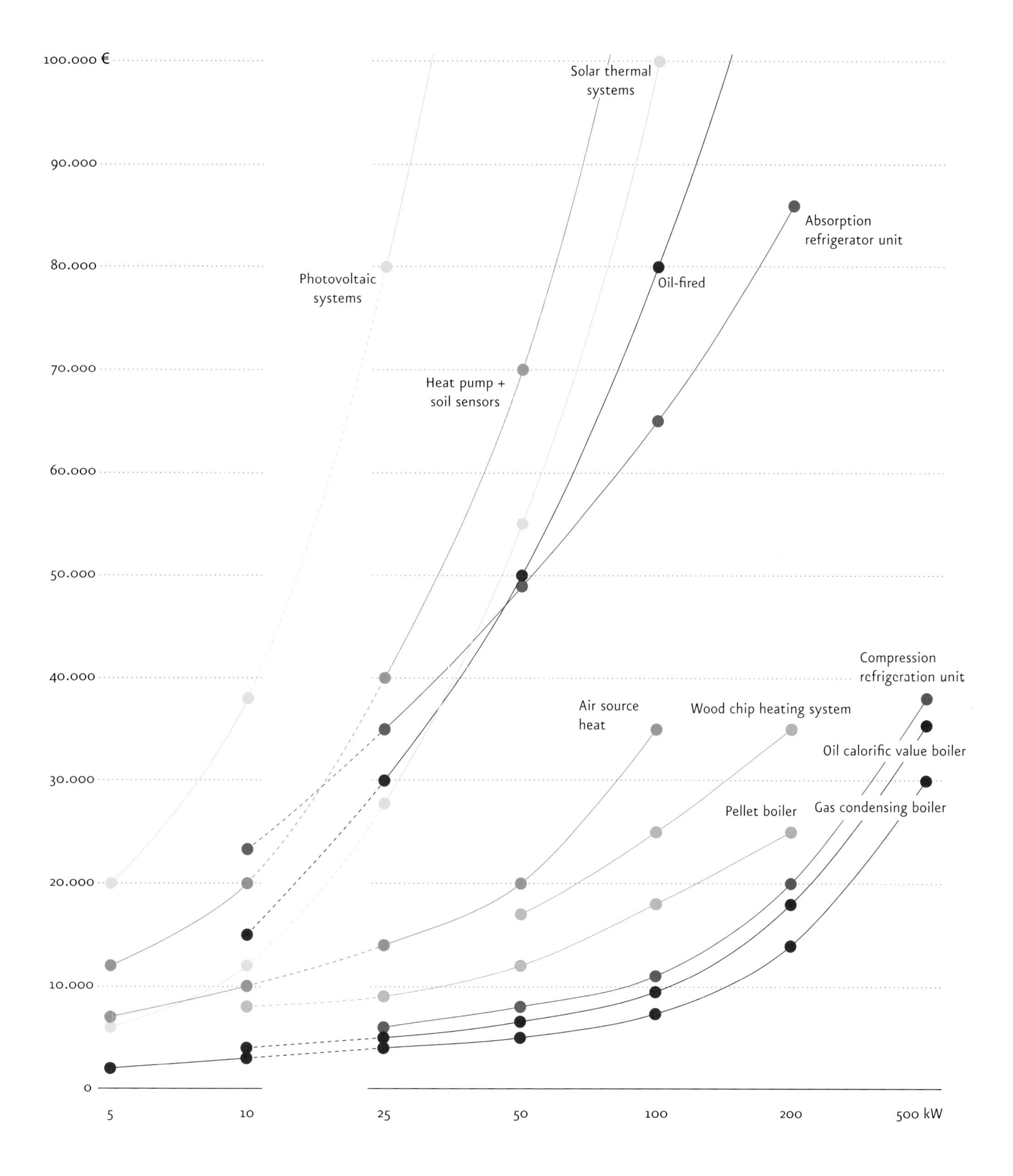

Fig. 7.5 The investment costs of energy generation systems

A representation of the specific investment costs in €/kW depending on the system's heating/cooling performance or electrical output. For the combined heat and power plant, the thermal performance is taken as the basis for this. The costs for the first setup and adjustment are included, as is the value-added tax. The costs for water and fuel storage must also be calculated. For hot water storage, the estimated cost is €250 for every 100 l of capacity. For energy sources with stored fuel, there will be approximately € 5,000–10,000 of added costs for fuel storage and transport. For refrigeration units, the recooling must also be calculated.

Climate and System Costs

The economic viability of investments in energy and room climate are closely related to the climate. Effects on maintenance and running costs also emerge on this basis.

Cool climate

↙ **heating energy demand** p. 144

heat recovery p. 144

combined heat and power plant p. 154

High ↙ heating energy demands make investment in very good heat insulation particularly viable economically, as this lowers energy costs and room conditioning systems and energy generation can be on a smaller scale. Solar thermal energy is economically viable in summer only with coverage ratios of up to 50%. Using soil for heating purposes is not economically viable. If there are cooling energy demands, soil offers a cooling source without energy costs. As a ventilation system should usually be provided to permit ↙ heat recovery, an underground duct will prove economically viable for preheating or precooling the air supply. The longer period in which heating is required offers favourable conditions for the use of ↙ combined heat and power plants. Wood-fired systems recommend themselves as wood is plentifully available and reasonably priced, and the demand for heat is greater.

Temperate climate

↙ **refrigeration unit** p. 154

solar thermal system p. 154

solar cooling p. 154

Good thermal insulation reduces heating energy demands. If mechanical ventilation is used, heat can be recovered. A good sun protection concept provides the basis for implementing a passive cooling strategy, thus reducing investment and running costs. If soil is used as a cooling source, then a ↙ heat pump is recommended for heating, as this will not generate additional costs for accessing the source energy. ↙ Solar thermal energy can cover a major proportion of hot water demands, and contribute heating support after a manageable payback period. Wood-fired heating systems make sense because wood is readily available and inexpensive, especially in the case of large-capacity units. If district heating is available, the heat not used in summer can be used for ↙ desiccant cooling, thus offering cooling at a reasonable price.

Subtropical climate

As the key issue here is summer cooling, the facade must be able to reduce irradiation efficiently, especially ↘diffuse irradiation. If the facade offers a certain degree of heat insulation, a heating system may not be necessary. Solar thermal systems can make an economically viable contribution to the heat supply for large parts of the year, and also supply solar cooling systems. It makes sense to build ↘photovoltaics into the building skin. If a ventilation plant is to be provided, an ↘earth pipe will reduce the amount of energy needed for heating, cooling and dehumidification. If ↘earth piles are used for cooling, then a ↘heat pump is an efficient heating source.

↘
global radiation
p. 142

photovoltaics
p. 154

earth pipe
p. 154

refrigeration unit
p. 154

Tropical climate

Effective measures for restricting solar gains mean considerable savings in terms of technology and energy costs. In the tropics, the principal role of room conditioning is cooling and dehumidification. If a ventilation plant is planned, then desiccant cooling combined with ↘solar energy is economically viable. Alternatively, a solar refrigeration unit can be driven by solar panel. The soil can be used for precooling and partial dehumidification by means of an underground duct. High radiation gains offer a good basis for using photovoltaics.

↘
solar thermal system
p. 154

Desert climate

The high irradiation levels require ↘sun protection concepts that limit solar gain in the room and thus reduce the amount of cooling energy required and the costs generated by technology and energy. Very high annual solar gain offers a good basis for using photovoltaics. Concentrating solar panels offer a high temperature level that can drive solar refrigeration units and desiccant cooling systems efficiently. According to the soil temperature, an underground duct can be used for precooling and in cases of high outdoor humidity for partial dehumidification of the incoming air. In zones with sharp day-night temperature swings, ↘night cooling combined with thermal mass is very effective. If outdoor humidity is low, ↘adiabatic cooling can be used to advantage.

↘
sun protection
p. 146

night ventilation
p. 152

cooling tower
p. 154

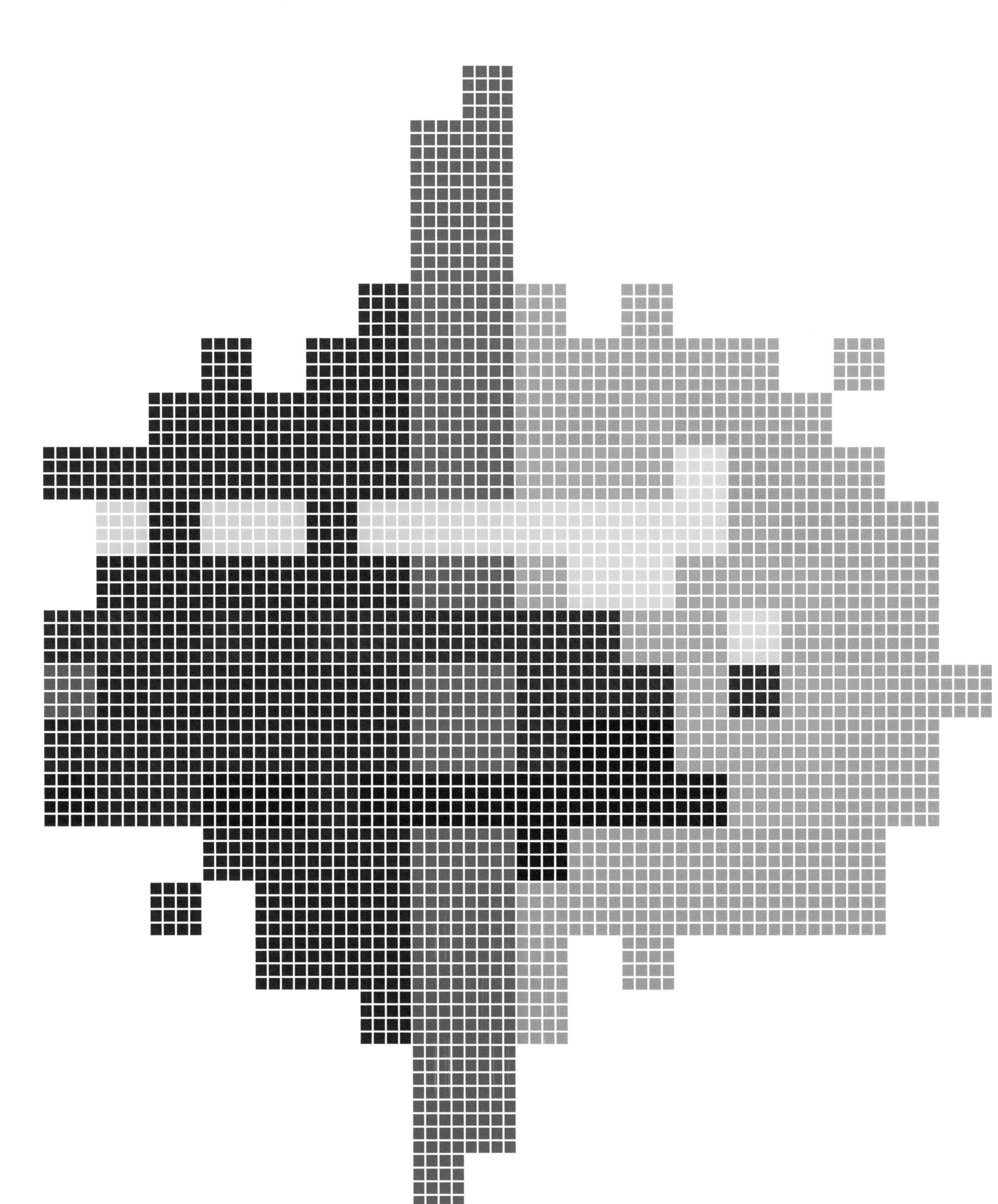

Glossary

Details of overall concept

A building is a unified system consisting of a facade, a building structure and building systems. The better integrated these are, the lower the energy expenditure will be. This means that a number of factors must be considered during the design phase, where many different possibilities are present. The design-related, functional and economic aspects interact with energy and room climate-related factors. To achieve a balanced building concept, the details must be refined and optimised as planning progresses and options are eliminated.

Interaction

Outdoor climate · Building Skin · Room conditioning · Room climate · Light · Building energy systems · Energy generation

Outdoor Climate

Absolute air humidity [g/kg]
The relationship of the quantity of water vapour present to the quantity of air present. The absolute humidity of outdoor air varies depending on the climatic zone and the time of the year. Where the outdoor air is too dry or too moist, it must be humidified or dehumidified to create comfortable conditions.

Condensation
Phase change from gas to liquid. When a substance reaches a particular temperature, it changes from a gaseous to a liquid state, releasing condensation heat. Conversely, in the **evaporation** process, a substance changes from a fluid to a gas. In doing so, it takes in heat from its surroundings, producing an effect that can be used to cool buildings.

Degree day value [Kd/a]
The product of the number of heating days in a year and the difference between the indoor air temperature of (for example) 20 °C and the average ↑outdoor air temperature during any particular heating day. Heating days are days when the average ↑outdoor air temperature throughout the day lies below the heating limit of (for example) 12 or 15 °C. The heating limit depends on the building's thermal protection. The degree day value is used to calculate ↑transmission and ↑ventilation heat losses.

Dew point temperature [°C]
Temperature at which the air is saturated with moisture and the relative air humidity reaches 100%. At any temperature lower than the dew point temperature, the water vapour ↑condenses. The dew point temperature is relevant because mould can form in the case of ↑thermal bridges. There is a danger that the temperature will drop below dew point temperature on the internal sides of glazing or where a surface cooling system is in place.

Enthalpy [J/kg]
The air's energy content. Enthalpy is a thermodynamic state variable resulting from the quantity of heat emitted or absorbed and taking into account temperature and humidity.

Global radiation [W/m²]
Solar radiation, partly directional and partly non-directional. It is the sum of **direct radiation** and **diffuse radiation**, and is created by scattering and reflection from air molecules, aerosol particles and other particles. When it meets an absorbent surface, heat is produced. The global radiation is the determining factor when establishing solar thermal gains via glazed surfaces and in calculating the yields of ↑photovoltaic systems and ↑solar thermal systems.

Outdoor air temperature [°C]
Absolute temperature of the outdoor air in °C. The difference between the existing outdoor temperature and the desired ↑indoor air temperature determines the ↑ventilation and transmission heat loss and gain. The outdoor air temperature is subject to fluctuations throughout the day and throughout the year, to a degree that is determined by the climate zone. Temperature differences, often described as ΔT, are given in Kelvin [K].

Position of the sun
Position of the sun relative to a particular location. Where south is 0°, the azimuth angle describes the quarter of the sky from which the sun shines. The angle between the sun and the horizon is called the angle of elevation. The movement of the sun influences the duration and intensity of the solar radiation on the ↑outer shell surfaces of a building.

Psychrometric Chart
Oblique coordinate system with the temperature on the X-axis and the absolute humidity on the Y-axis. It shows changes in the state of moist air, some of which are non-linear. Relative humidity can be read off from the rising curved lines, and enthalpy from the falling diagonals. They are based on Mollier's h,x diagram.

Relative air humidity [%]
The ratio of absolute humidity to saturation humidity. The saturation humidity depends on the air temperature, meaning that the relative air humidity is temperature-dependent. It is subject to fluctuations over the course of the day.

Soil temperature [°C]
The soil temperature at a particular depth. It depends on the composition, moisture content and depth of the soil. Just beneath the surface, the soil's temperature will be the same as the ↑outdoor air's average temperature over a month. Beyond a depth of approximately 10–15 m, attenuated seasonal temperature variations exist, and their maximum and minimum values show up as retarded in comparison with the annual exterior air tempera-ture. The annual maximum and minimum temperatures manifest themselves here 2 to 3 months after they occur above ground. The soil's temperature can be used directly for passive cooling, or for heat production by means of a ↑heat pump. Groundwater temperature will generally also be the same as the average temperature over a year. Groundwater utilisation enables higher extraction performances.

Test reference year
Climate values in an ideal-typical year. Typical climate values are used to calculate ↑heating and cooling loads and for thermal building simulations based on statistics recorded over a period of years. Among other values, these statistics include hourly changes in the ↑outdoor air temperature, the air pressure, the global radiation consisting of ↑diffuse and ↑direct radiation, the ↑air humidity and the ↑wind speed.

Wet bulb temperature [°C]
The lowest temperature at which water evaporation can be used for cooling, also known as the **limit of cooling temperature**. It is lower than the ↑outdoor air temperature and is dependent on air humidity. The greater the temperature difference, the drier the air. The wet bulb temperature provides information about the cooling potential of adiabatic cooling, which cools through the evaporation of water. It is important in determining the size of ↑recooling plants – in cooling provision for surface cooling systems, for instance. In practice, the minimum possible cooling temperature is never reached.

Wind pressure [N/m²]
Wind exerts pressure on a surface. The wind pressure is proportional to the square of the ↑wind speed. This information is vital to an optimal ventilation concept.

Wind speed [m/s]
The median speed of moving air. In meteorology, both the physical unit [m/s] and knots (1 kn = 0.514 m/s) are used as measurements. Measurements are taken at a height of 20–30 m. The Beaufort scale – a 12-step scale for classifying winds by their speed – is used. The wind speed influences a building's natural ventilation; a moderate level of wind can be useful for natural ventilation, but if winds are high, protected ventilation openings will be needed. The maximum wind speed also affects the installation of external ↑sun protection systems.

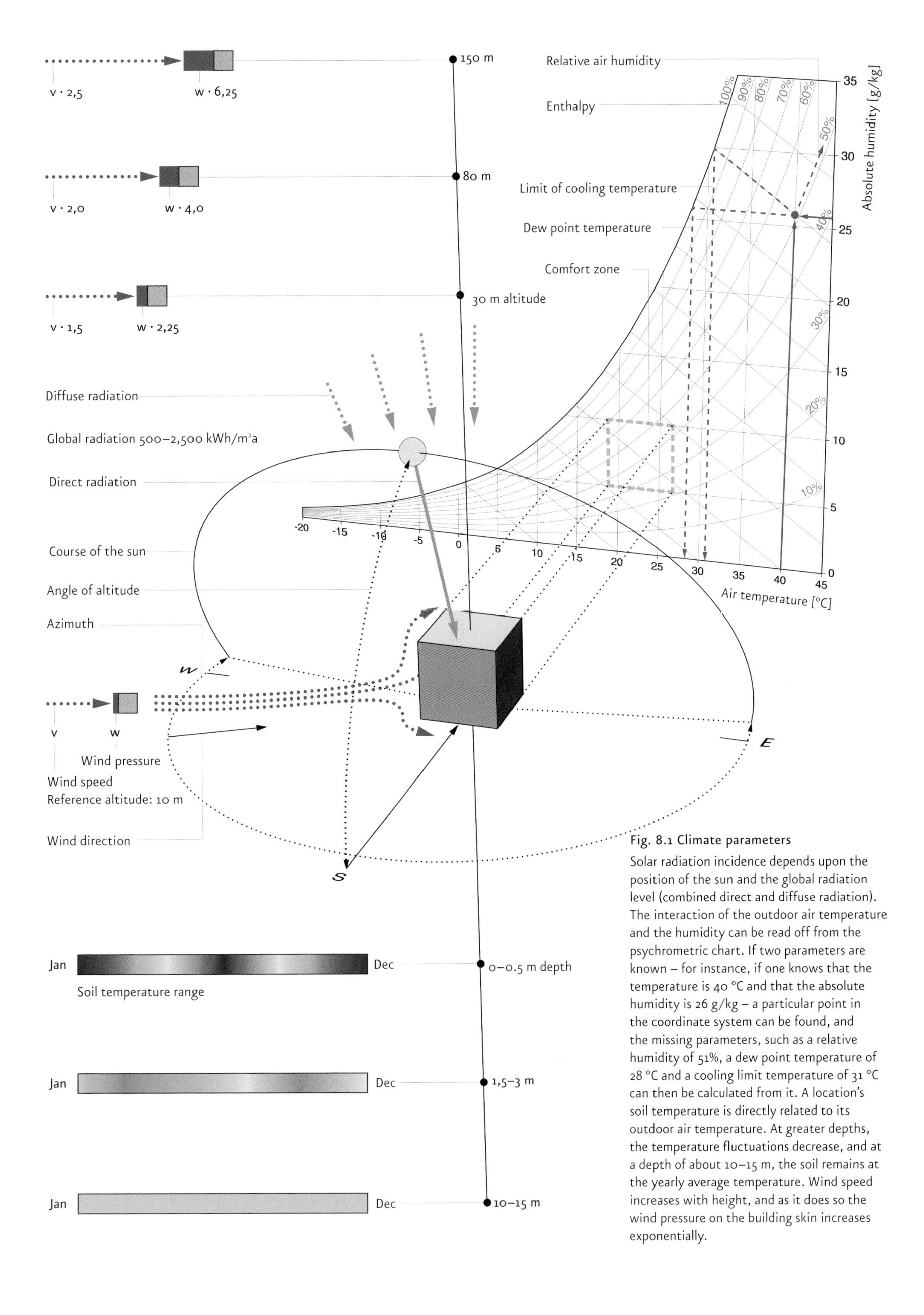

Fig. 8.1 Climate parameters

Solar radiation incidence depends upon the position of the sun and the global radiation level (combined direct and diffuse radiation). The interaction of the outdoor air temperature and the humidity can be read off from the psychrometric chart. If two parameters are known – for instance, if one knows that the temperature is 40 °C and that the absolute humidity is 26 g/kg – a particular point in the coordinate system can be found, and the missing parameters, such as a relative humidity of 51%, a dew point temperature of 28 °C and a cooling limit temperature of 31 °C can then be calculated from it. A location's soil temperature is directly related to its outdoor air temperature. At greater depths, the temperature fluctuations decrease, and at a depth of about 10–15 m, the soil remains at the yearly average temperature. Wind speed increases with height, and as it does so the wind pressure on the building skin increases exponentially.

Building Energy Systems

Cubature
The shape and volume of a building. The **ratio of the surface to the building volume** is known as the surface-to-volume ratio. Measures such as minimising the outer shell surface can help to reduce ↑transmission heat loss. Losses are also reduced in those parts of the heated building volume that are underground. The ↑daylight provision and the ↑natural ventilation options are determined by the building shape. The shading of individual facade areas also depends on cubature.

Electricity demand
The electricity demand for illumination and electrical devices and systems. These include devices for the delivery and provision of heat, cold and air, such as feed pumps, regulation and measuring technology, ↑heat pumps and ventilation systems.

End energy demand
The building's heating, hot water and cooling energy demand. In addition to the useful energy demand, which consists of the ↑heating energy demand, the ↑dehumidifying energy and the water heating demand, system losses must be compensated. These arise from control losses, distribution losses, storage losses and production losses within the building. In the same way, additional energy must be expended on the ↑cooling energy demand and the ↑dehumidifying energy.

Heating load / cooling load
The required performance of a cooling or heating system in order to maintain a particular ↑operative room temperature at a particular time. The maximum performance demands that arise when a period of heavy use coincides with unfavourable outdoor climate conditions are described as load peaks. When a system is required to perform at maximum, the situation is described as a full load.

Heat recovery
The use of heat from a building's exhaust air. Incoming air can be warmed very efficiently by exposing it to exhaust air in a heat exchanger. ↑Decentralised ventilation systems are ideal for this. Central ventilation systems handling incoming air and exhaust air generally require a more complex system of conduits. In a combined cycle system, a liquid circulated through tubes transfers the energy from the exhaust air to the incoming air over a greater distance. Heat can also be recovered directly via an exhaust air heat pump – in which case the energy could also be fed into a water-based heating system.

Heating energy demand
Sum of the ventilation heat losses and transmission heat losses minus ↑solar and ↑internal gains. Similarly, the **cooling energy demand** is calculated from solar and ↑internal heat gains and transmission and ventilation heat gains/losses.

Internal gains
The emitted heat of people and apparatuses within an indoor space. The critical parameters for heat emitted by people are the building's occupancy density and the lengths of time during which it is in use. Heat given off by electrical systems is calculated from their power consumption and by the length of time they are in use. In some cases, the heat they emit – the waste heat of server rooms, for instance – can be used to heat other rooms.

Orientation
The direction or point of the compass towards which the facade faces. The orientation influences ↑solar gains and therefore impacts on the sun protection strategy and on the yields solar energy systems installed on facades. The wind speed experienced by a facade, which influences the building's ↑natural ventilation, often depends on the facade's orientation.

Primary energy demand
The energy demand after losses outside the limits of the building's systems have been taken into account. The primary energy demand equals the energy demand plus the energy required for procuring, transporting and converting raw materials for energy generation. After these processes have taken place, the building has energy sources such as electricity, oil, gas, wood, district heating etc. at its disposal. The primary energy demand can be calculated by multi-plying the energy demand by a primary energy factor representing the energy sources. This factor also takes into account whether an energy source is renewable, either entirely or partially.

Solar gains
↑Global radiation that enters the room via transparent or translucent building components. Its absorption by surfaces within the indoor space creates heat. The radiation incidence and therefore the heat gain depend on the time of day and the time of the year, the location and the ↑orientation. The ↑facade's total degree of energy permeability (↑window surface percentage, ↑sun protection, ↑glazing) also influences solar gains. Where outdoor air temperatures are low, solar gains help to reduce the ↑heating energy demand. Undesired solar gains can cause overheating of indoor spaces.

Storage mass
The heat storage capacity of components within a 24-hour cycle. The influencing variables are ↑thermal conductivity and thermal capacity. Where the temperature of their surrounding environment is high, solid components can absorb heat and release it at a later point, when the temperature of their surroundings sinks below the temperature of the components. The storage and unloading or discharging process is slow, resulting in a **phase shift**. In order for them to act as a thermal buffer, a sufficiently large amount of the surface area of solid building components must be exposed and available within the indoor space. They must also be allowed to unload fully at night (by cooling). Intensified ↑night ventilation or ↑concrete core activation can be combined with a regenerative cooling source to cool the components at night. If solid building components are not available in sufficient quantities, then ↑phase change materials (PCM) can be used.

Transmission heat loss
Heat loss via the building skin. When the outdoor air is colder than the ↑indoor air, a flow of heat from the inside to the outside of the building takes place through the building components. The higher the temperature difference and the less efficient the thermal protection is, the higher the degree of heat loss. The main influences on the level of thermal protection are the ↑U-values and ↑thermal bridges. A facade surface's transmission heat loss is the product of the U-value of its components, its surface area, its temperature difference, and the period during which the heat flow takes place.

Ventilation heat loss
Heat loss through exchange of stale indoor air with fresh outdoor air. If the outdoor air is colder than the desired ↑indoor air temperature and the passive gains do not make up the difference, heating is required to compensate. ↑Heat recovery minimises ventilation heat losses. If there is a need for cooling, then the cool outer air can be used for this purpose; the rate of air exchange may be increased to achieve this if necessary. If the ↑outdoor air's temperature is above the maximum required ↑indoor air temperature, cooling is required. ↑Earth pipes are suitable for preparing the incoming air in temperature terms.

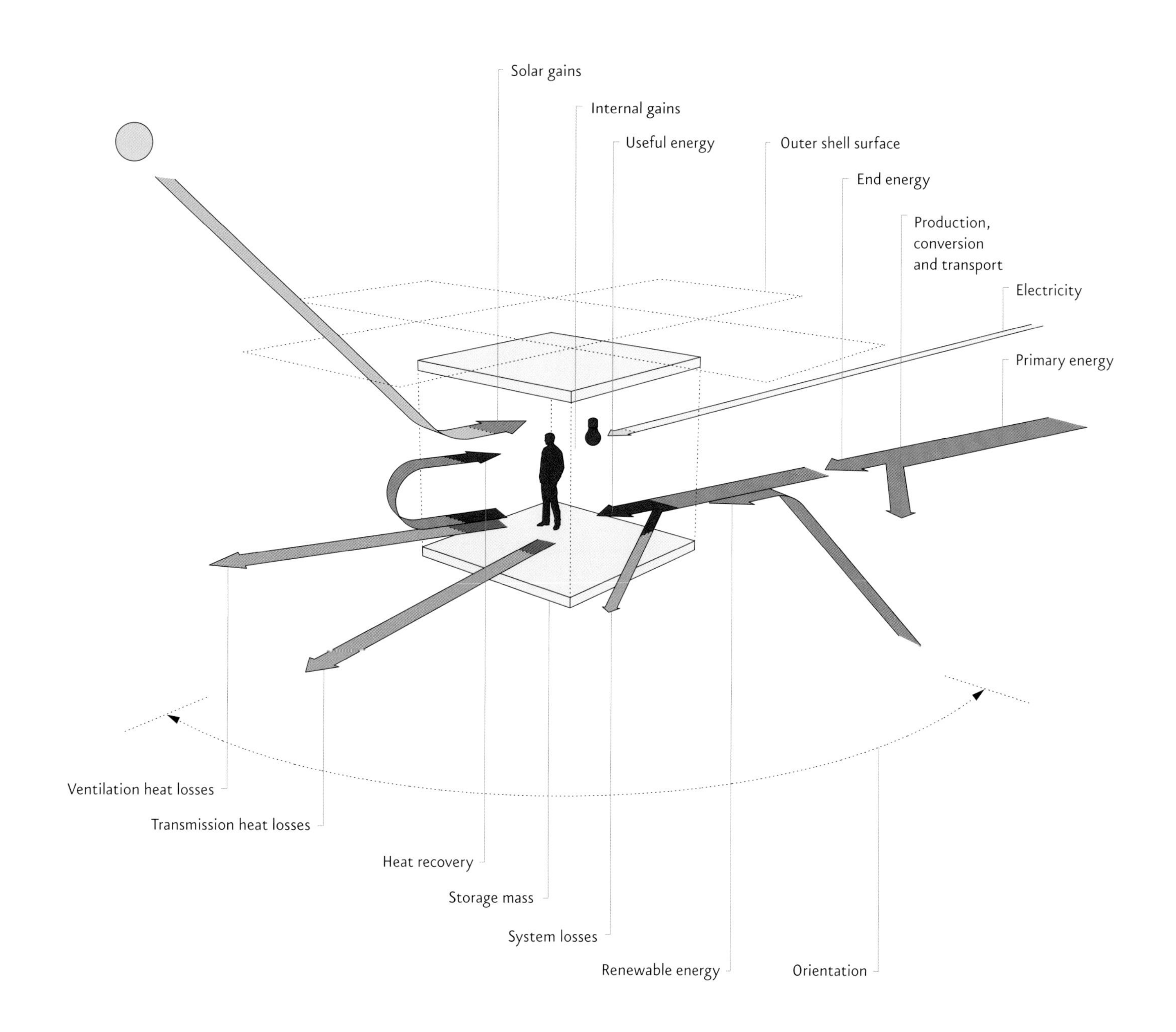

Fig. 8.2 Building energy flows

The composition, geometry and orientation of the building's outer shell surfaces influence its solar gains and transmission heat losses. Internal gains and ventilation heat losses are determined largely by the building's function. Various losses during the extraction of energy from raw materials before useable heating, cooling or electricity become available must be compensated. Losses from the conversion, production and transport of energy must be deducted from the primary energy. The remaining energy that is available to be used in the building is described as the end energy. Systems losses are deducted from the end energy; only a percentage of the energy originally invested is actually available for use. Using renewable energy within a building can reduce the primary energy expenditure.

Building Skin

Cold air decline
A thermally caused movement of air on the inner sides of tall ↑glazing elements. When ↑outdoor air temperatures are low, the inner sides of glass panes are colder than the indoor air due to their poor U-values, so that air close to these surfaces cools and sinks. The indoor/outdoor temperature difference, the window's height and the glazing's ↑U-value may create ↑air speeds and temperatures that are uncomfortable to those within the building. Countermeasures include improving the thermal properties of the ↑glazing, reducing window height or heating the facade or the edges of the floor.

Condensation settling
The ↑condensation of water at a temperature lower than the ↑dew point temperature. This may occur where the air humidity is high and where a significant difference exists between air temperature and surface temperatures. Condensation may precipitate on glass panes, on the inner sides of ↑thermal bridges and on the upper surfaces of ↑surface cooling systems. It may cause construction problems or health problems.

Facade-integrated photovoltaics
Production of electricity by means of solar cells mounted on the facade. Photovoltaic modules mounted on the facade can be used to produce energy if the orientation is suitable and the facade's shade level is low. Synergistic effects may be achieved by replacing other outer shell materials. Solar cells can also be introduced into panes of glass, where they can help to reduce radiation transmission. Depending on density, however, transparency and ↑daylight transmission will also be restricted. Potential reductions in performance due to overheating should be considered.

Glazing
The transparent components of the building skin. Installing **heat protection glass** prevents high ↑transmission heat losses and low surface temperatures on the inner sides of windows. Triple glazing with low-e coatings and gas fillings that reduce thermal conductivity and radiation exchange is the best solution available in energy terms. However, a window's weakest point in energy terms is the frame – a fact that makes smaller non-continuous windows inefficient for conserving energy. Undesired ↑solar gains can be reduced by installing **sun protection glazing**, which has a special coating that reflects a percentage of the ↑global radiation away. However, it also restricts ↑daylight transmission. This form of glass may distort colours as one looks out, and appear reflective when seen from the outside.

Glazing percentage [%]
The ratio of the glazed facade surface to the total facade surface. The transparent areas of the building skin must be large enough to ensure sufficient ↑daylight transmission and a view of the outdoor environment while not permitting too much ↑transmission heat loss via the glass surfaces. Even where the heat protection standard is high, almost five times as much heat is lost through the ↑glazing as via insulated, opaque surfaces. In summer and in areas that receive a large amount of solar radiation, a moderate window surface percentage is a significant factor in reducing ↑solar gains that might cause overheating of the building.

g-value [-]
This factor describes the permeability of glazing to the energy occasioned by solar radiation. The permeability of glass to solar radiation energy varies depending on the number of panes and the coating used. A percentage of the radiation is reflected outward, a percentage is admitted unchanged or diffused, and a further percentage is absorbed and emitted internally or externally as heat radiation. The g-value also depends on the angle of radiation incidence. Sun protection glazing with a very low g-value may also restrict visible light radiation permeability.

Natural ventilation
Air exchange via openings in the facade. Natural pressure differences caused by the wind or by temperature differences between indoors and outdoors can be used to create an exchange of air without deploying ventilators. As it does not treat incoming air, natural ventilation is possible only at particular times of day and at particular times of the year, depending on the climate zone. Natural ventilation can be used to provide a ↑healthy level of air exchange and, in some cases, to dissipate heat, while giving building users a connection with the outdoor space. The construction of the openings depends on the level of air exchange desired (their cross section), on conditions in the outdoor environment (noise and break-in protection), on how they are to be operated (manually or automatically), and on the climate (weather protection).

Sun protection
Construction measures that limit solar radiation energy input. The aim is to limit the ↑solar gains via glazing in summer while restricting ↑daylight input and the ability to see out of the window as little as possible. Different kinds of sun protection system are installed on different parts of the facade, are made from different materials and may be fixed, adjustable or responsive. The efficiency of a ↑sun protection system is quantified via the Fc-value [-], which describes the percentage of the incoming ↑global radiation that passes through. External systems are particularly efficient.

Thermal bridge
A thermal weak point in the building skin. At the points where two components meet, at the corners of the building and where the building skin is interrupted, the insulation layer is reduced, leading to increased heat loss. Thermal bridges may be localised points, such as where a support penetrates the building skin, or extended lines, such as the building's external corners.

Thermal insulation
A layer of materials with low thermal conductivity [W/mK] added to the facade to reduce heat losses. The smaller the heat conductivity value and the thicker the insulation level, the smaller the resulting ↑U-value. ↑Precipitation condensation may be a problem, depending on the position of the insulation and how snugly it fits against the inner side of the facade.

Total energy transmission of facade
The product of facade-specific factors, used to calculate ↑solar gains. The product of the window surface percentage, the sun protection Fc-value and the ↑glazing's g-value is used to quantify a facade's permeability to global radiation. The total degree of energy permeability multiplied by the sum of the radiation on the facade surface gives the ↑solar input.

U-value [W/m^2K]
The value used to measure the passage of heat through a building component. The heat transfer coefficient or U-value quantifies the heat flow through a building component surface area of $1\ m^2$ where the temperature difference between inside and outside is 1 K. A component's U-value is determined by its constituent materials and their ↑thermal conductivity, layer thicknesses and installation context.
The smaller the U-value, the more effective the building component is in insulation terms.

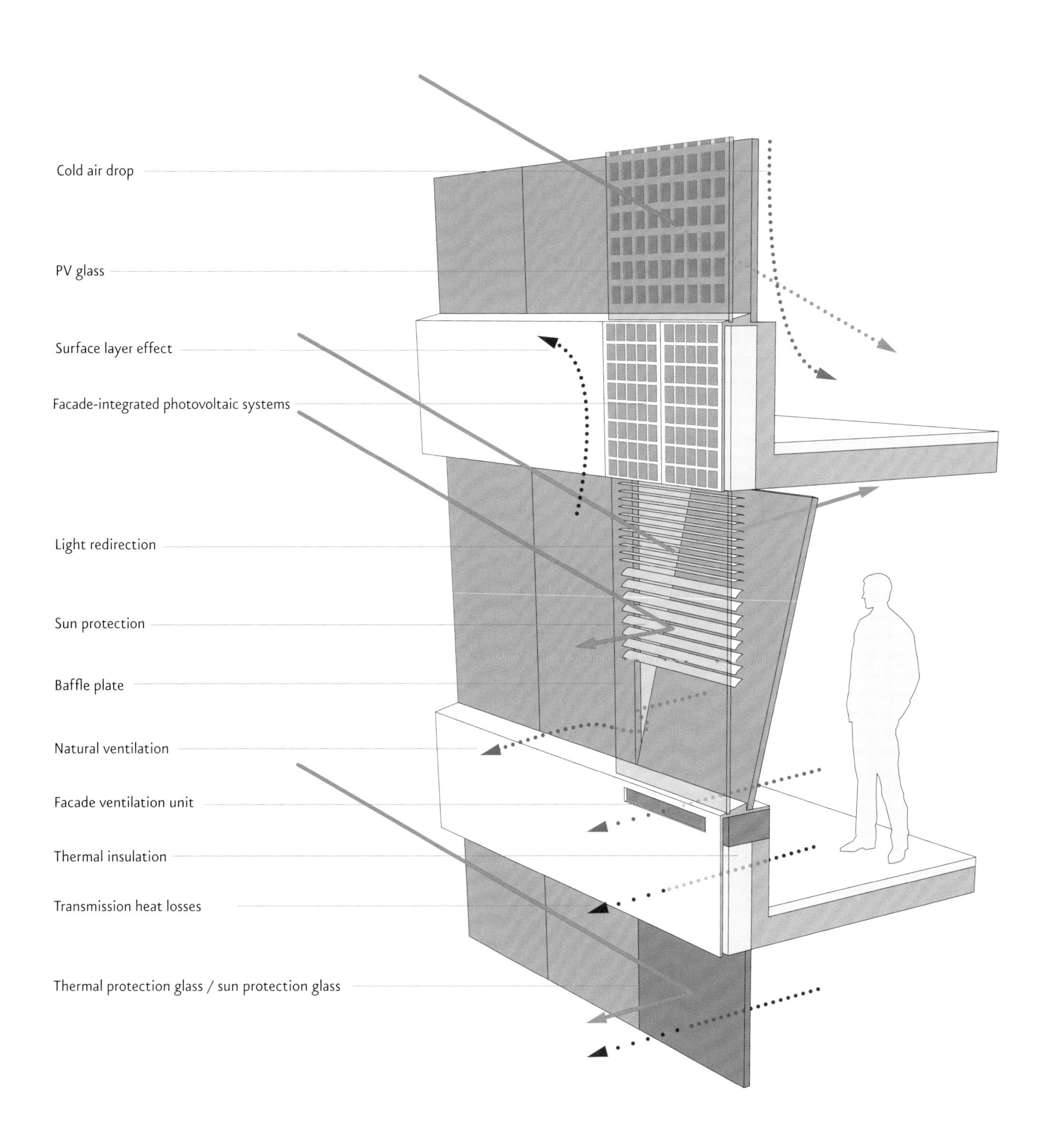

Fig. 8.3 The facade as an interface
In energy and climate terms, the facade is the interface between the indoor space and the outdoor space. It must therefore respond optimally to changes in the environmental climate, and be specifically adapted to its location. The more flexible the facade is in responding to the full range of environmental climate conditions, the less technology is required and the lower the energy expenditure is. Depending on what is required, it must make use of or block solar radiation. Sufficient daylight provision must be ensured. Transmission and ventilation heat losses should be minimised or harnessed and used for cooling. Beyond the energy balance, factors specifically relating to comfort must be considered.

Light

Daylight provision
The type and extent of daylight use-related interventions for a given building or room. Optimising daylight provision saves on the electricity used for artificial lighting. It also gives the users a good view and gives a natural and genuine colour to their surroundings. The height of window lintels is a significant factor in daylight provision; the higher the lintel, the deeper daylight penetrates into the space. Other factors include the size of windows, the glass's ↑daylight transmission, possible obstruction by nearby buildings and the configuration of the ↑sun protection. ↑Light redirection brings light deeper into rooms. In practice, a compromise must often be found between optimal sun protection (which means reducing the ↑window surface percentage) and maximum daylight utilisation. In certain circumstances, direct sunlight can lead to undesirable ↑glare.

Daylight quotient [%]
The specific value for the relationship between indoor and outdoor illuminance when the sky is obscured. The daylight quotient is the ratio of the ↑illuminance calculated from a point on the horizontal measuring plane within an indoor space to the horizontal illumination strength when the sky is obscured, and therefore the horizontal illumination strength when the sky is obscured. Analysing the daylight quotients gives the times when natural lighting is sufficient and the extent to which artificial ↑ light sources are needed in a particular zone.

Degree of daylight transmission [-]
Factor for quantifying the permeability of glass panes to visible wavelength radiation. In the case of ↑sun protection glass, a significant part of the solar radiation is reflected away to minimise the energy input. The more visible wavelength radiation is reflected away with it, the lower the degree of daylight transmission and the less available daylight within the indoor space.

Glare
The negative impact on sight of extreme differences in light density within the human field of vision. Disruptive sources of light include direct or reflected sunlight or lamps that are too bright. Glare protection on the inner side of a facade can be used to keep direct sunlight out of a workspace. Care should be taken that this does not reduce the ↑daylight input too much. In particular, the upper sections of windows should remain as permeable to light as possible.

Illuminance [Lux, lx], [lm/m²]
The quotient of the ↑light flux emitted by a light source that is encountered by a particular surface and the surface area that is illuminated. The illuminance tells us whether enough light is available in a particular zone for a specific use. The reference value for workplace lighting is 500 lx at working level.

Light flux [Lumen, lm]
The overall visible wavelength radiation power of a light source point. The quotient of light flux and the total input power of a lamp are described as the light yield [lm/W].

Light intensity [candela, cd], [lm/sr]
The element of a lamp's ↑light flux that is emitted in a particular direction. The direction is defined by the solid angle [steradian, sr].

Light redirection
The refraction, reflection, or diffusion of light into the deeper parts of the room by elements outside of or inside of the facade, or at facade level. Daylight redirection systems create a more even illumination of rooms and improve ↑daylight provision in the deeper parts of the room. A good daylight redirection system can reduce undesired reflections and ↑glare. The differentiation criteria for light redirection systems are: whether they redirect diffuse or direct light and whether they are fixed or adjustable. Different systems create different degrees of synergy with the sun protection system.

Light sources
Artificial light sources. Thermal radiators such as incandescent light bulbs and halogen light bulbs give off light as a particular material is heated. Discharge lamps use the electrical discharge of gases to produce light. There are two types of discharge lamp: low and high pressure. Light-emitting diodes (LED) are electroluminescence radiators; they use semiconductors that convert electricity directly into light. There are significant differences between these various types of lamp in terms of light yield, colour rendering, activation behaviour and lifespan. Lighting planning must therefore take into account the demands for each room and choose lamps that are appropriate for each location. Using energy-saving light sources and sensors that switch the lights off when there is plenty of daylight and when no-one is present can significantly reduce a building's electricity consumption and ↑internal heat loads.

Luminance or illumination intensity [cd/m²]
The ratio of ↑illumination strength to the visible, light-emitting surface of a light source. If one is not looking at the surface vertically, then only the projection of the surface is considered. Light density is used in describing large-area light sources (such as monitors) and in calculating the brightness of reflective surfaces (such as white walls and the surfaces of tables).

Natural lighting
The use of daylight to light an indoor space. The sizes and arrangement of the window surfaces and the configuration of the sun protection are the significant factors in optimising **daylight gains**. Broad window strips provide even illumination, and a high lintel facilitates efficient ↑daylight provision at all depths of the room. ↑Light redirection can be used to optimise illumination. A light redirection zone should be provided so that building users have sufficient access to daylight even when sun protection is in place.

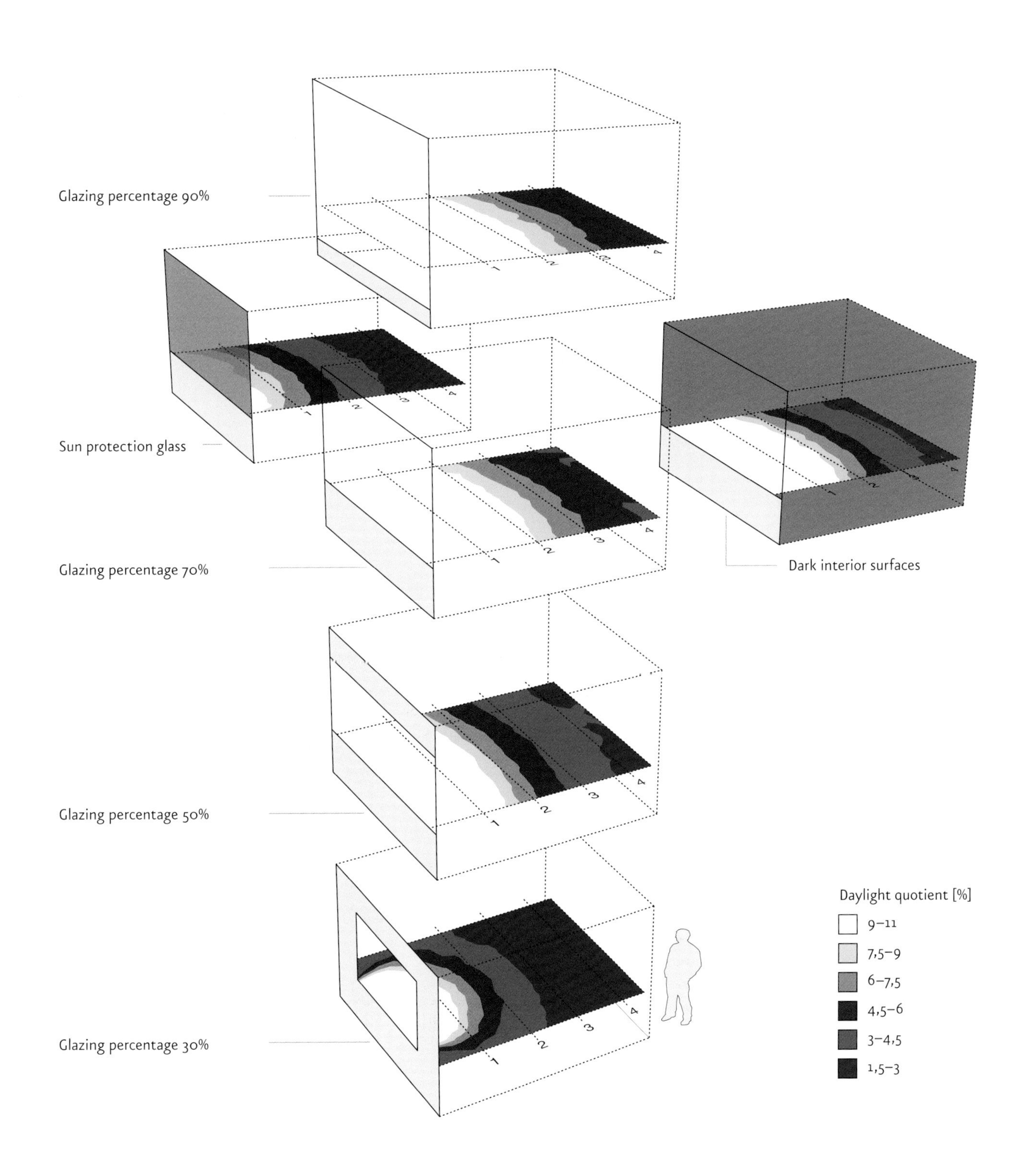

Fig. 8.4 The interaction of facade and daylight

The provision of daylight within an indoor space is mainly determined by the glazing percentage, the window's geometry, the glazing's degree of daylight transmission and the degree of reflection of the inner surfaces. This diagram shows changes in daylight quotients at the height of the working level. They are affected by the glazing percentage in the office space, which is 4.5 m deep. Also shown is the impact of sun protection glazing (daylight transmission: 40%), and of darker interior surfaces (half reflectance) where the window surface percentage is 70%. The daylight quotient gives the relationship of outdoor illumination strength to indoor illumination strength where the sky is obscured. The average outdoor illumination strength is about 12,400 lux in Moscow, 14,400 lux in Munich, 16,300 lux in Shanghai, 25,900 lux in Bangalore and 25,500 lux in Dubai.

Room Climate

Air quality
The degree of air contamination, of pollutants and odorants. Human breathing uses up oxygen and increases the CO_2 content of the air within a room. When dealing with the odour load, the air quality is given in decipols [dp]. This value depends on the number of sources of odours within a room (e.g. people) and the fresh air input. Each room has its own healthy **air exchange rate**, which will depend on what it is being used for and how many occupants it has. If the outdoor air in a particular location has a high dust load, filters can be used to clean the incoming air. Where this is the case, the basic rate of air exchange can no longer be met via window ventilation, and a mechanical ventilation system is required.

Air speed [m/s]
The value of the air speed within a room. An air speed above a certain value is generally considered uncomfortable. The maximum acceptable value depends on other factors, such as the air temperature. Air flows may be caused by ↑air conditioning systems or by ↑natural ventilation. Major differences in temperature between surfaces and indoor air can also create noticeable air streams. The degree of turbulence describes the homogeneity of the air stream: the higher the degree of turbulence, the more likely it is to give rise to uncomfortable air speeds.

Comfort
A collective term for the evaluation of all room climate values and other non-quantifiable values that influence the contentment of people within an indoor space. Measurable values that affect comfort include the ↑operative indoor temperature, ↑indoor air humidity, ↑air speed, ↑noise impact, ↑illuminance and ↑air quality. Non-measurable values include the view, the comprehensibility level of the heating, cooling and ventilation systems, and the options users are given for changing the room climate to suit themselves.

Heat/cold transfer
Installations inside the building used for heating and cooling. There are several different forms of temperature control with different principles of operation: heat radiation (e.g. ↑underfloor heating), convection (e.g. ↑convectors), and the inflow of preconditioned air (e.g. air conditioning). Radiation-based **surface cooling and heating systems** need large temperature-controlled surfaces in order to function. Convection systems create a thermally driven air stream that increases the discharge of heat or cold into the indoor air. Convection systems should be configured in such a way that they do not create high air speeds, especially when ventilation systems are present to amplify the air stream. The same is true when centrally conditioned air is to be pumped into a room. The maximum and minimum possible surface and air outlet temperatures are subject to comfort-related parameters, and these limit the system's maximum performance. To prevent ↑condensation forming on cooling surfaces when air humidity is high, either the cooling performance must be reduced or the incoming air must be dehumidified.

Humidifying/dehumidifying
Regulation of the indoor air's water vapour content. If the outdoor air is too dry or too moist, air exchange will create a humidifying or dehumidifying demand. The ↑relative air humidity can be changed by heating or cooling the air. The air humidity value that is considered to be comfortable will depend on the ↑operative room temperature. The incoming air humidity can be regulated in a central ventilation and air conditioning system, with the use of cold or heat. Dehumidifying systems inside the building require condensate drainage.

Room acoustics
The sound-related physical properties of an indoor space. An indoor space will have certain reverberation time and noise level reduction demands, depending on its function. The significant factors are the indoor space's geometry and the acoustic properties of its surfaces. The need to provide sound-absorbing surfaces often conflicts with the need to include exposed solid ceilings as a thermal mass in order to regulate the temperature. If this is the case, wall surfaces and furniture can be covered with absorbent material, or free-hanging absorber elements can be used.

Noise load
The negative impact on an indoor space of noise from internal or external noise sources. The maximum acceptable level of noise in an indoor space will depend on its function. The air noise transfer from one indoor space to another can be reduced by solid or soundproofed separating walls. Structure-borne noise transfer can be prevented by adding footfall sound insulation. Continuous facades will require noise protection measures. The negative impact of noise coming from outside the building can be counteracted by noise protection glazing and protected ventilation openings (e.g. baffle plates).

Operative room temperature
The perceived temperature of an indoor space is given by the **room air temperature** and the average temperature of the surfaces enclosing indoor space. Components whose temperature is different from the air temperature due to inertia and actively heated or cooled surfaces within an indoor space influence the temperature that people experience. Radiation warmth combined with low air temperature can create the same feeling of warmth as a higher air temperature without any additional ↑heat radiation. Conversely, higher room air temperatures can be balanced out by cool surfaces. The temperature range an individual considers to be comfortable depends on what they are doing, the clothes they are wearing, cultural factors, the outdoor climate, and the room air humidity.

Radiation asymmetry
Difference in the perceived radiation temperature in two opposite areas between which a person spends time. The thermal radiation field of a human body may be non-uniform due to relatively cold and warm surfaces and due to solar radiation. Asymmetrical radiation conditions caused by (for instance) increased ceiling radiation temperatures or cold wall or window surfaces may cause thermal discomfort. People are more acutely aware of radiation asymmetry created by warm ceilings than they are of cold or hot walls.

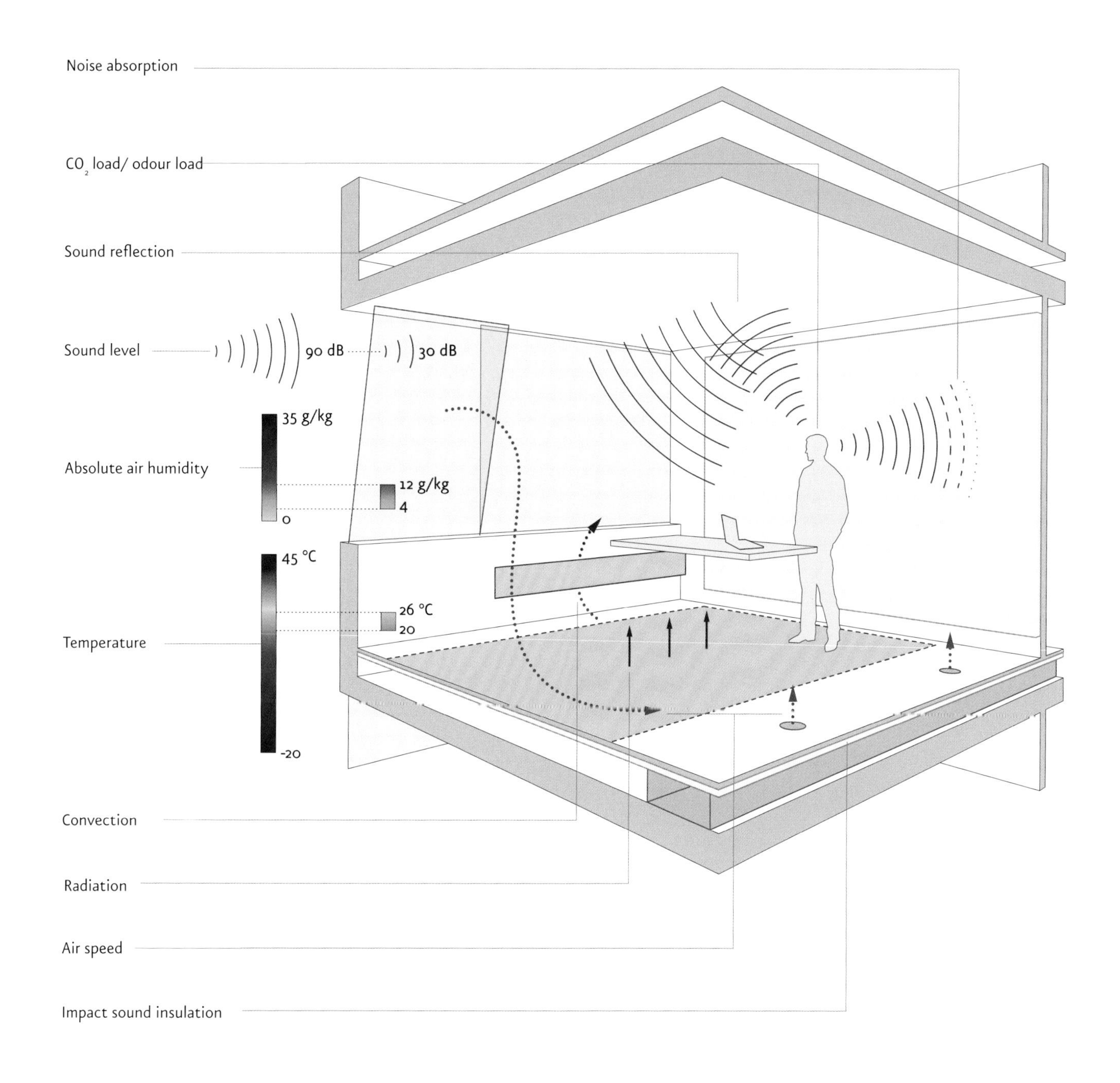

Fig. 8.5 Room climate

The idea of an optimised facade concept is to create an internal climate that offers a high degree of comfort, regardless of outdoor conditions. For each indoor space, measures must be put in place to regulate the indoor temperature, the indoor air humidity, the indoor acoustics and the indoor air quality and to avoid high air speeds or radiation asymmetries. These measures must be appropriate to the indoor space's function and to the building's location. The ability to open elements of the facade to let the outer world in, the view and the comprehensibility of technology are "soft", non-quantifiable comfort factors – which, however, have a major influence on the wellbeing of individuals.

Room Conditioning

Airflow
Distribution of incoming air throughout the building and, in some cases, collection of the exhaust air. At building level, the ventilated zones can be connected individually to incoming air channels (and, if required, exhaust air channels). If overflow apertures are included, several zones can be connected in a row. In this system, the exhaust ventilation is located in the area with the lowest hygiene requirements. If an incoming air system with no exhaust is installed, the exhaust air escapes via openings in the facade.
The function of an exhaust system is the reverse of this. If an exhaust system is used instead of an incoming air system, however, the incoming air, which streams in at room level via ventilation elements, cannot be centrally preconditioned. The spatial arrangement of the inflow and exhaust elements and the outflow velocities and temperatures are different for mixed ventilation and source ventilation systems. The minimum and maximum inflow temperatures are limited by ↑comfort parameters. High ↑air speeds should be avoided in areas where people spend their time.

Concrete core activation
The use of concrete ceilings to provide surface cooling/ surface heating by means of water running through tube loops set into the concrete. Thermal storage masses create a↑phase shift, allowing cool night air to be used for cooling during the day via a↑recooling plant. This reduces the cooling energy demand by evening out the peak loads. Renewable energy sources can also be utilised efficiently in the case of heating, due to the moderate↑system temperatures.

Convector
Transfer of heat or cold by ↑convection. Air is temperature-controlled between two heat exchanger plates and introduced into the indoor space by means of a convection current. Due to the directional nature of the air stream, convectors can be used either to heat or to cool air. If both heating and cooling are required, then fan coil units are needed.

Cooling ceiling (or heating ceiling)
A water-based↑surface cooling system installed close to the ceiling. The cold or heat it distributes is transmitted mainly as radiation. When the system is suspended so that the indoor air plays around it, there is also an element of convection.
To avoid condensation forming, cooling ceilings are generally combined with a↑dehumidifying system. Reliably available renewable cooling sources can be easily integrated into this system.

Decentralised ventilation system
The conditioning and transport of outdoor air via a facade-integrated system. Air is sucked in and travels through the ventilation system and past the heat exchanger, which warms it. If exhaust air is also handled by this system, heat recovery can be included in the process. If the cooling performance is above a certain level and the outdoor air is moist, condensate drainage may be required.

Induction unit
Reheating or recooling of centrally preconditioned air within the indoor space. The incoming air from the pipes is cooled or warmed by means of a cooling/heating register. Due to the induction effect, indoor air is sucked in and also cooled, increasing the unit's performance.

Night ventilation
The process of enhancing nightly heat exchange in order to cool solid building components. Night ventilation works efficiently if there is enough free↑storage mass or↑PCM available, if a high degree of air exchange is possible during the night, and if the↑outdoor air temperatures are low enough during the night. The ventilation openings must be protected against the weather and against break-ins. They must also have a large enough unobstructed cross section.

PCM (phase change material)
Encapsulated material with a high thermal storage potential used in phase transition. At increased temperatures, the material melts, absorbing amounts of heat that are very large relative to the material's mass. This allows the↑operative indoor temperature to be kept at a certain level for a greater length of time, despite heat inputs. The cooling effect is maintained until the material is completely melted. Once the environment temperature drops beneath a certain level, the material can discharge the heat. PCM can be used as a powder in plasterboard, or as a coating. It can also be deployed as a granulate in bags – on the top of cooling ceilings, for instance.

Split unit
An electrically operated, decentralised room climate system used for heat and cold production. The external unit contains a compressor and a waste heat ventilator; the compressor compresses a refrigerant, which enters the indoor unit via a refrigerant conduit. Inside the indoor unit, it evaporates, and the indoor space is cooled by convection by means of a further ventilator. Split units can also act as heaters when operated in reverse.

System temperatures
The temperature levels of a heating or cooling system's inflow air and return flow air. Different types of system with different operating principles require different **inflow temperatures.** Convective systems such as induction units or convection heaters require high inflow temperatures.↑Surface cooling systems can cope with moderate temperatures, making them more suitable for combining with renewable heat sources. The same is true of cooling systems.

Underfloor heating/cooling
Floor temperature control via tube loops with water running through them beneath the floor covering. For the system to work, a sufficiently large area of the floor must be activated and the layers of floor material above the heating loops must conduct heat. The limits on maximum surface temperatures restrict the system's performance. Combining underfloor heating with renewable energy sources is an efficient solution, because these require only moderate↑system temperatures. Under some circumstances, it is possible that the heating performance will not be sufficient to cancel out the↑cold air decline along the facade. If this is the case, an extra convector should be added. For reasons of comfort, only a small degree of cooling can be performed via the floor.

Ventilation and air conditioning system
An indoor technological air-handling system for delivering and conditioning air. A ventilation and air conditioning system consists of several components, generally arranged one behind the other. It can deliver, filter, warm, cool, humidify and dehumidify air. The ventilation system often has an integrated heat recovery unit. These units are located in one or more ventilation centres, with a network of ventilation shafts and channels to deliver incoming air to individual rooms. If an air heat exchanger is being used to provide↑heat recovery, the exhaust air must be returned to the central unit. There must be enough space available within the building for the central units and the air channels. Short direct channels save on installation costs and on operating energy. If large volumes of air are required, a way of supplying this air without compromising comfort must be found.

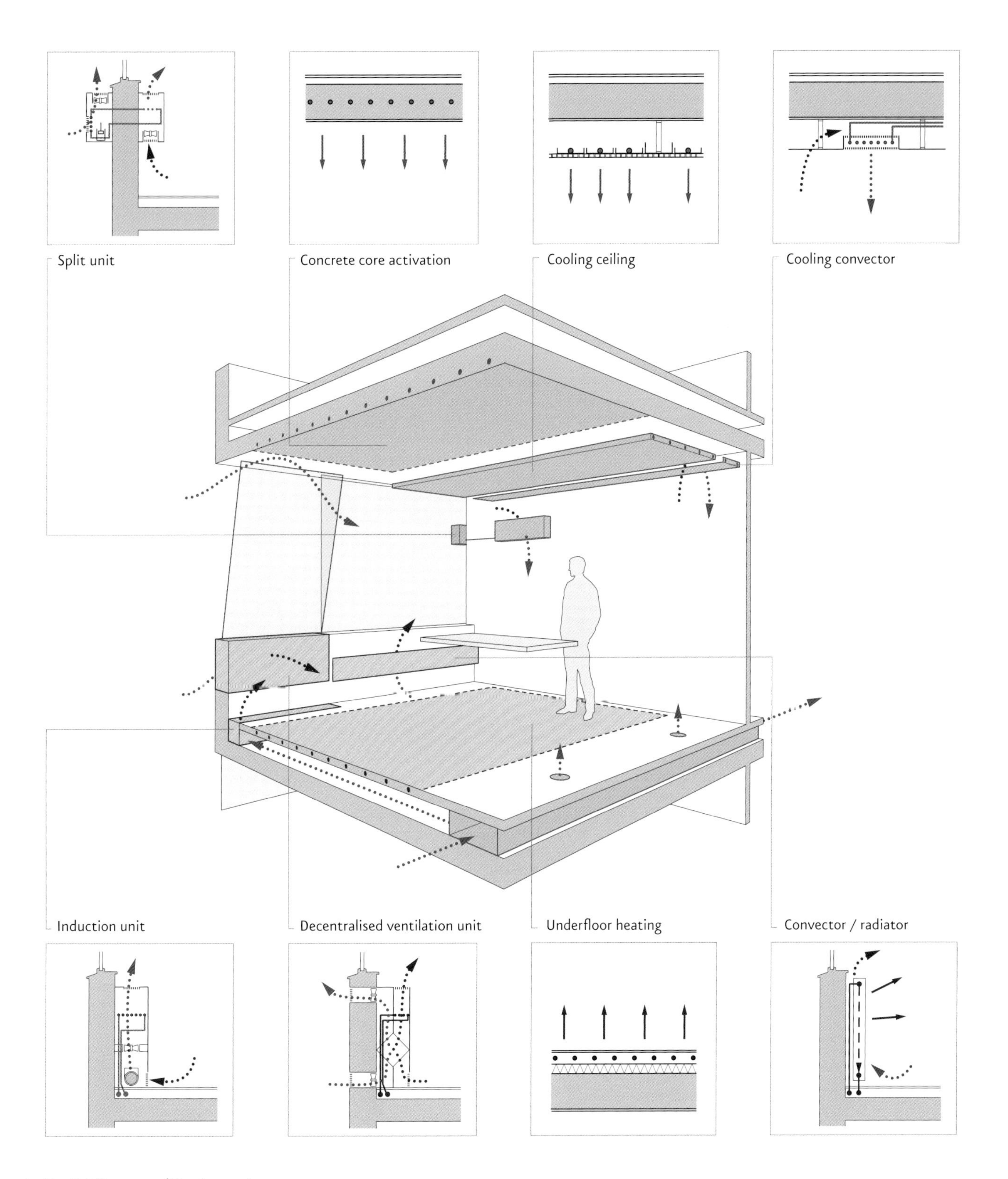

Fig. 8.6 Room conditioning systems

The kind of room conditioning system that should be used depends on the building's function, the properties of its facade and the local outdoor climate conditions. The building's function gives the comfort requirements, the internal heat loads and the fresh air requirement. The facade influences solar heat gains and determines the feasibility of natural ventilation. The outdoor climate dictates whether the building will have to be heated or cooled, humidified or dehumidified. To conserve energy, it is advisable to restrict air exchange to the healthy exchange level and to use water-based systems to transport heat and coolness. If solar thermal technology or the soil's energy potential is to be used, it makes sense to incorporate surface heating systems or cooling systems.

Energy Generation

Combined heat and power plant (CHP)
A power station for producing electricity and heat. Oil, gas and renewable resources such as biogas, biodiesel or biomass are used as fuel. The principle of cogeneration allows the energy content of the fuel to be harnessed with almost no loss. It is wise to equip a combined heat and power plant for as many ↑full load hours as possible and to combine it with an additional heat production unit that is flexible and can supplement it during ↑peak loads. The electricity produced is generally fed into the mains grid.

Condensing boiler
A system for efficient combustion of fuel to produce heat. In a condensing boiler the ↑condensation heat of the emitted gases is utilised in addition to the heat produced by burning. This means that the exhaust gas conduits have to be humidity-resistant and pressure-tight. Condensing boilers are the ideal gas and oil burning system in energy terms.

Cooling tower
A technology that harnesses the cooling potential of the outdoor air for a direct cooling system or for ↑recooling. In locations where ↑outdoor temperatures are sufficiently low, a cooling tower provides a reliably available cooling source. In locations where outdoor temperatures do not remain low, the cool night temperatures can be stored in a ↑concrete core activation system for phased release. **Recooling plants** may be operated as dry or wet systems (in a wet system, the temperature of the cooling medium is further reduced by water ↑evaporation). The effectiveness of **adiabatic cooling** depends on both the outdoor air temperature and the ↑outdoor air humidity. Cooling towers are also used to provide recooling for ↑refrigeration units.

Degree of efficiency [%]
Ratio of energy output (useable energy) to energy input for technological systems. The degree of efficiency describes the efficiency of a system and quantifies conversion energy loss. The degree of efficiency is a factor for ↑heat recovery systems, for furnaces, ↑photovoltaic systems, and ↑light sources. For ↑heat pumps or ↑refrigeration units, the term COP (coefficient of performance) is used. The **annual coefficient of performance**, however, is a better measure of the efficiency of the whole system. It describes the relationship of useable, input energy to output energy over a year.

Earth piles/groundwater utilisation
Technologies that allow the soil to be used as a heating or cooling source. The temperature level of the ↑soil or the groundwater can be used directly for cooling via a heat exchanger or indirectly for heating using a ↑heat pump. Groundwater is utilised directly via suction and injection wells. Alternatively, tube registers with water running through them can be laid underground. The energy is made available from a central heat exchanger, and can be used to prewarm or precool the incoming air via a register in the ventilation system, or be fed into the ↑surface heating or surface cooling system. This technology can also be used to optimise ↑recooling for ↑refrigeration units.

Earth pipe
An underground channel that harnesses the heat or coolness of the soil. An earth pipe can be used to prewarm or precool incoming air. This system can only function in combination with a mechanical ventilation system. It is economical to lay the earth pipe in the area excavated for the construction of the building or inside a double wall in a cellar or underground garage. Earth pipes are generally configured for cooling. For the system to perform well, the difference between the ↑soil temperature and the ↑outdoor air temperature must be sufficiently great. The efficiency of the earth pipes depends on the soil properties.

Photovoltaics
The direct conversion of sunlight into electrical energy by solar cells. Efficiency is approximately 15% dependent on the technology. Beyond a cell temperature of 25 °C, it decreases as the temperature rises. Due to the high investment costs, photovoltaics are generally best suited to areas that experience a high level of radiation and surfaces that are exposed to a high degree of radiation. It is possible to integrate photovoltaic systems into a roof or facade construction, and this approach sometimes permits a synergy that makes the system more economical.

Refrigeration unit
A system that expends electricity or thermal energy to produce low temperatures. A refrigeration unit uses operating energy to extract thermal energy from a medium; this thermal energy must be released again in another location with a higher energy level. ↑Cooling towers, structures that exploit the cooling potential of the outdoor air, are suitable for this **recooling process**. The ratio of cooling performance to the power consumed in operating the system is described as the coefficient of performance, or ↑COP. **Heat pumps** are devices that work in the opposite way. Energy for a heating system must be taken from a source at a lower temperature. A renewable heat source (such as the soil) can be used. The lower the temperature difference between the renewable energy source and the required heating or cooling temperature is, the more efficient the process is and the lower the amount of additional operating energy required.

Solar cooling
A combination of ↑solar collectors and thermally operated ↑refrigeration units. An absorption refrigerator converts the heat produced by the collectors so that it can be used for cooling. This system requires high collector temperatures, making it suitable for areas with high levels of solar radiation. Where a high proportion of the radiation is direct rather than diffuse, concentrating collectors can be used. The system can be made more economical by using the absorber filed to produce heat at times when cooling is not required. **Desiccant cooling systems** (DEC) use the warmth of the collectors to dehumidify the incoming air without changing its temperature. The air can then easily be humidified and cooled by means of evaporation cooling.

Solar thermal system
Technology that converts solar radiation into heat. Heat from **solar collectors** is transmitted to a carrier medium (usually water) and channelled into a ↑storage unit. Because a ↑heating energy demand and high levels of solar radiation do not generally occur at the same times of year, solar heating is practical only in areas with a low heating need and a minimum degree of solar radiation all year round.

Storage
A system for storing heat or coolness. Many renewable heating or cooling concepts require an energy store. Stores allow energy generation systems to produce energy unaffected by the load fluctuations created by the consumer. When production exceeds immediate need, the spare energy is stored so that it can be used later at a time of peak load.

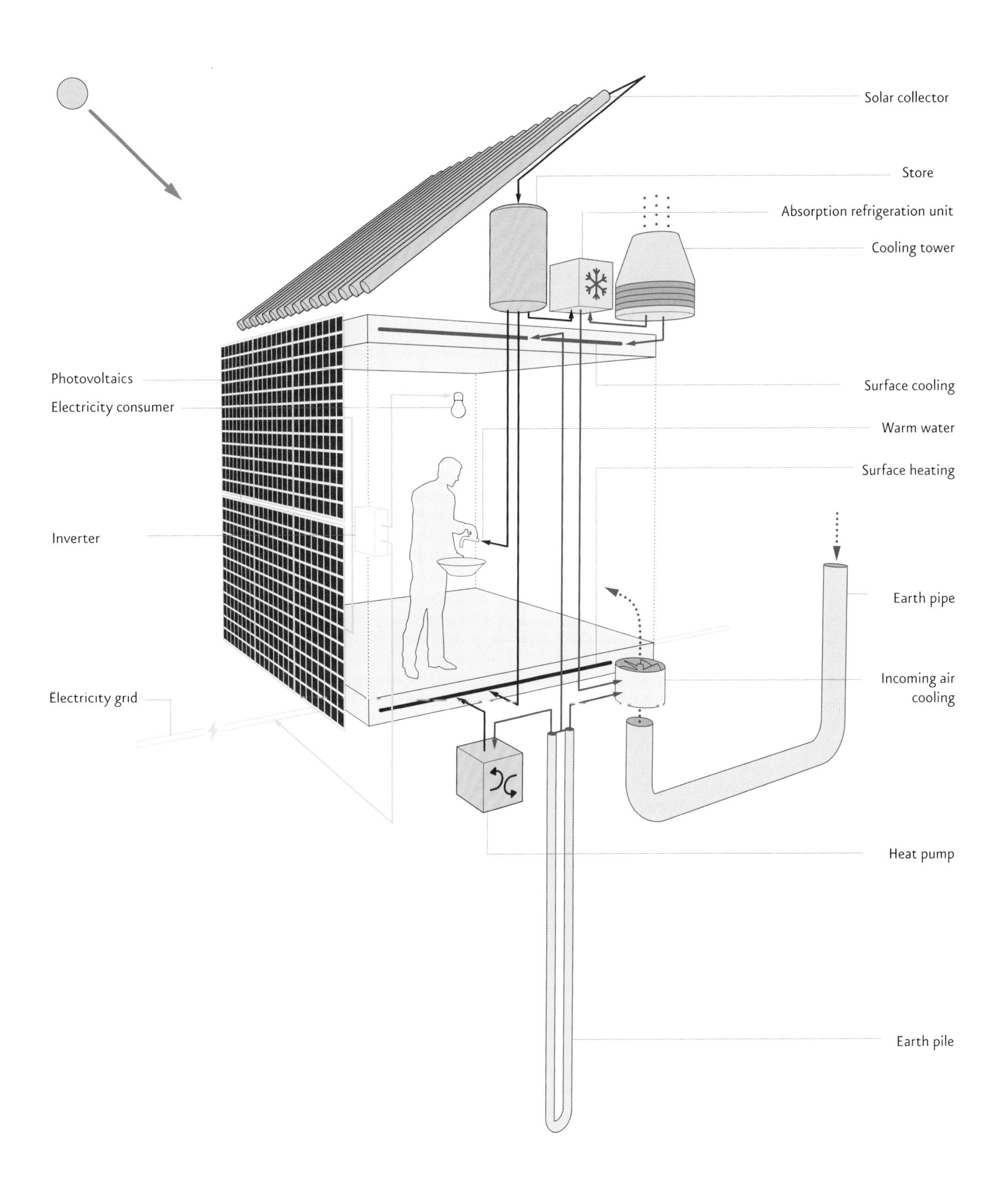

Fig. 8.7 Energy generation systems

The energy generation system used depends on the heat, cold or dehumidifying requirement and on the room conditioning system's inflow temperatures. Location-specific factors include the intensity of the solar radiation and how it changes over time, and the outdoor air and soil temperatures. The better adapted to the room conditioning concept an energy generation system is, the more efficient and economical it will be.

Appendix

Cool

City	Latitude [°]	Longitude [°]	Height above sea level [m]	Average temperature [°C]	Maximum temperature [°C]	Minimum temperature [°C]	Maximum daily variation [K]
Detroit US	42.330	-83.080	182	9.2	34.5	-18.4	17.5
Kiev UA	50.420	30.500	108	7.7	32.0	-17.8	18.9
Montreal CA	45.520	-73.570	22	6.3	31.6	-26.0	18.5
Moscow RU	55.750	37.700	152	5.0	30.6	-25.5	17.9
Toronto CA	43.666	-79.383	76	7.6	32.4	-21.3	15.7
Voronezh RU	51.670	39.220	152	6.1	30.5	-25.1	19.6
Boston US	42.330	-71.070	0	10.7	34.2	-14.7	16.5
Nagano JP	36.650	138.170	365	11.5	34.2	-9.4	20.7
New York US	40.750	-73.980	10	12.4	35.2	-13.7	18.1
Beijing CN	39.930	116.400	30	11.8	36.4	-14.3	15.1
Philadelphia US	40.000	-75.170	31	12.1	36.5	-14.1	18.9
Pyongyang KP	39.033	125.783	35	9.6	33.3	-19.9	16.6
Anchorage US	61.160	-150.000	0	2.5	24.9	-22.9	19.4
Gothenburg SE	57.750	12.000	60	7.3	26.9	-17.4	14.8
Helsinki FI	60.220	25.000	12	4.7	27.1	-24.8	16.2
Oslo NO	59.930	10.750	154	5.3	25.2	-18.9	14.7
Stockholm SE	59.350	18.080	15	6.7	28.9	-19.9	14.5
Calgary CA	51.080	-114.080	1.056	4.2	30.4	-31.2	27.0
Lhasa CN	29.653	91.119	3.650	7.5	25.5	-12.9	18.7

The heating/cooling degree day and humidifying/dehumidifying gram day values given on the following pages and on p. 37 are based on the following:

Heating degree days [Kd/a]:
Heating days * (20.0 °C - $T_{average}$)
for heating days: $T_{average}$ < 12 °C

Cooling degree days [Kd/a]:
Cooling hours * ($T_{absolute}$ - 18.0 °C) : hours of use
for cooling days: $T_{absolute\ use\ time}$ > 18,0 °C

Humidifying gram days [gd/kga]:
Humidifying hours * (8.0 g/kg - $x_{absolute}$) : hours of use
for humidifying hours: $x_{absolute\ use\ time}$ < 8.0 g/kg

Dehumidifying gram days [gd/kga]:
Dehumidifying hours * ($x_{absolut}$ – 8.0 g/kg) : hours of use
for dehumidifying hours: $x_{absolute\ use\ time}$ > 8.0 g/kg

Average humidity [g/kg]	Maximum humidity [g/kg]	Minimum humidity [g/kg]	Average radiation [W/m²]	Maximum radiation [W/m²]	Sum of radiation [kWh/m²a]	Heating degree days [Kd/a]	Cooling degree days [Kd/a]	Humidifying gram days [gd/kga]	Dehumidifying gram days [gd/kga]
6.2	21.1	0.8	158.2	1,035.0	1,385.8	3,809.6	497.9	732.4	249.4
5.8	17.7	0.6	134.3	913.0	1,176.5	4,122.7	265.7	729.6	157.7
5.2	19.4	0.4	154.3	1,009.0	1,351.7	4,754.9	408.8	882.9	155.7
5.1	17.7	0.0	113.7	914.0	996.0	5,100.8	196.7	926.7	167.0
5.6	16.6	0.5	154.7	1,047.0	1,355.2	4,263.3	324.0	794.1	139.7
5.7	17.0	0.4	137.1	919.0	1,201.0	4,761.0	311.7	747.6	168.1
6.0	19.6	0.7	162.7	1,045.0	1,425.3	3,216.8	508.5	760.2	212.4
7.6	21.6	1.4	151.9	1,068.0	1,330.6	3,056.4	652.1	569.9	483.1
6.5	21.0	0.8	160.2	1,011.0	1,403.4	2,817.1	697.9	718.2	259.7
6.9	23.9	0.5	169.2	917.0	1,482.2	3,222.3	903.7	806.7	501.0
6.9	23.2	1.0	165.6	988.0	1,450.7	2,914.7	750.6	665.3	363.5
6.9	21.3	0.5	146.5	980.0	1,283.3	3,801.2	599.6	748.4	478.5
3.7	11.0	0.4	100.1	850.0	876.9	6,023.3	16.2	1,126.9	10.7
6.1	15.3	0.9	107.3	922.0	939.3	4,059.1	75.1	549.1	133.4
4.8	13.6	0.4	110.2	847.0	965.4	5,148.6	91.9	861.4	69.2
4.6	13.8	0.6	101.4	906.0	888.3	4,878.9	71.1	927.3	32.2
5.2	14.5	0.6	111.8	868.0	979.4	4,395.7	121.6	798.9	70.5
4.0	13.7	0.2	155.2	1,051.0	1,359.6	5,336.1	213.2	1,107.3	29.7
5.5	16.5	0.6	219.6	1,306.0	1,923.7	3,894.5	100.8	902.5	194.9

Temperate

City	Latitude [°]	Longitude [°]	Height above sea level [m]	Average temperature [°C]	Maximum temperature [°C]	Minimum temperature [°C]	Maximum daily variation [K]
Budapest HU	47.500	19.080	130	11.0	34.6	-12.2	18.3
Bucharest RO	44.450	26.170	79	10.5	33.9	-14.3	19.3
Milan IT	45.470	9.200	98	11.7	31.9	-6.9	17.9
Paris FR	48.870	2.330	42	11.0	31.1	-8.3	15.5
Zagreb HR	45.800	15.970	146	11.3	33.1	-10.2	14.2
Ankara TR	39.920	32.830	872	11.6	36.1	-13.9	18.5
Madrid ES	40.410	-3.710	608	13.9	37.5	-2.4	16.0
Berlin DE	52.530	13.420	44	9.3	33.2	-15.1	20.1
Munich DE	48.130	11.580	536	8.0	28.7	-15.2	15.4
Warsaw PL	52.250	21.000	90	7.8	31.6	-17.5	17.8
Zurich CH	47.380	8.550	471	8.5	31.1	-10.4	16.3
Bergen NO	60.380	5.330	0	7.9	23.7	-7.7	13.7
Dublin IE	53.330	-6.250	0	9.8	23.3	-2.2	13.0
Glasgow UK	55.850	-4.250	56	8.4	23.1	-7.8	15.3
London UK	51.500	-0.170	36	10.6	28.2	-3.5	12.7

Average humidity [g/kg]	Maximum humidity [g/kg]	Minimum humidity [g/kg]	Average radiation [W/m²]	Maximum radiation [W/m²]	Sum of radiation [kWh/m²a]	Heating degree days [Kd/a]	Cooling degree days [Kd/a]	Humidifying gram days [gd/kga]	Dehumidifying gram days [gd/kga]
6.0	16.4	1.2	137.5	978.0	1,204.5	2,989.7	497.2	657.2	113.6
6.6	18.0	1.0	161.5	1,051.0	1,414.7	3,233.2	649.1	562.8	225.2
7.3	20.3	1.9	142.2	1,007.0	1,245.7	2,794.1	518.4	477.5	301.9
6.8	17.0	1.9	116.2	920.0	1,017.9	2,773.6	241.6	474.3	159.2
7.1	18.6	1.6	136.5	1,002.0	1,195.7	2,862.6	432.7	507.3	262.5
6.6	19.0	1.3	193.5	1,079.0	1,695.0	2,872.9	713.4	552.3	166.5
7.1	16.7	2.5	187.6	1,028.0	1,643.4	2,175.9	712.6	460.9	179.6
5.8	16.9	1.0	116.4	953.0	1,019.7	3,458.0	325.8	672.1	98.0
5.8	15.1	1.1	131.7	970.0	1,153.7	3,895.6	177.1	683.4	113.1
5.8	15.7	0.9	114.4	934.0	1,002.1	3,995.4	222.4	671.4	126.5
6.0	15.2	1.2	126.5	1,105.0	1,108.1	3,740.7	157.3	628.7	118.1
5.3	12.8	1.4	86.8	868.0	760.4	3,956.4	28.6	754.9	40.0
6.2	13.0	2.4	107.8	906.0	944.3	3,059.9	27.8	505.5	53.6
5.8	13.1	1.9	99.3	936.0	869.9	3,662.1	18.3	598.5	35.6
6.5	15.5	2.6	107.6	914.0	942.6	2,854.6	137.9	504.4	90.1

Subtropics

City	Latitude [°]	Longitude [°]	Height above sea level [m]	Average temperature [°C]	Maximum temperature [°C]	Minimum temperature [°C]	Maximum daily variation [K]
Hanoi VN	21.020	105.870	46	22.9	37.5	6.7	14.2
Hong Kong HK	22.270	114.170	0	23.2	34.5	6.9	12.1
Taipeh TW	25.020	121.450	419	19.8	32.5	5.1	12.6
Xiamen CN	24.450	118.080	30	20.8	36.2	4.2	14.9
Houston US	29.830	-95.330	13	19.9	36.9	-5.6	21.0
Shanghai CN	31.230	121.470	8	15.8	36.3	-4.7	14.0
Tokio JP	35.670	139.750	16	15.6	34.8	-2.0	13.6
Algiers DZ	36.750	3.000	116	17.3	38.6	1.0	17.7
Brisbane AU	-27.500	153.000	19	20.5	35.4	4.3	18.6
Buenos Aires AR	-34.670	-58.500	0	17.3	32.3	4.0	12.7
New Orleans US	30.000	-90.050	0	20.7	34.4	-1.2	19.3
Perth AU	-31.970	115.820	0	18.4	39.1	4.9	22.0
Sydney AU	-33.920	151.170	0	17.9	32.1	5.6	14.0
Tel Aviv IL	32.080	34.770	0	19.4	34.7	4.8	15.7
Adelaide AU	-34.930	138.600	149	16.4	39.6	4.0	28.0
Barcelona ES	41.420	2.170	121	16.1	31.7	0.7	13.2
Istanbul TR	41.030	28.950	2	14.1	32.7	-3.9	13.1
Melbourne AU	-37.750	144.970	82	14.1	36.6	-0.4	22.7
Montevideo UY	-34.870	-56.170	30	16.5	33.3	0.8	16.9
San Francisco US	37.750	-122.450	0	14.1	30.1	4.2	15.1

Average humidity [g/kg]	Maximum humidity [g/kg]	Minimum humidity [g/kg]	Average radiation [W/m²]	Maximum radiation [W/m²]	Sum of radiation [kWh/m²a]	Heating degree days [Kd/a]	Cooling degree days [Kd/a]	Humidifying gram days [gd/kga]	Dehumidifying gram days [gd/kga]
16.1	27.2	6.1	154.3	1,055.0	1,351.7	121.4	1,902.4	2.2	2,330.9
14.2	26.4	3.9	154.3	1,112.0	1,351.7	84.3	1,820.6	46.7	1,642.2
13.7	24.1	5.2	155.2	1,094.0	1,359.6	349.7	1,160.3	15.9	1,554.3
14.7	26.6	5.1	157.3	1,039.0	1,377.9	348.4	1,517.3	9.3	2,037.3
11.3	23.2	2.3	184.6	1,043.0	1,617.1	772.6	1,668.7	174.3	1,072.6
10.2	27.6	1.9	146.3	1,009.0	1,281.6	1,922.9	971.1	359.9	990.1
8.3	23.5	1.4	134.2	1,023.0	1,175.6	1,771.7	843.2	533.5	595.2
9.4	19.6	3.9	188.7	996.0	1,653.0	683.5	1,070.9	141.7	547.2
10.3	24.8	4.1	218.3	1,227.0	1,912.3	41.7	1,645.9	132.5	737.3
8.9	21.0	3.6	194.9	1,193.0	1,707.3	580.3	726.5	189.3	417.8
11.5	23.7	2.2	189.3	1,133.0	1,658.3	443.1	1,518.2	156.3	1,053.5
8.3	19.6	4.1	221.2	1,194.0	1,937.7	201.8	1,152.8	196.8	233.3
9.2	19.5	3.4	191.1	1,124.0	1,674.0	147.6	812.7	186.2	499.8
9.7	19.6	3.8	222.7	1,059.0	1,950.9	156.4	1,326.4	181.5	602.0
7.1	18.0	3.4	203.7	1,110.0	1,784.4	810.9	775.7	396.8	129.7
7.6	17.5	2.6	180.7	1,013.0	1,582.9	1,036.6	634.1	384.0	246.1
7.4	18.4	2.1	166.5	1,064.0	1,458.5	1,976.4	595.7	427.5	263.4
7.1	20.8	3.3	176.4	1,162.0	1,545.3	1,435.8	605.1	384.2	174.8
8.5	18.7	3.6	175.0	1,194.0	1,533.0	824.7	787.9	210.7	335.5
6.8	12.7	3.4	196.2	1,093.0	1,718.7	792.5	187.9	378.1	57.6

Tropics

City	Latitude [°]	Longitude [°]	Height above sea level [m]	Average temperature [°C]	Maximum temperature [°C]	Minimum temperature [°C]	Maximum daily variation [K]
Bangkok TH	13.730	100.500	0	27.9	35.4	19.0	12.6
Jakarta ID	-6.130	106.750	0	27.2	34.9	21.0	12.0
Kuala Lumpur MY	3.130	101.700	152	26.3	34.8	20.4	12.2
Manaus BR	-3.100	-60.000	45	26.5	34.6	20.4	10.4
Port au Prince HT	18.550	-72.330	0	27.4	35.0	20.0	11.2
Singapore SG	1.280	103.850	30	26.5	33.5	20.8	10.3
Bangalore IN	12.970	77.580	762	24.2	36.6	14.3	14.7
Kinshasa CD	-4.360	15.300	350	25.5	35.5	15.9	12.9
San Salvador SV	13.708	-89.202	680	22.9	32.8	13.7	14.2
Santa Cruz BO	-17.750	-63.230	388	23.2	33.9	6.5	16.7
Yaoundé CM	3.850	11.520	731	23.7	32.1	17.5	11.1
Brasilia BR	-15.920	-47.670	960	21.3	32.7	9.3	16.9
Caracas VE	10.540	-66.930	1.051	20.8	28.6	13.1	12.3
Kigali RW	-1.930	30.070	1.417	21.0	32.8	9.9	20.5
San José CR	9.930	-84.080	1.140	20.5	30.6	12.9	15.2
Miami US	25.870	-80.250	2	24.3	34.2	6.6	13.0
Mumbai IN	18.980	72.850	0	27.6	37.6	16.2	15.4
Rio de Janeiro BR	-22.880	-43.280	152	23.1	34.4	12.5	12.9
Santa Clara CU	22.420	-79.970	102	25.8	35.5	12.0	14.3
Bogotá CO	4.630	-74.080	2.560	13.3	23.6	2.0	20.0
Cuzco PE	-13.524	-71.985	3.420	11.7	23.3	-1.4	21.1
Quito EC	-0.224	-78.512	2.810	14.1	23.5	6.1	15.0

Average humidity [g/kg]	Maximum humidity [g/kg]	Minimum humidity [g/kg]	Average radiation [W/m^2]	Maximum radiation [W/m^2]	Sum of radiation [kWh/m^{2}a]	Heating degree days [Kd/a]	Cooling degree days [Kd/a]	Humidifying gram days [gd/kga]	Dehumidifying gram days [gd/kga]
17.6	25.1	8.2	201.5	1,084.0	1,765.1	0.0	3,086.0	0.0	2,514.0
18.5	25.3	13.2	199.6	1,149.0	1,748.5	0.0	3,028.9	0.0	2,871.1
17.9	24.9	12.3	188.9	1,152.0	1,654.8	0.0	2,790.0	0.0	2,762.9
18.3	24.1	12.8	205.1	1,159.0	1,796.7	0.0	2,732.1	0.0	2,837.9
15.1	22.2	8.4	228.1	1,107.0	1,998.2	0.0	3,114.2	0.0	16,128.7
18.9	25.0	13.2	186.3	1,080.0	1,632.0	0.0	2,714.8	0.0	2,993.7
15.9	26.7	9.4	231.2	1,168.0	2,025.3	0.0	2,350.7	0.0	2,160.8
16.0	23.0	9.6	184.9	1,187.0	1,619.7	0.0	2,593.0	0.0	2,134.9
14.2	22.1	7.5	214.6	1,208.0	1,879.9	0.0	1,842.1	0.1	1,637.5
13.8	22.9	5.6	209.8	1,285.0	1,837.8	62.9	2,019.9	8.3	1,509.4
16.6	24.3	11.5	205.1	1,187.0	1,796.7	0.0	2,005.2	0.0	2,385.4
12.3	21.0	5.2	204.6	1,259.0	1,792.3	0.0	1,721.4	26.2	1,155.3
13.6	19.9	8.2	185.1	1,209.0	1,621.5	0.0	1,233.2	0.0	1,476.5
13.3	20.7	7.7	207.4	1,306.0	1,816.8	0.0	1,711.7	0.0	1,422.9
12.1	18.8	6.6	213.2	1,208.0	1,867.6	0.0	1,368.2	1.5	1,092.7
13.8	23.8	5.4	201.5	1,072.0	1,765.1	9.6	2,211.3	15.0	1,484.0
16.4	27.2	7.2	214.5	1,057.0	1,879.0	0.0	3,155.9	0.4	2,210.2
14.3	24.1	8.1	193.0	1,205.0	1,690.7	0.0	1,912.3	0.0	1,712.2
16.3	26.0	7.8	185.8	1,156.0	1,627.6	0.0	2,639.6	0.0	2,202.4
10.1	14.3	5.4	179.4	1,310.0	1,571.5	262.9	121.1	2.3	641.9
8.4	14.4	3.5	255.7	1,441.0	2,239.9	1,886.3	122.2	174.8	276.2
10.3	15.5	6.0	189.6	1,231.0	1,660.9	141.8	107.6	20.6	583.9

Deserts

City	Latitude [°]	Longitude [°]	Height above sea level [m]	Average temperature [°C]	Maximum temperature [°C]	Minimum temperature [°C]	Maximum daily variation [K]
Abu Dhabi AE	24.470	54.420	0	27.2	44.9	11.1	16.9
Doha QA	25.220	51.530	30	26.6	45.4	10.1	15.9
Dubai AE	25.230	55.280	0	27.1	43.6	11.9	13.4
Hyderabad PK	25.380	68.400	61	27.6	41.7	9.5	15.4
Mecca SA	21.430	39.820	336	26.4	41.0	12.6	15.2
Manama BH	26.200	50.570	0	26.6	41.7	12.6	10.8
Sharjah AE	25.330	55.430	46	26.3	44.5	8.5	17.7
Alexandria EG	31.220	29.920	0	20.1	33.1	6.8	14.4
Kairo EG	30.050	31.250	84	21.3	39.6	5.1	15.4
Marrakech MA	31.630	-8.010	460	19.6	43.7	4.0	17.6
Alice Springs AU	-23.800	133.900	545	21.2	42.0	-0.2	21.2
Medina SA	24.500	39.580	762	27.5	46.0	8.0	14.4
Riyadh SA	24.650	46.770	701	25.5	43.9	4.9	16.8
Las Vegas US	36.170	-115.170	680	19.5	44.9	-3.4	18.8
Teheran IR	35.670	51.430	1.140	17.0	39.9	-6.9	15.8
Yazd IR	31.920	54.370	1.219	19.1	42.9	-6.1	16.5
Almaty KZ	43.320	76.980	976	9.0	36.5	-21.8	23.5
Denver US	39.750	-105.000	1.622	10.2	34.2	-20.5	23.1
Kabul AF	34.516	69.195	1.800	12.1	37.4	-11.0	21.7
Salt Lake City US	40.750	-111.920	1.309	11.0	38.2	-14.6	22.9

Average humidity [g/kg]	Maximum humidity [g/kg]	Minimum humidity [g/kg]	Average radiation [W/m²]	Maximum radiation [W/m²]	Sum of radiation [kWh/m²a]	Heating degree days [Kd/a]	Cooling degree days [Kd/a]	Humidifying gram days [gd/kga]	Dehumidifying gram days [gd/kga]
12.5	27.7	5.2	232.2	1,034.0	2,034.1	0.0	3,318.4	25.4	1,098.0
12.3	28.2	5.1	194.7	1,063.0	1,705.6	0.0	2,949.0	30.2	1,066.4
13.3	30.3	4.6	231.3	1,031.0	2,026.2	0.0	3,122.1	32.0	1,341.2
14.7	27.9	4.1	227.4	1,012.0	1,992.0	0.0	3,247.7	75.1	1,718.7
14.0	24.2	6.6	254.5	1,068.0	2,229.4	0.0	3,135.1	2.8	1,514.4
11.5	23.2	4.6	237.6	1,006.0	2,081.4	0.0	2,657.8	48.0	867.1
13.5	28.4	5.1	228.6	1,047.0	2,002.5	0.0	3,185.1	28.0	1,351.8
10.2	20.1	3.8	231.5	1,045.0	2,027.9	25.9	1,304.1	126.2	642.2
8.5	17.8	3.3	228.5	1,104.0	2,001.7	81.7	1,799.0	290.8	313.4
8.3	17.1	3.7	212.5	1,060.0	1,861.5	388.8	1,543.7	248.8	246.0
7.1	23.3	2.1	257.2	1,217.0	2,253.1	485.4	2,133.2	540.0	169.2
6.2	13.9	2.5	274.5	1,132.0	2,404.6	0.0	3,455.0	593.2	17.7
6.0	19.9	2.3	249.9	1,101.0	2,189.1	119.7	3,033.7	660.6	37.5
4.0	15.2	1.2	234.6	1,080.0	2,055.1	1,245.6	1,914.0	1,126.6	16.4
4.8	13.8	1.5	209.9	1,104.0	1,838.7	1,935.6	1,465.7	906.5	8.5
4.4	11.7	1.3	230.1	1,166.0	2,015.7	1,468.4	1,917.4	1,020.4	1.1
5.2	15.0	0.6	153.6	1,060.0	1,345.5	3,984.8	663.5	818.5	61.9
4.9	16.2	0.6	191.1	1,137.0	1,674.0	3,484.6	651.2	954.7	69.1
5.8	13.2	1.4	225.4	1,192.0	1,974.5	2,964.2	846.5	720.4	66.8
5.0	15.4	1.0	202.9	1,119.0	1,777.4	3,345.8	818.5	894.3	29.4

Literature and Links

[Argos] Argos – software for calculating thermal bridges following EnEV and DIN 4108. www.zub-kassel.de/software/argos

[ASHRAE-55] ASHRAE Standard 55: Thermal Environmental Conditions for Human Occupancy. Atlanta, ASHRAE, 2009

[Behling et al. 2000] Behling, S.; Behling, S.; Schindler, B.: *Solar Power. The Evolution of Sustainable Architecture*. Munich, New York 2000

[BINE-Info] Online information service for transferring information from research into practice. www.bine.info

[Blüthgen, Weischet 1980] Blüthgen, J.; Weischet, W.: *Allgemeine Klimageographie*. 3rd edition. Berlin 1980

[Brandi 2005] Brandi, U.: Detail Praxis. *Tageslicht – Kunstlicht*. Munich 2005

[Brunner et al. 2009] Brunner, R.; Hönger, C.; Menti, U.; Wieser, C.; Unruh, T.: *Das Klima als Entwurfsfaktor*. Lucerne 2009

[ClimaDesign] ClimaDesign. Lehrstuhl für Bauklimatik und Haustechnik. TU Munich. www.climadesign.de

[ClimateTool] ClimateTool – Interactive planning tool for building-specific analysis of any site. www.climate-tool.com

[Daniels 1997] Daniels, K.: *The Technology of Ecological Building. Basic Principles and Measures, Examples and Ideas*. Basel, Boston, Berlin 1997

[Daniels 2000] Daniels, K.: *Gebäudetechnik. Ein Leitfaden für Architekten und Ingenieure*. Munich 2000

[DIALux] DIALux – free software for professional lighting planning. www.dial.de/CMS/German/Articles/DIAL/DIAL.html?ID=1

[Dibowski, Wortmann 2004] Dibowski, G.; Wortmann, R.; AG Solar Nordrhein-Westfalen: *Luft-Erdwärmetauscher L-EWT*. Jülich 2004

[Doswald 1977] Doswald, F.: *Planen und Bauen in heissen Zonen*. Zurich 1977

[Ebert et al. 2010] Ebert, T.; Essig, N.; Hauser, G.: *Detail Green Books. Zertifizierungssysteme für Gebäude*. Munich 2010

[Ellis 1960] Ellis, F. P.: "Physiological Responses to Hot Environments". In: *Medical Research Council Report No. 298*, H.M.S.O., 1960

[Epass Helena] Epass Helena – software for calculations using EnEV 2009, DIN V 18599, DIN V 4108 and DIN V 4701. www.zub-kassel.de/software/epass-helena-enev-2009

[ESP-r] ESP-r dynamic building and grounds simulation program. www.esru.strath.ac.uk/Programs/ESP-r.htm

[Fanger 1982] Fanger, P. O.: *Thermal Comfort. Analysis and Applications in Environmental Engineering*. Florida 1982

[Flagge, Herzog 2001] Flagge, I.; Herzog, T.: *Architektur und Technologie*. Munich 2001

[Forkel 2008] Forkel, M.: www.klima-der-erde.de

[Gaines, Jäger 2009] Gaines, J.; Jäger, S.: *Albert Speer & Partner. Ein Manifest für nachhaltige Stadtplanung*. Munich 2009

[GeoDataZone 2010] GeoDataZone, Das Lexikon der Erde. www.geodz.com

[Gerhart 2003] Gerhart, J.: "Effects of Wind". In: Eisele, J.; Kloft, E.: *High-Rise Manual*. Basel, Boston, Berlin 2003

[Göbel 2004] Göbel, P.: *Wetter und Klima*. Cologne 2004

[Goris et al. 2010] Goris, A.; Heisel, J.: *Schneider, Bautabellen für Architekten*. Neuwied 2010

[Gösele et al. 1996] Gösele, K.; Schüle, W.; Künzel, H.: *Schall, Wärme, Feuchte*. Wiesbaden, Berlin 1996

[Häckel 1999] Häckel, H.: *Farbatlas Wetterphänomene*. Stuttgart 1999

[Häckel 2005] Häckel, H.: *Meteorologie*. 5th edition. Stuttgart 2005

[Hausladen, Tichelmann 2009] Hausladen, G.; Tichelmann, K.: *Interiors Construction Manual*. Basel, Boston, Berlin 2009

[Hayner et al. 2010] Hayner, M.; Ruoff, J.; Thiel, D.: *Faustformel Gebäudetechnik: für Architekten*. Munich 2010

[Hegger et al. 2006] Hegger, M.; Auch-Schwelk, V.; Fuchs, M.; Stark, T.; Rosenkranz, T.: *Construction Materials Manual*. Basel, Boston, Berlin 2006

[Hegger et al. 2008] Hegger M.; Fuchs M.; Stark T.; Zeumer M.: *Energy Manual. Sustainable Architecture*. Basel, Boston, Berlin 2008

[Herzog et al. 2005] Herzog, T.; Krippner, R.; Lang, W.: *Facade Construction Manual*. Basel, Boston, Berlin 2005

[Heyer 1972] Heyer, E.: *Witterung und Klima. Eine allgemeine Klimatologie*. 7th edition. Leipzig 1972

[Hindrichs, Daniels 2007] Hindrichs, D.; Daniels, K.: *Plusminus 20°/40° Latitude*. Stuttgart, London 2007

[Hindrichs, Heusler 2006] Hindrichs, D.; Heusler, W.: *Façades. Building Envelopes for the 21st Century*. 2nd edition. Basel, Boston, Berlin 2006

[Hupfer, Kuttler 2006] Hupfer, P.; Kuttler, W.: *Witterung und Klima. Eine Einführung in die Meteorologie und Klimatologie*. Begründet von Ernst Heyer, 12th edition. Wiesbaden 2006

[h,x-Diagramm] h,x diagrams for different heights. www.dolder-ing.ch/wissen/Lueftung-Klima/h-x-diagram/Mollier_h-x-diagramm_pdf-vorlagen-dowload.htm

[Hyde 2006] Hyde, R.: *Climate Responsive Design*. 3rd edition. Cornwall 2006

[IBP-Fraunhofer] Fraunhofer-Institut für Bauphysik. www.ibp.fraunhofer.de

[IDA] IDA – software for dynamic building simulation. http://equa.se.linweb57.kontrollpanelen.se/en/software/idaice

[ILK] ILK_hx-Diagramm – freeware (Excel-Tool) for showing processes in the Mollier h,x diagram. www.ilkdresden.de/index.php?id=833

[Kaltenbach 2004] Kaltenbach, F.: *Detail Practice. Translucent Materials*. Basel, Boston, Berlin 2004

[Kaltschmitt 2006] Kaltschmitt, M.; Streicher, W.; Wiese, A.: *Renewable Energy. Technology, Economics, Environment*. Berlin 2010

[Keller et al. 2010] Keller, B.; Rutz, S.: *Pinpoint, Key Facts and Figures for Sustainable Buildings*. Basel 2010

[Klimafibel 2007] Urban development climate primer for Baden-Württemberg, in cooperation with the Amt für Umweltschutz. Stuttgart 2007. www.staedtebauliche-klimafibel.de

[Kohler et al. 2009] Kohler, N.; König, H; Kreissig, J.; Lützkendorf, T.: *Detail Green Books. Lebenszyklusanalyse in der Gebäudeplanung*. Munich 2009

[Köppen-Geiger] Effective climate calculation using Köppen-Geiger. http://koeppen-geiger.vu-wien.ac.at.

[Koschenz, Lehmann 2000] Koschenz, M.; Lehmann, B.: Thermoaktive Bauteilsysteme tabs. EMPA. Dübendorf 2000

[Köster 2004] Köster, H.: *Dynamic Daylighting Architecture: Basics, Systems, Projects*. Basel, Boston, Berlin 2004

[Lang 2001] Lang, W.: "Is it all 'just' a facade? The functional, energetic and structural aspects of the building skin". In: Schittich, C. (ed.): *In Detail. Building Skins*. Basel, Boston, Berlin 2002

[Lauber 2005] Lauber, W.: *Tropical Architecture*. Munich, Berlin, London, New York 2005

[Lenz et al. 2010] Lenz, B.; Schreiber, J.; Stark, T.: *Detail Green Books. Nachhaltige Gebäudetechnik*. Munich 2010

[Liedl 2011] Liedl, P.: *Interaktion Klima-Mensch-Gebäude: Planungswerkzeuge für die Konzeption von Verwaltungsgebäuden in unterschiedlichen Klimaregionen im Kontext von Energie und Raumklima mit detaillierter Klimaanalyse*. Dissertation. TU Munich, 2011

[Lippsmeier 1980] Lippsmeier, G.: *Building in the Tropics*. 2nd edition. Munich 1980

[Meteonorm] Meteonorm – Global Solar Radiation Database. Version 6.0. www.meteonorm.com

[Meyers 2005] *Meyers Grosses Länderlexikon*. Mannheim 2005

[Milne, Givoni 1979] Milne, M.; Givoni, B.: "Architectural Design Based on Climate". In: Watson, D.: *Energy Conservation through Building Design, Chapter 6*. New York 1979

[Mommertz 2009] Mommertz, E.: *Detail Practice. Acoustics and Sound Insulation*. Basel, Boston, Berlin 2009

[NASA 2006] *National Aeronautics and Space Administration: The Earth Observer*. Nov./Dec. 2006. Volume 18, Issue 6. 2006

[NASA 2008] National Aeronautics and Space Administration. www.nasa.gov

[Oesterle et al. 1999] Oesterle, E.; Lieb, R.; Lutz, M.; Heusler, W.: *Doppelschalige Fassaden, Ganzheitliche Planung*. Munich 1999

[Olgay 1963] Olgay, V.: *Design With Climate. Bioclimatic Approach to Architectural Regionalism*. New Jersey 1963

[Oliver 2003] Oliver, P.: *Dwellings*. London 2003

[PCM express] PCM express – free planning and simulation program for the use of phase change materials (PCM). www.valentin.de/produkte/pcm

[Pfundstein et al. 2004] Pfundstein, M.; Rudolphi, A.; Spitzner, H.; Gellert, R.: *Detail Practice. Insulating Materials*. Basel, Boston, Berlin 2004

[Pistohl 2009] Pistohl, W.: *Handbuch der Gebäudetechnik*. Düsseldorf 2009

[Pültz 2002] Pültz, G.: *Bauklimatischer Entwurf für moderne Glasarchitektur*. Berlin 2002

[PV-Kalkulation] Online PV calculation (including optimal angle of inclination) for locations in Europe and Africa. http://re.jrc.ec.europa.eu/pvgis/apps4/pvest.php

[PV*SOL] PV*SOL – Dynamic simulation program with 3D visuals and shading analysis for grid-connected photovoltaic plants. www.valentin.de/produkte/photovoltaik

[Radiance] Radiance: Dynamic daylight simulation program. www.al-ware.com/index.php?CATID=523&SUBCATID=562#3DLi

[Recknagel et al. 2007] Recknagel, H.; Sprenger, E.; Schramek, R.: *Taschenbuch für Heizung und Klimatechnik 07/08*. Munich 2007

[Recknagel et al. 2010] Recknagel, H.; Sprenger, E.; Schramek, E.: *Taschenbuch für Heizung und Klimatechnik 2011/2012*. Munich 2010

[Richarz et al. 2008] Richarz, C.; Schulz, C.; Zeitler, F.: *Detail Practice. Energy-Efficiency Upgrades*. Basel, Boston, Berlin 2007

[Roberts, Guariento 2009] Roberts, S.; Guariento, N.: *Building Integrated Photovoltaics. A Handbook*. Basel, Boston, Berlin 2009

[RWE 2010] RWE Energie Aktiengesellschaft: *Bau-Handbuch 2009*. Heidelberg 2010

[Schönauer 2000] Schönauer, N.: *6000 Years of Housing*. New York 2000

[Schönwiese 2003] Schönwiese, C.-D.: *Klimatologie*. 2nd edition. Stuttgart 2003

[Schultz 2002] Schultz, J.: *Die Ökozonen der Erde*. Stuttgart 2002

[SolarCoolingLight] SolarCoolingLight – Freeware for pre-dimensioning solar cooling systems. www.solair-project.eu/218.0.html#c1010

[TAS] TAS – Dynamic simulation program on a modular basis. www.edsl.net/main/

[Top-Wetter] Top-Wetter: Meteorological calculations. www.top-wetter.de/calculator

[Treberspurg 1999] Treberspurg, M.: *Neues Bauen mit der Sonne. Ansätze zu einer klimagerechten Architektur*. Vienna, New York 1999

[TRNSYS] TRNSYS – Dynamic building and grounds simulation program on a modular basis. www.transsolar.com/software/docs/trnsys/trnsys_uebersicht_de.htm

[T*SOL] T*SOL – Dynamic simulation program for detailed examination of thermal solar systems and their components. www.valentin.de/produkte/solarthermie

[U-Wert] U-value calculation for materials and building components. www.u-wert.net

[Vitra Design Museum 2007] Vitra Design Museum: *Leben unter dem Halbmond*. 2nd edition. Weil am Rhein 2007

[Walter, Lieth 1967] Walter, H.; Lieth, H.: *Klimadiagramm-Weltatlas*. Jena 1967

[Webb 1960] Webb, C.G.: *Thermal Discomfort in an Equatorial Climate*. London 1960

[Weller et al. 2009] Weller, B.; Hemmerle, C.; Jakubetz S.; Unnewehr, S.: *Detail Practice. Photovoltaics*. Basel, Boston, Berlin 2010

[Wellpott 2006] Wellpott, E.; Bohne, D.: *Technischer Ausbau von Gebäuden*. Stuttgart 2006

[World Ocean Atlas 2010] World Ocean Atlas: National Oceanographic Data Center NODC. www.nodc.noaa.gov

[Wüstenrot Stiftung 2009] Wüstenrot Stiftung: *Energieeffiziente Architektur*. Stuttgart 2009

[ZUB-Kassel] Zentrum für Umweltbewusstes Bauen e. V. www.zub-kassel.de

[DIN ISO 2533] DIN ISO 2533: Standard atmosphere. Berlin 1997

[DIN 5034] DIN 5034: Daylight in interiors. Part 1, 2, 3. Berlin 1999, 1985, 2007

[DIN EN ISO 7726] DIN EN ISO 7726: Ergonomics of the thermal environment – Instruments for measuring physical quantities. Berlin 2001

[DIN EN ISO 7730] DIN EN ISO 7730: Ergonomics of the thermal environment. Berlin 2006

[DIN 12524] DIN 12524: Thermal and humidity-protection qualities. Tabulated rated values. Berlin 2000

[DIN EN 12665] DIN EN 12665: Light and lighting. Basic terms and criteria for specifying lighting requirements. Berlin 2002

[DIN EN 15251] DIN EN 15251: Indoor environmental input parameters for design and assessment of energy performance of buildings addressing indoor air quality, thermal environment, lighting and acoustics. Berlin 2007

[DIN 33403-2] DIN 33403-2: Climate in the workplace and in the working environment. Part 2: Influence of the climate on human heat balance. Berlin 2000

[DIN 33403-3] DIN 33403-3: Climate in the workplace and in the working environment. Part 3: Assessing the climate in warm and hot areas on the basis of selected climate summary measures. Berlin 2001

[DIN V 18599] DIN V 18599: Energy efficiency of buildings – Calculation of the net, final and primary energy demand for heating, cooling, ventilation, domestic hot water and lighting. Berlin 2007

Index

Authors and Acknowledgements

Univ.-Prof. Dr.-Ing. Gerhard Hausladen

1947	Born in Munich
1967	to 1972 Studied mechanical engineering at the Technische Universität München (TUM)
1972 to 1980	Academic staff member and academic assistant in the building services and building physics department at the TUM
1980	Doctorate in engineering
1980 to 1985	Technical director of a medium-sized industrial company in the heating technology field
1986	Founded his own engineering practice for building services, building physics and energy technology
1992 to 2001	Professor of technical building equipment at the University of Kassel
1998	Founded the Zentrum für Umweltbewusstes Bauen e.V. (ZUB) at the University of Kassel
1998 to 2001	Board of the ZUB at the University of Kassel
from 2001	Professorial chair in the department of building climatology and building services at the TUM
from 2007	Chair of the ClimaDesign e. V. board

www.climadesign.de; www.ibhausladen.de

Dr.-Ing. Petra Liedl

1976	Born in Weiden i.d. Opf.
1995 to 2001	Studied architecture at the TUM
2002 to 2007	Academic assistant in the department of building climatology and building services at the TUM International research and teaching visits
2007 to 2010	Doctoral grant at the International Graduate School of Science and Engineering (IGSSE) at the TUM
2008 to 2009	Associate of the "Neue Verantwortung" foundation, "Sustainable technology leadership" group, Berlin
2011	Doctorate in engineering on the subject of "Interaction Climate-Man-Buildings": development of the interactive planning tools ClimateTool and SkinTool and a building climatology-related climate classification Dr. Marschall-Preis 2011 from the Faculty of Architecture, TUM
from 2006	Work with the Ingenieurbüro Hausladen
from 2007	Founder member and member of the ClimateDesign e.V. board Lecturer at universities and academies specialising in ClimateDesign international

www.climate-tool.com

Prof. Dr.-Ing. Mike de Saldanha

1966	Born in Munich
1982 to 1985	trained as a power electronics engineer with Siemens in Munich
1987 to 1994	Studied architecture in Munich und Kassel
1994 to 1996	Studied energy and environment in Kassel
1995	Solar mobile expedition to North Africa
from 1995	Self-employment in the energy and solar fields
from 1997	Many years of work in the Ingenieurbüro Hausladen
1998 to 2001	Academic assistant at the University of Kassel
1998	Founder member of the Zentrum für Umweltbewusstes Bauen e.V. in Kassel
2002 to 2006	Academic assistant in the department of building climatology and building services at the TUM
2002	Founder member of the Masters course in climate engineering and member of the academic committee at the University of Krems
2005	Conception and establishment of the ClimaDesign Masters course at the TUM
2006	Doctorate in engineering at the TUM on the subject of "Interaction of skin, space and structure"
from 2006	Proprietor of the atelier.ClimaDesign
from 2010	Chair of building technology + energy technology in the architecture and interior design department at the Hochschule Darmstadt

www.atelierclimadesign.de; www.simulationsstudio-darmstadt.de

We would like to thank Michael Kehr (Dipl.-Ing.) most warmly for greatly assisting this book project in a number of ways, for his creative input into the graphics featured in this book and for his meticulous specialist cooperation. We would also like to thank Sandro Pfoh (Dip.-Ing) for his assistance in the rendering of graphics.

Our sincere thanks also go to Georg Hausladen (M.Sc.) for providing photographs of the vegetation in each individual climate zone for use in this book.

Our thanks also go to Siemens Real Estate and especially Bernd Heibel, Rainer Kohns and Otto Reich for the chance to work with them on a study on climate-friendly office buildings worldwide.

Particular thanks go to Annette Gref, Berit Liedtke, Sarah Schwarz and Werner Handschin at the Birkhäuser Verlag for a lively exchange of ideas, professional editing and excellent co-operation. They have looked after this book project wonderfully well in terms of both content and technical matters, and have made many helpful suggestions.

Concept Gerhard Hausladen, Petra Liedl, Mike de Saldanha
Texts Gerhard Hausladen, Petra Liedl, Mike de Saldanha
Editors Annette Gref, Berit Liedtke, Sarah Schwarz
Translation from German into English Michael Robinson
Copy editing Monica Buckland
Project management Annette Gref, Berit Liedtke,
Sarah Schwarz

A CIP catalogue record for this book is available from the Library of Congress, Washington D.C., USA.

Bibliographic information published by the German National Library. The German National Library lists this publication in the Deutsche Nationalbibliografie; detailed bibliographic data are available on the Internet at http://dnb.d-nb.de.

This book is also available in a German language edition (ISBN 978-3-0346-0727-8).

P.O. Box, 4002 Basel, Switzerland

Part of De Gruyter

Printed on acid-free paper produced from chlorine-free pulp.
TCF ∞
Printed in Germany

ISBN 978-3-0346-0728-5

9 8 7 6 5 4 3 2 1 www.birkhauser.com